IMPERIALISM

and

IDEALISM

IMPERIALISM
—— *and* ——
IDEALISM

American Diplomats in China,
1861–1898

David L. Anderson

INDIANA
UNIVERSITY
PRESS

BLOOMINGTON

Research for this book was partially funded by a grant from the Johnson Fund of the
American Philosophical Society

Manufactured in the United States of America

Library of Congress Cataloging in Publication Data

Anderson, David L.
    Imperialism and idealism.

    Bibliography: p.
    Includes index.
    1. United States—Foreign relations—China.
2. China—Foreign relations—United States.   3. United
States—Foreign relations—1865–1898.   4. United States—
Foreign relations—1861–1865.   5. China—Politics and
government—1862–1899.   6. Americans—China—History—
19th century.   I. Title.
E183.8.C5A735   1985   327.73051   84-48544
ISBN 0-253-32918-3
1 2 3 4 5   89 88 87 86 85

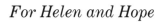

For Helen and Hope

CONTENTS

	Preface	ix
ONE	Imperialism and Idealism: America's China Policy Dilemma	1
TWO	"Fair Diplomatic Action": Anson Burlingame and the Cooperative Policy in China	16
THREE	"Determined Moral Pressure": J. Ross Browne and Burlingame's Policy	38
FOUR	Disillusionment and Frustration: Frederick F. Low and Benjamin P. Avery in China	62
FIVE	The Diplomacy of Expediency: The China Career of George F. Seward	90
SIX	Attempts at an Independent Policy: James B. Angell and John Russell Young in Peking	115
SEVEN	Two China Policies: Charles Denby versus the State Department	144
EIGHT	Epilogue: The Dilemma Becomes the Policy in John Hay's Open Door Notes	171
	Appendix: United States Ministers to China, Secretaries of State, and Presidents, 1861–1901	193
	Notes	195
	Bibliography	222
	Index	233

ILLUSTRATIONS

Map of China	Frontispiece
Imperial Palace, Peking	6
Five-Clawed Dragon, Imperial Palace	7
Anson Burlingame	17
Prince Kung	23
J. Ross Browne	47
Frederick F. Low	67
Palace of Heavenly Purity	79
Benjamin P. Avery	82
George F. Seward	91
James B. Angell	117
John Russell Young	127
Charles Denby	145
USS *Monocacy*	157
Bronze Lion, Imperial Palace	182

PREFACE

HISTORICALLY, official United States policies toward China have been ambivalent and inconsistent because of tension between American ideals and self-interests. During both the nineteenth and the twentieth centuries, Washington frequently professed support for the principle of China's independence in international affairs, but simultaneously American officials pursued privileges and advantages for the United States that undermined China's sovereignty. In searching for the origins of this ambiguity, this book focuses on the lives and careers of the first eight American diplomats to reside in Peking. This biographical approach is based on the notion that these individual envoys were in various ways representative of some fundamental and paradoxical elements in America's historical and cultural identity that in turn shaped the dualities in American China policy. Since the days of John Winthrop and the Puritans, a basic dichotomy between self-interest and self-sacrifice had existed in American thought, and the American diplomatic ministers carried this tradition to Peking.

The first of these envoys was Anson Burlingame, an antislavery reformer who idealistically attempted to transform Western coercion into cooperation with the Chinese. His successor, J. Ross Browne, was a professional writer and a skeptic who concluded that force, not forbearance, was the only realistic Western policy in Asia. The six United States ministers who followed Burlingame and Browne continued to wrestle with the same alternatives: Should the United States join the other Western nations in diplomatic and military efforts to extract privileges and concessions from China or should it seek to secure American interests by actively defending the integrity of the weak Chinese government? For the eight American envoys in Peking between 1861 and 1898, this dilemma manifested itself as a varying mixture of selfish imperialism and selfless idealism. These two concepts sometimes converged and sometimes competed, but they gave United States actions in China a decided ambivalence. The dilemma remained unresolved in 1899–1900, when Secretary of State John Hay incorporated both imperialism and idealism into his Open Door Notes. Hay's famous notes perpetuated the contradictions inherent in the preceding forty years of American diplomacy in China and bequeathed to his twentieth-century successors a paradoxical policy formula in Asia.

The scope of this study purposely has been limited to the year-by-year diplomatic routine of the chief American representatives in China. This approach assumes that, in the four decades before the Open Door Notes, United States China policy was often whatever these individuals said it was. Less often, the State Department or American public opinion became directly involved in specific issues, but even then the result was sometimes a policy tug-of-war between the minister and Washington. Since the policies of each envoy were essentially the product of his own personality and his particular interpretation of events, the American position in China usually shifted with a change in ministers and hence was markedly inconsistent.

The research has concentrated on American archival sources, because the basic purpose of this study is to examine the careers and policy determinations of these non-Chinese-speaking American representatives and to assess Hay's Open Door Notes in the context of American diplomatic traditions. For the Chinese side of the diplomatic relationship, secondary sources based on Chinese archival materials have been used.

Portions of this book have been previously published in three historical journals. I wish to thank the editors of *Diplomatic History* for permission to use part of my article "Anson Burlingame: American Architect of the Cooperative Policy in China, 1861–1871," which appeared in vol. 1, no. 3 (Summer 1977). *California History* has allowed me to reprint portions of two articles: "The Diplomacy of Discrimination: Chinese Exclusion, 1876–1882," in vol. 57, no. 1 (Spring 1978), and "Between Two Cultures: Frederick F. Low in China," in vol. 59, no. 3 (Fall 1980). *Civil War History* has consented to the publication of portions of my article "Anson Burlingame: Reformer and Diplomat," in vol. 25, no. 4 (December 1979).

Many people have provided me with invaluable assistance in the writing of this book. I am indebted to my wife, Helen, above all others, for her help as well as her constant encouragement and support. I wish to thank Norman Graebner for reading the manuscript and making valuable suggestions. John Israel provided useful advice in the early stages of this project. The staff of Indiana University Press deserves a special note of gratitude. Charlotte Gaines of Indiana Central University assisted in the preparation of the map. Numerous librarians and archivists have provided their highly professional services. Finally, I am grateful to the American Philosophical Society for a grant that helped fund my research.

IMPERIALISM
—— *and* ——
IDEALISM

CHAPTER ONE

Imperialism and Idealism

AMERICA'S CHINA POLICY DILEMMA

DURING THE YEARS 1861–1898, the United States sent eight ministers plenipotentiary to China. Anson Burlingame, the first of these envoys and the first American diplomat to reside in Peking, respected China as a sovereign nation and a venerable civilization, and he advocated a policy of patient, peaceful dealings with the Chinese. J. Ross Browne, who followed Burlingame, considered the Chinese backward and stubborn; he favored forceful and united foreign pressure for change in China. The methods of these two ministers—conciliation and coercion—represented the extremes in the American options in China. The policies of their successors generally fell somewhere between the two. Frederick F. Low and Benjamin P. Avery in the early 1870s tried variations of both approaches but achieved few results with either. George F. Seward in the late 1870s made expediency his only policy standard. James B. Angell and John R. Young in the early 1880s attempted to establish an independent American position between the Chinese and the other foreigners. Charles Denby, the last of the group, favored assertive and joint foreign action in China but was repeatedly restrained by the State Department. Overall, the efforts of these envoys gave American policy in China during the four decades preceding John Hay's Open Door Notes an obvious ambivalence that reflected a basic dilemma: Should the United States follow the other Western nations in forcing its will upon China or instead pursue a

[1]

different course premised on respect for Chinese sovereignty? This quandary originated in the competing forces of Western imperialism and American idealism—the two impulses that shaped United States China policy in the nineteenth century.

Tension had always existed between American idealism and more pragmatic assessments of national interest. This basic dichotomy in United States foreign relations had evolved from the historical circumstances of the birth and development of the American nation. From its earliest colonial origins, America had been the setting for a new Zion— "a City upon a Hill" in John Winthrop's immortal phrase—and simultaneously the scene of an elemental struggle for survival in a dangerous wilderness. The early American settlers pursued the ideals of self-government, equality, and opportunity at the same time that they faced the realities of dense forests, cold winters, and hostile foes. Being both spiritual and worldly, they condemned self-indulgence, but not self-interest. The American frontier was a "human whirlwind" in search of wealth and opportunity, and when the wilderness had been transformed into farms, towns, and eventually a new nation, the American people emerged with a sense of moral righteousness. Their secular success confirmed their spiritual faith, but it also produced internal tensions between the pursuit of good and the pursuit of gain. This ambiguity in American values and goals permeated United States conduct abroad as well as at home.[1]

A nation's self-image is always complex and often contradictory. For the United States that basic identity has been shaped by a combination of national aggrandizement and altruistic motives—two objectives that clash but that also complement one another. Among the citizens of the new United States, there was a great sense of pride and self-satisfaction in the presumed uniqueness of American democracy and republicanism. Regardless of the actual economic, social, and political origins and consequences of the American Revolution, a myth of the revolution emerged quickly among Americans that they had achieved a singular accomplishment. They perceived their own nation to be the freest, most democratic, most republican, and most progressive polity ever created. They believed that they had come closer to a virtuous and equitable society than anyone ever before in the long history of mankind, and the magnitude and importance of their success imparted to them a concomitant responsibility. Many Americans considered it a duty to share their superior creation with others. This sense of mission, combined with the previously developed sense of survival, formed a potent prescription for the expansion of American influence in the world.[2]

The outward thrust of the United States was imbued with the same dichotomies that already existed in the minds of Americans. Collectively and individually, Americans were a "people of paradox." They were both moralistic and materialistic, liberal and conservative, democratic and oligarchical, idealistic and pragmatic, altruistic and self-interested, politically naive and clever, interventionist and isolationist. These dualities could be complementary, but most often they presented Americans with choices. The policy options developed by the United States diplomats in China from 1861 to 1898 often reflected this ambiguous tradition.[3]

The eight American ministers in Peking from Burlingame through Denby shared with the majority of their countrymen opposing perceptions of the United States and China based more on idealism than realism. Most Americans had never seen Asia, but they believed that it lagged far behind the United States. Because American citizens conceived of their own nation as the epitome of progress and freedom, they assumed that China, with its archaic imperial government and its hoary Confucian traditions, was the antithesis of all that the United States had achieved. The enormous cultural gap between China and the United States prompted Americans to view the potential for progress in China as almost endless. The desire to bring China into the modern world was evident in both of the two principal types of Americans interested in China—merchants and missionaries. Merchants sincerely believed that capitalism as it had evolved in the West was the dynamic force behind social as well as economic progress. Similarly, missionaries considered Christianity to be a doctrine of both salvation and civilization. Since most merchants were Christians and most missionaries accepted the principles of capitalism, there was no inherent conflict in the two efforts, and in fact the two groups labored side by side in the best American tradition of the compatibility of prayer and profit. Charles Denby described one of these connections between commerce and Christianity: "As the condition of the Chinese improves, his wants will increase. Fancy what would happen to the cotton trade if every Chinese wore a shirt! Well, the missionaries are teaching them to wear shirts."[4] The inextricable link between American ideals and interests made the line between altruism and selfishness very thin in China.[5]

Imperialism denotes, among other things, the arrogance and chauvinism characteristic of those societies that consider themselves technologically and culturally superior to others. This definition fits United States policies in China from 1861 to 1898. Among Americans in China, imperialism was inherent in their efforts to promote progress, their sense of competitiveness with the British and other Europeans, their search for economic bonanzas, and their humanitarian desire to reform and uplift the Chinese. Because of the dualities that existed in American thought and traditions, however, these motives and objectives in China presented the United States diplomatic representatives with some difficult choices. Should the minister allow, for example, Americans to build a railroad line without official Chinese permission, on the grounds that such a project would serve as an example of the benefits of Western technology? Should missionaries be protected if in their quest for converts they traveled beyond areas approved by the imperial authorities? In numerous cases such as these, American ideological and economic aggressiveness often clashed with American ideals of equality and self-determination. Although Americans ascribed to themselves a purity of motives that made them appear either naive or hypocritical, they faced a genuine dilemma in China: How could the sometimes converging but more often competing considerations of idealism and imperialism be reconciled?[6]

The unique circumstances confronting Western diplomats in China magnified the American dilemma. Peking was one of the world's most isolated capitals. Its inhabitants had little, if any, first-hand knowledge of the world beyond its massive walls. Located over 100 miles inland from the nearest seaport and distant from a navigable river, Peking was not on any major trade or travel routes and had no telegraphic communication. The American ministers in the nineteenth century approached Peking by a difficult water and land route. They transferred from deep-water ships to small launches at Taku for the 50-mile trip up the Peiho River to Tientsin. Although gateways to the capital, these two cities, connected by the shallow, crooked Peiho, were unimpressive provincial outposts in comparison to the bustling

Yangtze Valley port of Shanghai, the favorite of foreigners. Beyond Tientsin the river became even more shallow. Flat-bottomed houseboats propelled by boatmen with poles carried the ministers and their parties the next 120 miles to Tungchow. The final leg of the journey— 14 miles overland—was the most arduous of the trip. The road to the capital was in such disrepair that it served as an obstacle rather than a conveyance. Most foreigners managed to secure ponies or sedan chairs, but at least one minister arrived in Peking in one of the dilapidated, springless carts used by most Chinese. The recipient of this dubious distinction reported that the novel vehicle "on several occasions came very near dislocating my vertebrae."[7]

Viewed from a distance, Peking appeared to be a majestic city. Massive walls with pagoda-topped gates guarded the capital. The wall around the southern or Chinese City was thirty feet high and almost as thick. The adjoining northern or Tartar City had an even more imposing wall, which was fifty feet high and sixty feet thick at the base. Looking down from one of these walls was like surveying a huge park of lush, green trees cut at spacious intervals by broad avenues and interspersed with the yellow- and green-tiled roofs of imperial and official buildings. In the center of the Tartar City stood the Imperial and Forbidden cities, the residences of the emperor and his retainers.[8]

Closer inspection, however, revealed Peking also to be a city of incredible filth, stench, and poverty. Beneath the trees and between the rectilinear avenues were meandering dirt paths packed with a wretched humanity and lined with tiny hovels that served as homes. Beggars abounded. The streets were open sewers containing the desiccated refuse of centuries. The acrid odor overwhelmed the outsider. A witty French priest once explained why there was not more cholera in such an unsanitary place. "Cholera!" he exclaimed, "it could never enter. It would be asphyxiated at the gate."[9]

Western diplomats in Peking experienced not only the physical isolation and discomforts of the city but also the extreme ethnocentrism of the Chinese officials. The roots of East Asian society—the Confucian family and social order, the writing system, the imperial bureaucracy—lay in ancient China. The Chinese capital was the political and intellectual hub of an old and highly cultivated civilization that extended beyond China's borders to such satellite kingdoms as Korea, Vietnam, and Mongolia. From the Chinese perspective, Peking was

Hundreds of graceful and elegant buildings with their expansive
courtyards made up the Imperial Palace in Peking—also known as
the Forbidden City.

the center not only of East Asia but of all the world, and this Sinocentrism was evident in Chinese terminology. The emperor was *T'ien-tzu*
(the son of heaven), who ruled *T'ien-hsia* (all under heaven) from
Chung-kuo (the Middle Kingdom or China).[10]

The Chinese world view assumed Chinese superiority. Just as the
emperor ruled his subjects in China through a hierarchic, nonegalitar-
ian system, theoretically he conducted foreign relations the same way.
Although China did not exercise actual dominion over its surrounding
states, it maintained the myth of Chinese suzerainty through traditional forms such as ceremonial tribute missions from the neighboring
kingdoms to Peking. While Westerners refused to concede to even
symbolic Sinocentrism, the ancient tradition continued to shape the
Chinese government's thinking and expression throughout the
nineteenth century. In the imperial government's official records, its
relations with the United States and the European countries were
called "barbarian affairs" *(i-wu)*. The assumption of cultural superior-

ity manifested itself in Chinese recalcitrance toward the Western envoys and their diplomatic efforts.[11]

Far removed from ready contact with home, surrounded by squalor, and constantly frustrated by an arrogant and seemingly unyielding government, the foreign diplomats and their families in Peking gravitated together into a tight group. When Anson Burlingame arrived in 1862, all the foreigners in Peking, including missionaries, numbered less than one hundred among a Chinese population of one-and-a-half million. Burlingame acquired a modest Chinese dwelling across the street from the Russian legation and within a few hundred feet of the British and French. The four legations were situated in walled

The five-clawed dragon, a decorative motif throughout the Imperial Palace, was the symbol of the emperor, the son of heaven who ruled all under heaven.

compounds large enough to allow their inhabitants to live comfortably and avoid daily contact with their surroundings. Among these foreigners a convivial and informal camaraderie existed.[12]

By 1898 the number of legations in Peking had grown to eleven and the number of foreigners to several hundred. The so-called Legation Quarter of the city near the Hata Gate expanded to include churches, schools, banks, and other unofficial foreign buildings and residences. The American legation included several buildings and covered about an acre of land, although its size was still modest in comparison to the seven-acre British compound. Business and society were more formal among the foreigners than they had been in the early 1860s. The Westerners still avoided association with the Chinese, and the legations remained an isolated, alien enclave in Peking.[13]

The interdependence and intimacy of the foreign community in Peking in the nineteenth century created a policy problem for the United States. Consistent with George Washington's Farewell Address and its admonition for international impartiality, American foreign policy had followed a tradition of no close connections and alliances with other countries. In Peking, however, multinational cooperation was part of the daily life of the American minister. In an effort to overcome Chinese recalcitrance, the Western diplomats tended to work together, and hence an independent policy was difficult for the American envoys to maintain.

The foreign-treaty system in China created even greater pressure for international cooperation than did the intimacy of the diplomatic community. Sino-Western relations before 1861 had produced a series of unequal treaties dictated to the Chinese at gunpoint. The British victory over China in the Opium War of 1839–42 led to the Treaty of Nanking, which represented the first codification of a Western nation's legal and commercial rights in the Middle Kingdom. Although the United States and France had not cooperated with Britain in the military and naval actions against China, both of these nations followed the British lead and made their own treaties with the emperor's government. In the American Treaty of Wanghia, signed in 1844, the American negotiator Caleb Cushing was careful to include a most-favored-nation provision, which ensured that the United States received the same terms from the Chinese as had the European nations. Beginning with the Cushing Treaty, American diplomacy endeavored to secure an open door in China for American commerce. The United States displayed a concern for China's political integrity by not adopting the British military tactics, but the American treaty indicated that Washington desired equal commercial advantages.[14]

In the pre-1861 period, the United States government had no explicit policy of cooperation with Britain and France. Two American commissioners to China in the 1850s, Humphrey Marshall and Robert McLane, personally believed that the United States should cooperate with France and Russia in an effort to check the aggressive tendencies of Britain. Commissioner Peter Parker favored cooperation with the British in a scheme in 1856–57 to threaten the Chinese into revising the treaties. If the Chinese failed to comply, Parker advocated that the United States take possession of Formosa, Britain seize the Chusan Islands, and France acquire Korea. The State Department vetoed Parker's plan but did instruct his successor, William B. Reed, to cooperate with the British and French in any peaceful discussions with the Chinese. This instruction had little significance, however, because Britain and France were at war with China when Reed arrived at his post.[15]

The Anglo-French war against China began in 1856 during a dispute over a sailing vessel, the *Arrow*. The Arrow War, as it was called, had its origin in repeated Western demands for more treaty concessions from China and produced the Treaties of Tientsin of 1858. The United States, Britain, France, and Russia made separate treaties with the Chinese. The emperor's representatives signed the American and Russian treaties first, because the United States and Russia had not participated in the military action and because the provisions of their treaties were extremely moderate in comparison to the demands of the other two nations. The Chinese soon agreed to the more comprehensive British and French treaties, however, because the imperial forces were simply no match for the Europeans. Following further hostilities in 1860, Britain and France concluded an additional convention with the Chinese at Peking. These documents finalized the Sino-Western treaty system that Britain, France, and the United States had first established in 1842–44, following the Opium War.[16]

As of 1861, the following treaty provisions governed relations between China and the Western nations: (1) Great Britain, France, Russia, and the United States had the right to maintain resident ministers in Peking. (2) Fifteen Chinese cities were open to foreign trade under the supervision of foreign consuls. (3) Chinese tariffs were subject to mutual agreement among China and the other nations. (4) Foreigners had the right to travel in the interior of China. (5) Foreign missionaries were entitled to protection by Chinese authorities. (6) The Chinese government owed indemnities to the foreigners who had sustained losses during the recent hostilities. (7) Foreign consuls exercised sole judicial authority over foreign residents in China, i.e., extraterritoriality. (8) Each Western signatory enjoyed most-favored-nation treatment on any concession granted by China to any other nation. These stipulations represented the heart of the treaty system.[17]

The most-favored-nation provision interlocked the Western treaties and meant that the Western nations encountered China as a legally unified group. This multinational character of Western diplomacy contravened the idea of separate national policies in China. Among the Western nations, however, the British role was conspicuous in shaping the course of Sino-Western relations before 1900, and, indeed, Great Britain did dominate many aspects of the Western commercial, military, and diplomatic presence in China. The United States and the other Western nations often found themselves participating in a diplomatic system managed primarily from London. Caleb Cushing went to China in 1844 because the United States insisted on its own separate treaty, yet Cushing modeled his Treaty of Wanghia on the British Treaty of Nanking. The Chinese, in fact, encouraged the United States to follow the British lead in an attempt to maintain the fiction that any concessions were the gift of the emperor, not the British navy. In the Treaties of Tientsin, the United States again cooperated with Britain, along with France and Russia, to gain additional concessions from the Chinese. This pattern in America's nineteenth-century China policy has been termed "jackal" diplomacy, which required only knowing how and when to say "me, too."[18]

America's practice of following Britain and using the most-favored-nation principle was sensible given the limited power and interests of the United States in China. America had no territorial ambitions in China, and the Middle Kingdom posed no threat to American security. What the United States desired was the opportunity to carry on a relatively small but profitable trade with the Chinese and the protection of its citizens in China. Given the modest nature of its involvement with China, the United States had no reason to make an extensive independent commitment to ensure the maintenance of these goals. Instead, American policymakers sought to work both with the Chinese government and with other Western nations to protect the limited interests of the United States.

In the 1860s, Secretary of State William H. Seward and Minister Burlingame made cooperation with the other Western powers their official policy. Secretary of State John Hay's Open Door Notes of 1899 and 1900 represented, among other things, another attempt to obtain the cooperation of the other treaty nations in preserving the concept of mutual respect for treaty rights. The concept of Western cooperation that is common to Cushing's treaty, Seward's diplomacy, and Hay's notes gives these policies the appearance of consistency. Consequently, historians of American diplomacy in China who focus on the treaty system—especially on the most-favored-nation clause contained in the treaties—impart to American policy a continuity not only over the years of the nineteenth century but also with the policies of the other Western nations.[19]

Did the policies of the Seward-Burlingame era actually continue through the decades and reappear in Hay's notes?[20] The cooperative policy that Burlingame and Seward inaugurated in the 1860s identified American interests with the enduring welfare of the Chinese government and with continued agreement among the Western nations. Burlingame attempted to implement this approach through cooperation with both the Chinese and his Western colleagues. Could the United States fully cooperate, however, with the Chinese and the foreigners at the same time? Respect for China's political integrity could not always be reconciled with the treaty system that constantly undermined Chinese sovereignty. Cooperation could be with the Westerners against China or with the Chinese against European pressures, but in most cases it could not be both. What kind of cooperation, then, was the United States to sanction? Cooperation was a vague concept. In the years preceding the Open Door Notes, each of the U.S. ministers redefined cooperation, and their definitions were not consistent. J. Ross Browne disagreed sharply with his predecessor Burlingame's efforts to include the Chinese in the cooperative framework and advocated Western unity against the imperial government. The other ministers generally took positions somewhere between those of Burlingame and Browne, and by the time that Hay became secretary of state, he had a whole range of policy suggestions and precedents in China from which to choose. The Open Door Notes did couple the idea of cooperation among the treaty nations with concern for China's sovereignty, but the intervening forty years since the Seward-Burlingame initiative had revealed the incompatibility of these precepts. Hay's notes were a product of American policy contradictions, not continuities.

There was diversity not only among the United States diplomats themselves but also between them and their European counterparts. Although the United States participated fully in the treaty system, both Chinese officials and European diplomats recognized that the American representatives were not simply Yankee imitators of their European colleagues. The British, in particular, noticed that the American envoys, most of whom were not career diplomats, were "more unbuttoned" and had "less affectation" than Her Majesty's foreign-service officers. The Europeans observed that the Americans in China tended to maintain a slightly naive enthusiasm for simple republican virtues that in the United States itself were disappearing. The European diplomats also were aware of the Americans' appearance of "disinterestedness" in China. The Chinese considered the Americans more approachable and less class-conscious than the Europeans. They also viewed the United States as less troublesome and more peaceable than the other Western nations, and the Chinese even harbored some hopes that, because of the successful American Revolution against Britain, the American barbarians might provide some balance against the British barbarians. Although these hopes were usually disappointed, some mandarins still formed favorable opinions of the United States. In general, the "highmindedness and popularity" of the American diplomats caused consternation among some Europeans and created in Chinese eyes a better image of the United States than of the other powers.[21]

Understanding the men who served as United States representatives in China is as essential to interpreting American China policy as is a legal analysis of the treaty system. These diplomats, who came from a wide variety of backgrounds, not only implemented but in large measure determined their nation's policies in the Middle Kingdom. Following the Cushing Treaty, individual American envoys proposed various diplomatic initiatives, but the State Department itself did not always articulate formal policies for China. Most secretaries of state were too involved with other foreign and domestic issues to give much thought to America's limited interests in China. Because Peking was a distant capital on the periphery of Washington's official attention, the State Department usually gave its representatives in China very general instructions that allowed the recipient considerable discretion. Slow means of communication also left the envoys on their own much of the time. The diplomatic officers in China made virtually every decision requiring even the slightest degree of prompt attention, because to confer with Washington by mail required three to six months. Even after telegraphic communication to Shanghai became available in the early 1870s, messages went to East Asia via London and were so expensive to transmit that the American government limited the use of cablegrams to only the most urgent cases. In the years before Hay's Open Door Notes, Seward and other secretaries of state certainly contributed to policy development, but the United States minister in Peking often found the decision making left in his hands.[22]

The varying approaches to China by the American ministers from Burlingame in the 1860s to Denby in the 1890s revealed their differing assumptions about the possibilities of reconciling Eastern and Western civilizations. Burlingame and others believed that a common ground could be found, but men such as Browne considered the two cultures to be too antagonistic to resolve their differences peacefully. All of the American ministers, however, shared a common Western desire to try to make China into something it was not, namely, more like the West. Burlingame and his successors thought in terms of expanding American influence, not empire, but the implicit fact of imperialism was never far removed from American policy.

In 1861 America faced a struggle for its existence as a unified nation, but by the end of the century the United States had survived the Civil War, political scandals, and economic depressions and had emerged as a powerful and united country. The period from the Civil War to the Spanish-American War also saw the United States develop a highly productive industrial economy and assume a position of increasing prominence and influence in international affairs. China, too, began the 1860s fighting a costly civil war—the Taiping Rebellion. Although the imperial government survived this crisis, the ruling Ch'ing Dynasty encountered increasingly severe problems during the remainder of the century. Among the most serious of these challenges was the mounting foreign encroachment on China's sovereignty and territorial integrity. By 1900, China faced a struggle for its existence as a unified nation. As the United States gained power, stability, and prestige, China lost all three.

The changes in the two countries were related. Americans composed part of that foreign presence that contributed to China's problems. The United States certainly did not owe its phenomenal economic growth in the late nineteenth century to its modest trade with China, but the United States stood behind Britain alone in the amount of foreign trade conducted in the Middle Kingdom. The appeal of the China market played a key role, according to some historians, in the United States' acquisition of the Philippine Islands in 1898.[23] Other historians have attributed American expansion in the Pacific to a New Manifest Destiny, which they describe as "a national and 'racial' inheritance, a deep and irresistible inner necessity." Such sociological and psychological interpretations include China as part of the non-white world to which the United States owed a moral obligation to bestow "liberty and hope and happiness."[24]

The task of the United States ministers plenipotentiary in China from 1861 to 1898 was to forge policies out of the commercial, religious, and cultural complexities of the Sino-Western encounter. These eight Americans were a varied group: New England congressman, satirical author, California governor, editor of a literary journal, consular official, college president, New York journalist, and Indiana lawyer. All of these envoys considered China to be socially, politically, spiritually, and technologically backward. In their frustration with Chinese reluctance to recognize the West's self-proclaimed commercial and cultural benefits, some of them came to believe that only force could change China's hidebound ways. They all assumed that China was not physically strong enough to resist the application of Western military and naval force. Although they did not advocate war with the imperial government, some of the ministers recommended that the United States cooperate with the other Western nations to coerce China into reforming its culture and opening its markets and materials to the rest of the world. Disagreeing with this approach, others argued for peaceful cooperation with China, as well as with the other nations, to protect American interests. Their lack of consensus over the course of United States conduct in China revealed the deeply rooted American dilemma over idealism and imperialism. Still unable to resolve the dilemma, John Hay formalized it into a policy in the Open Door Notes, which in turn shaped much of America's twentieth-century conduct in Asia.

CHAPTER TWO

"Fair Diplomatic Action"

ANSON BURLINGAME AND THE
COOPERATIVE POLICY IN CHINA

AMONG THE GROUP of pioneer American diplomats in China, Anson Burlingame stands out, not because he was the first to reside in Peking but because of his long-enduring impact on United States policies in China. Burlingame's approach to Sino-Western relations was known as the "cooperative policy," which meant cooperation *with* the Chinese as well as cooperation among the Western representatives in China. Burlingame was the opposite of the "gunboat" diplomatist and consciously endeavored to transform Western policy methods in China from force to forbearance. He did not model his actions on British or other Western policies. Instead, his efforts as a diplomat reflected his background as a reformer long active in the antislavery struggles in America in the 1840s and 1850s. Burlingame instinctively recoiled against the bigoted attitudes and injustices inherent in Western coercive practices in China. In 1867 the Chinese recognized his conciliatory policy by naming him as their first official envoy to the Western nations. As a diplomat in the service of first the United States and then China, he became a self-proclaimed harmonizer of the Eastern and Western civilizations. His idealism was not equaled by that of any of his American successors in Peking, but it established one of the policy options for American diplomats in China in the second half of the nineteenth century.

Accompanied by two Chinese co-envoys (Chih-kang and Sung Chia-ku), Anson Burlingame officially represented China in the United States and Europe from 1867 to 1871, after having served for six years as the first United States minister to reside in Peking. *Library of Congress.*

Burlingame had no diplomatic experience before going to China, but he was endowed with two of a diplomat's greatest assets—an extraordinarily attractive personality and a natural gift of eloquence. The son of a lay preacher, he grew up on the Ohio and Michigan frontier in the 1820s and 1830s. He first demonstrated his lifelong talent for stump oratory while a student at the Detroit branch of the fledgling University of Michigan. A popular student, he was prominent in college politics. After graduation he went to work in a Detroit law office. He quickly acquired a large circle of friends among the city's leading citizens and was frequently invited to address lodge meetings and other groups. In later years young Burlingame was remembered in Detroit as having "a charming and persuasive manner, and promising talents as an orator."[1] The twenty-two-year-old Burlingame left Michigan in 1843 to broaden his horizons at Harvard Law School. After graduation from Harvard, he remained in Massachusetts as a permanent, and soon prominent, resident of Cambridge. In Boston, as in Detroit, his winning personality carried him into the elite circles of society. Many of his closest friends were the young and enthusiastic antislavery reformers known as Free Soilers. Richard Henry Dana, Jr., a member of this group, observed that Burlingame "is a warm hearted, full blooded fellow, and everybody likes him."[2]

Burlingame's public career began in 1848, when he joined Charles Sumner and others from Massachusetts in support of Martin Van Buren's unsuccessful Free Soil candidacy for president. Burlingame contributed his considerable ability as a speaker to Massachusetts's effort against the fugitive-slave provision of the Compromise of 1850. During the 1850s he also championed other reform causes, such as the promotion of American aid to the Hungarian revolutionary Louis Kossuth. Burlingame's social-reform activities brought him public notice, which first carried him into state politics and, finally, in 1855 took him to the United States House of Representatives.[3]

During his first congressional term, Burlingame's youthful spirit and sincere commitment to just principles propelled him into the role of a Northern regional hero. In the spring of 1856, Senator Charles Sumner, Burlingame's friend and fellow antislavery advocate, delivered an important Senate speech against slavery in Kansas. Congressman Preston Brooks of South Carolina considered portions of the speech personally insulting to his kinsman South Carolina senator Andrew P.

Butler. Brooks retaliated against Sumner by beating him severely with a cane while the senator sat at his desk in the Senate chamber. In a House speech, Burlingame denounced in his ringing oratorical style this brutal infringement of Sumner's freedom of speech. Brooks quickly challenged Burlingame to a duel. Burlingame accepted, and as the man challenged, the former Michigan frontiersman chose rifles as the weapons and the Canadian side of Niagara Falls as the site. Brooks refused to travel to a location so deep in hostile Northern territory. Burlingame had hoped for this result, but to the Northern public it appeared that the cowardly Brooks had backed down from an almost certainly fatal confrontation with rifles. Burlingame's skillful handling of "Bully" Brooks gave the New Englander a reputation in the North as "a northern man who would fight."[4]

Burlingame's "manly and honorable" conduct during the Brooks affair, his extraordinarily attractive personality, and his speaking talents made him one of the most popular and effective orators for the new Republican party. In 1860 he spent so much time away from Massachusetts stumping for Abraham Lincoln that he neglected his own reelection bid and lost his House seat. President Lincoln repaid his zealous advocate with a diplomatic appointment to Vienna. Before Burlingame assumed his new post, however, the Austrian monarchy objected to his past association with Kossuth and declared him persona non grata. The Lincoln administration then changed Burlingame's assignment to Peking. The fighter for causes set off to tackle his most difficult challenge: to bridge the cultural gap between the Eastern and Western civilizations.[5]

The new minister arrived at the Portuguese colony of Macao on the southern coast of China in October 1861, a month before his forty-first birthday. Largely because the winter made Peking inaccessible, he did not proceed to the Chinese capital until the following July. Since the United States had no legation building, he bought a small house in Peking with half of his first year's salary. The other half had been used to pay his transportation to China. He had no staff other than Samuel Wells Williams, the missionary-turned-diplomat who served as secretary of the legation. In the hills twelve miles west of Peking, Burlingame established a summer legation at Sanshanan (Temple of the Three Hills). He named it "Tremont Temple," after the favorite Free Soil meeting place in Boston.[6]

The new minister's lack of diplomatic experience did not handicap him as much in Peking as it might have elsewhere. Diplomacy in the Chinese capital in the early 1860s was conducted on a personal and informal basis. In addition to Burlingame, the only other diplomatic representatives permanently stationed in Peking were the British, French, and Russian ministers. The total of legation personnel, missionaries, and other Westerners in the capital city numbered less than one hundred, and the small group of Western diplomats was a close personal as well as professional community. In a private letter to Secretary of State William H. Seward, Burlingame wrote that "my colleagues are all my warm friends."[7] In this situation Burlingame, the congenial and engaging politician with the natural talent of persuasion and eloquence, easily assumed a predominant role among the Westerners in the Chinese capital.[8]

Burlingame formed an especially close personal friendship with Sir Frederick Bruce, the British minister. Bruce, a bachelor, visited Burlingame and his wife almost every day. The two men would sit for hours, smoking and talking about a wide variety of subjects. These visits frequently included dinner and continued into the evening with card games, poetry reading, or more discussion if some diplomatic issue were pressing. Historical assessments premised on national power and interest have consistently given Britain the leading position in Western affairs in China. The special relationship between Burlingame and Bruce, however, challenged the usual assumptions. The likable American minister and his opinions had much more weight in Peking than the power and interest of the United States indicated. In their daily talks, the two envoys often discussed the treaty system and Chinese sovereignty. The missionary-educator W. A. P. Martin, who personally observed the Burlingame-Bruce relationship, wrote: "Each imagined that he was leading the other. Like double stars, their influence was mutual, but in power of persuasion Bruce was no match for Burlingame."[9]

Burlingame overcame quickly his lack of knowledge of China. Before receiving his appointment to the post in Peking, he had never taken any interest in Asia. He had made only one recorded reference to China on the floor of the House of Representatives. Employing an orator's stereotype, he had remarked that when he was ready to depart from practicality, he would "join the immovable civilization of

China, and take the false doctrines of Confucius for my guide, with their backward-looking thoughts."[10] After arriving in China, he began to understand that such comments were symptomatic of the gulf of misunderstanding that separated the Eastern and Western civilizations. Both Chinese and Westerners were basically ignorant and disrespectful of each other's culture. Consequently, Westerners had often resorted to coercion of the Chinese in an effort to overcome stubborn and haughty Chinese resistance to Western intrusions into China. In the face of Western threats and force, the Chinese became even more recalcitrant. Burlingame later recalled: "When I came to China, in 1861, the force policy was the rule. It was said 'the Chinese are conceited barbarians, and must be forced into our civilization;' or, in the energetic language of the time, it was said, 'you must take them by the throat.'"[11] In this clash of cultures, Burlingame recognized some of the same racial and social prejudices that had surrounded the slavery issue in the United States. At home he had always opposed the coercion of one race by another, and in China he continued to adhere to that same principle.[12]

The 1860s were a crucial period in the history of both the United States and China, and Anson Burlingame became a connecting link between the domestic events in the two countries. In America the abolitionist and Free Soil crusades for human equality had precipitated a civil war that wrought sweeping changes in American life. Those same American reform forces were carried to China in 1861 by Burlingame, and once in China he found a new cause to champion. The Ch'ing Dynasty, which had ruled China since 1644, was finally suppressing the bloody Taiping Rebellion, which had raged since 1850. This domestic upheaval and the foreign invasions of China during the Opium War of 1839–42, the Arrow War of 1856–58, and the British-French occupation of Peking of 1860 had dealt the imperial government several near-fatal blows. In an attempt to revive itself, the dynasty embarked upon the T'ung-chih Restoration in 1862.[13] For slightly more than a decade, the restoration leaders made a valiant effort to reach an accommodation with the modern West while trying to preserve the basic values and institutions of China's centuries-old tradition. This struggle for reform within tradition appealed strongly to Burlingame's idealistic spirit.

Shortly before Burlingame's arrival in Peking, the Chinese government had created the Tsungli Yamen, China's first Western-style foreign office. This effort to reform its diplomatic methods represented an attempt by the emperor's court to defend China's interests under the unequal treaties. Initially the Tsungli Yamen consisted of only three prominent Chinese officials and had only a weak and informal role in the government. The mandarin in charge of this new office, however, was Prince Kung, the de facto head of the Chinese government. Under his leadership the Tsungli Yamen quickly became the chief contact between the Western representatives and the imperial government. Traditionally, the Chinese had assumed that all other nations were morally and culturally inferior to the Middle Kingdom and had treated other countries as tributary states. Most Chinese officials in the 1860s still adhered to this hierarchical and Sinocentric world view. The Tsungli Yamen met stiff domestic opposition, because it represented a new, more direct, and egalitarian mode of international relations. Burlingame recognized that Prince Kung's efforts were a dramatic innovation in Chinese foreign policy, and the American became a sympathetic supporter of the prince's reform efforts.[14]

Burlingame believed that attention had to be given to the manner of conducting diplomacy in China before questions of trade, residence, and other legal issues arising under the treaties could be successfully resolved. To move beyond the pattern of Western coercion and Chinese recalcitrance, a new relationship of mutual respect for each other's civilization had to be established. Burlingame perceived that the basic conflict was one of cultures. The Chinese idea of a hierarchical world order arranged below a morally superior China collided with the Western concept of theoretically coequal states. The values of the industrial-commercial West often directly opposed the values of agrarian China. Burlingame made the critical assumption that these differences were reconcilable.[15]

The American minister remained cautious of British intentions in China, although he knew that Bruce personally concurred with his desire to see conciliation replace coercion in Western policy. As recently as 1860, Britain and France had occupied Peking militarily, and in 1859 Bruce himself had given the order for the British fleet to force its way past the Chinese forts at Taku, the port serving Tientsin and Peking. In March of 1862, however, Secretary of State Seward instructed Burlingame to follow the lead of Britain and France in China,

As head of the Tsungli Yamen, Prince Kung was the principal Chinese official with whom Western diplomats dealt in the 1860s and early 1870s. *Stuart Collection, Rare Books and Manuscript Division, The New York Public Library, Astor, Lenox and Tilden Foundation.*

since the American Civil War prevented any independent course of action by the United States.

Seward's March 6, 1862 instruction to Burlingame indicated the secretary of state's thinking on cooperation with the Europeans:

> Great Britain and France are not only represented in China by diplomatic agents, but their agents are supported by land and naval forces, while, unfortunately, you are not. The interests of this country in China, so far as I understand them, are identical with those of the two other nations I have mentioned. There is no reason to doubt that the British and French ministers are acting in such a manner as will best promote the interests of all the western nations. You are therefore instructed to consult and cooperate with them. . . . Our domestic affairs are improving very rapidly, and I trust we shall soon be able to send a war steamer to your support.[16]

Seward reasoned in terms of power and interest. Britain, France, and the United States shared a similar interest in China—namely, the desire to carry on trade on equitable terms. As Seward saw the situation, the two European nations had power (troops and ships) in Asia, and America did not. He assumed that the other countries would initiate policy and the United States would simply cooperate with them, or, in other words, follow their leadership. If American naval vessels had been available for service in China, Seward's policy might have been different. With the government at home fighting a war for survival, however, he decided that cooperation was the only feasible course for the United States.[17]

Seward's instruction pleased Burlingame, but the minister's enthusiasm for cooperation contrasted sharply with the secretary's acquiescence to the policy. Burlingame reasoned in philosophical terms. Political and social beliefs, not power and interest, formed the policy standards of this long-time crusader for freedom and democracy. For him the dictates of morality and friendship required cooperation in China—not only with the other Westerners but with the Chinese as well. Furthermore, Burlingame refused to defer to the representatives of any other countries in deciding what American policy in China would be. In acknowledging Seward's instruction, Burlingame agreed to cooperate with but not necessarily follow the Europeans:

> To be neutral [in China] is to be indifferent, not only to the rights of our citizens but to the interests of civilization. If at any future time the

English or French, or either of them, should menace the integrity of the Chinese territory, then the very fact that we had acted with them for law and order would give us greater weight against such a policy. There is great temptation for them to aggress [against the Chinese]. . . . If the treaty powers could agree among themselves to guarantee the neutrality of China and together secure order in the treaty Ports and give their moral support at least to that party in the Empire which would most favor a stable government, the interests of humanity would be subserved.[18]

Burlingame and Seward may have been using the same words, but they were not speaking the same language. Historians have frequently linked the cooperative policy that soon developed in Peking with Seward's name. Actually, Seward and Burlingame made very different assumptions about American policy and defined cooperation differently. Seward deserves little credit for the cooperative policy as it actually manifested itself in China.[19]

In pursuit of his objective of peaceful East-West accommodation, Burlingame in June 1863 initiated a formal system of cooperation among the Western nations in China. In round-robin negotiations, he secured an agreement from ministers Bruce, Jules Berthemy of France, and L. D. Balluzeck of Russia to respect China's territorial integrity and assist China in entering the family of nations. Although many foreign merchants and missionaries in the treaty ports hoped to exploit the unstable conditions in China created by the Taiping Rebellion, "the four Bs," as the ministers were called, believed that their nations' interests were best served by a stable government in Peking. Under Burlingame's leadership the ministers sought cooperation with the officials of the new T'ung-chih emperor.[20]

Specifically, Burlingame gained the agreement of his three Western colleagues in Peking to the following: (1) to claim only their nations' treaty rights in the ports and not to claim any concessions that violated China's sovereignty or territorial integrity; (2) not to take part in China's internal affairs; but (3) to sustain jointly their treaty rights against any who violated them, including the Taiping rebels; (4) to give moral support and military advice to the government; but (5) not to place foreign officers on the field of battle; (6) to aid the government in protection of its revenues against pirates with a cosmopolitan naval force under the command of the Englishman Sherard Osborn; (7) to aid

China in organizing a national army according to European principles; and (8) to support the Chinese custom-house system as it had been administered by the Englishman Horatio Nelson Lay. These points represented the first tangible manifestations of the cooperative policy.[21]

In the course of securing agreement to this list of self-denying statements, unique in the history of Sino-Western relations, Burlingame naturally held his most extended discussions with his friend Bruce. Bruce gave his unqualified support to Burlingame's efforts to initiate a cooperative approach to the resolution of Sino-Western issues. The Englishman's reasons for endorsing cooperation, however, were not necessarily identical to those of the American. Burlingame tended to stress the interests of civilization and humanity more than specific American interests. Bruce, on the other hand, expressed more concern about the precise interests of Britain. Noting Russian and French expansion in the Amur-Ussuri region and in Indochina, he viewed cooperation as providing a diplomatic basis for checking these rivals of Britain. The cooperative plan appeared to be a less costly alternative than military force for protecting British interests. Bruce realized that diplomacy alone might not provide foreigners adequate security. Like Burlingame, he argued that gunboat tactics to resolve foreign grievances only undermined the authority of an already weak imperial government and made life in China even more chaotic and insecure for foreigners.[22]

The cooperative policy, this new coordinated Western effort to meet the Chinese government halfway, did not mean the end of Sino-Western antagonism. Although the newly created Chinese foreign office, the Tsungli Yamen, seemed receptive, many Chinese officials remained obdurately antiforeign. The Western nations happened to be represented in 1863 by a unique group of men who trusted each other and the Tsungli Yamen. "Our only hope" for improved Sino-Western relations, Burlingame wrote to the secretary of state, "is in forbearance and perfect union among ourselves."[23] To maintain this policy, Burlingame hoped that the four Western governments would somehow formalize the agreement made among their ministers. Privately he urged Seward to "sustain the policy we have agreed to and do what you can to secure its adoption by the other treaty powers at home."[24]

Within a few years, Burlingame himself would go to Europe and America seeking the same thing on behalf of the Chinese government.

In approving Burlingame's efforts, Seward indicated that he was well aware that the cooperative policy depended on the personalities of the "enlightened representatives" in Peking. He feared "that the beneficial policy thus agreed upon would fall into disuse, if those ministers, or any of them should at any time give place to less intelligent and able statesmen."[25] Despite his doubts about the durability of Burlingame's policy, the secretary of state praised his minister in Peking and wished him good luck. There was little else, however, that Seward could do. With the Union victories at Vicksburg and Gettysburg in July 1863, the Civil War in America had reached a critical stage. Since Seward was preoccupied with the war, Burlingame was more than ever on his own in far away Peking.

Under Burlingame's leadership and inspiration, the cooperative policy in China got off to an auspicious beginning. The foreign representatives and Chinese officials worked together to solve several practical problems arising under the treaties. Some of these cases were confined to discussion among the parties of some legal technicality in the implementation of the treaties. On other occasions, however, diplomatic questions threatened to result in hostilities that could have extinguished all hopes of peaceful cooperation. In each case Burlingame rallied his Western and Chinese colleagues to the maintenance of the liberal and deliberative principles of the cooperative policy.

Only a few days after the Western representatives had formalized their agreement to cooperate, Prince Wittgenstein, the newly arrived Prussian minister, sought permission to reside in Peking, although no existing treaty gave him that right. He asked Burlingame to approach the Chinese government on his behalf. Acting with his three colleagues in Peking, Burlingame made the request. The members of the Tsungli Yamen claimed that they were willing to approve it but feared that antiforeign officials might attack the government for granting more than was required by treaty. Whether or not conservative opinion was the reason for the Tsungli Yamen's position, Burlingame expressed understanding of the government's "difficulties" and asked the prince to wait until a more propitious time to renew the request. The

Prussian accepted this outcome without protest and agreed to trust the judgment of the ministers in Peking as to when to inquire again. The sensitivity of Burlingame and the other ministers to the Chinese position was remarkable, since Western diplomats in China during the nineteenth century more commonly joined together to press demands upon the government instead of advising the petitioner to wait until a time more suitable to the Chinese. To Burlingame the cooperative policy meant cooperation with China as well as with the Western nations.[26]

Numerous other examples from the State Department archives reveal how Burlingame put his concept of cooperation into practice. One instance was the case of the American merchant ship *Lucky Star*. The vessel went aground on the coast of China in June 1863, and the people on the shore plundered the wreck. Charles Nelson, the ship's master, sought to make a claim against the Chinese government for his losses. Burlingame refused to present the case to the Tsungli Yamen, because Nelson had insufficient evidence to support the amount of his claim. Also, Nelson had not complied with Article XIII of the American Treaty of Tientsin, requiring the claimant to give evidence of official misconduct by the local authorities. Burlingame in this and other cases expressed his respect for China as a sovereign nation.[27]

The United States minister's unwavering commitment to cooperation with the government in Peking met some serious challenges at times from other Westerners in China—including Americans. One such case was the affair of Henry Andrea Burgevine, which began as an apparent success for the cooperative approach but ended severely testing the policy's very foundations. Burgevine was an American soldier of fortune with a proven record of military ability but with an allegiance only to himself. His career in China started in the ranks of General Frederick T. Ward's Ever-Victorious Army, a Chinese army with foreign officers organized to fight the anti-Ch'ing Taiping rebels. Burgevine quickly became one of Ward's chief subordinates and most successful commanders. When Ward died in battle in September 1862, Burgevine secured the appointment as his successor. There had been opposition to Burgevine's promotion, because each of the Western ministers in Peking desired to see one of his own countrymen lead the Ever-Victorious Army. Interceding for Burgevine, Burlingame argued that since Ward was an American and since an Englishman

(Sherard Osborn) would be commanding a Chinese naval force, an American should remain at the head of the army. Ultimately the other ministers agreed to accept Burgevine, and Burlingame hailed the resolution of this seeming impasse as a great victory for the cooperative spirit.[28]

Almost immediately the new commander of the Ever-Victorious Army ran into serious trouble with the Chinese government. Charging him with stealing public funds and numerous other crimes, the government offered a reward for his execution. Burlingame liked Burgevine personally and believed that corrupt local officials, whom Peking refused to defy, had framed the American. With the help of Bruce and after extended correspondence with the Chinese government, Burlingame managed to clear the mercenary of all charges. In the interim, however, the clearly unprincipled Burgevine had joined the rebels against the government. He later returned to the government lines under the protection of the Ever-Victorious Army's new British commander, Major Charles G. (Chinese) Gordon, but maintained that he had not deserted the rebels and that he remained hostile to the government. Threatened with a trial by American consul general George F. Seward at Shanghai, Burgevine fled China. He soon returned, however, and Seward arrested him. The exasperated consul general informed his uncle, the secretary of state, that Burgevine "is determined to be a martyr and sorry am I that I cannot but advance his wishes."[29] Even the usually patient Burlingame gave up on Burgevine and notified the State Department that he would now work as hard to defeat the American adventurer as he had once done to sustain him.[30]

Although Burgevine had gained release from custody in Shanghai by promising to leave China, he reappeared on Taiwan trying to contact the rebels. Local Chinese officials captured him but refused to turn him over to the American consul as required by the extraterritoriality provisions of the treaties. The government declared Burgevine a traitor and announced that he would be executed. Acting as chargé d'affaires in Burlingame's absence, Samuel Wells Williams agreed, in keeping with the cooperative spirit of the times, to let the Chinese hold the prisoner while he requested instructions from Washington. Before Secretary Seward could reply, in the summer of 1865 Burgevine drowned "accidentally" while being transported inland by his captors.[31]

The Burgevine case brought one of the basic tenets of the cooperative policy—recognition of China's sovereignty—into direct conflict with one of the cornerstones of the treaty system—extraterritoriality. Burlingame and Williams believed Burgevine to be guilty of treason against the Chinese government. With a civil war raging in the United States, the two Americans were receptive to the government's claim of China's right to protect itself against rebellion. Secretary of State Seward previously had informed America's diplomatic representatives: "The nation has a right, and it is its duty, to live. . . . In taking this ground, the United States claim only what they concede to all other nations."[32] Because Burgevine was an American citizen, however, the extraterritoriality provisions of the treaties protected him without qualification from any form of punishment by the Chinese authorities. Although Secretary Seward had agreed before learning of the drowning to accept Chinese jurisdiction, Burgevine's sudden demise left the legal question unresolved. The secretary of state had stipulated that his consent was given voluntarily "upon the grounds of national honor," and not because of any treaty provision. Seward never acknowledged the legality of any of China's claims to Burgevine and later indicated that he considered the American to have been murdered. Chargé d'affaires Williams, who shared Burlingame's assumptions about cooperation, believed the Chinese claim of accidental drowning.[33]

While the Burgevine case dramatized the East-West legal complications inherent in the cooperative policy, the simultaneous controversy over the Lay-Osborn flotilla threatened to destroy completely the fragile cooperative framework. Horatio Nelson Lay, the English head of the Chinese customs service, arranged to procure a flotilla of modern English warships for the Chinese government's coastal defenses. The four Western ministers in Peking had endorsed this plan in their June 1863 statement of cooperation with the Chinese government. Initially the crews were to be English sailors under the command of Sherard Osborn, an English officer, but eventually the force was to be cosmopolitan. Burlingame expressed doubts about the wisdom of an all-English operation but assented to the scheme because of his complete confidence in his good friend Bruce. Despite his objections to the details, the American minister welcomed the idea of an efficient Western navy in the service of China. He believed that the flotilla would enable the Chinese authorities not only to resist the rebels but also to enforce China's maritime regulations. He knew that many Americans who had grown accustomed to weak application of customs laws would protest, but Burlingame believed that respect for China's sovereignty was in the best interest of all the countries involved.[34]

The plan proceeded smoothly until the flotilla arrived in China in the fall of 1863. The Chinese government refused to accept the ships on Lay's terms, and a diplomatic crisis ensued. Bruce immediately prepared to support his countryman Lay, struck the flag of the British legation, and broke communications with the Peking government. Discussions continued, however, through the American legation. Finally, after three tense days, Sir Frederick stopped pacing the floor in Burlingame's house and announced his decision to remain neutral in the conflict between the Chinese government and its agent Lay. Bruce's reversal marked an important triumph for both Burlingame personally and his policy. War would have made cooperation a dead letter.[35]

Burlingame played a critical role in this episode, which was central to the cooperative policy. Lay had demanded a veto over any orders given Osborn by the Chinese government. Prince Kung, head of the Tsungli Yamen, had refused the fleet on these terms, which were manifestly inconsistent with Chinese sovereignty. Lay had then asked that Bruce and his Western colleagues "menace" the government into acquiescence to his demand. Burlingame not only provided the critical communication link between Bruce and the Tsungli Yamen but also served as the British minister's confidant. He consistently urged the Englishman to adhere to the peaceful doctrines of cooperation and not to heed Lay's counsels of force. Even after Bruce decided to withhold support from Lay, the American continued to act as intermediary. The Tsungli Yamen solicited Burlingame's advice on the disposition of the warships and the removal of Lay. Fearing that the flotilla might fall into the hands of Japanese feudal lords, Chinese pirates, or the Confederates in America, Burlingame arranged for the Chinese to return the ships to England through Bruce. In addition, he assured the Chinese government that the Western representatives would not interfere in the naming of Robert Hart to replace Lay as head of the customs service.[36]

The American minister also went to the aid of his colleague Bruce against anticipated criticism from British officials who advocated a forceful policy toward the Chinese government. Burlingame summarized the situation:

> There are two schools of Englishman. One would "take the Chinese by the throat" and take the country *a la* India. The other would deal fairly by them—would maintain the integrity of the Chinese Empire leaving every nation the inspiration of fair opportunity. Sir Frederick Bruce belongs to the latter school. . . .[37]

Seeking to protect both his friend and the cooperative policy, Burlingame asked Seward to commend Bruce's conduct to the British government and to publish the details of the Lay-Osborn affair. The secretary of state complied with the request, terminating a crisis that began on the brink of war between England and China and ended with a reassertion of the peaceful doctrines of cooperation.[38]

In 1864 Burlingame requested a leave of absence, after having been away from the United States for over three years. He departed from China in May 1865 and did not return to the American legation in Peking until September 1866. Although he was absent from his post for many months, he continued to work for the principles of cooperation as he traveled first to London and then to Washington. In the British capital he conveyed to Her Majesty's government the Tsungli Yamen's urgent concerns about an unresolved problem stemming from the Lay-Osborn flotilla. Britain had not repaid the Chinese government for Osborn's ships, although the vessels had been returned to England over a year earlier. Conservative officials in Peking, who were hostile to the very existence of the Tsungli Yamen, were holding its members personally responsible for the public funds spent on the flotilla and as yet unrecovered. If the remittance was not received soon, the ministers of China's foreign office, with whom the cooperative policy had been conceived, would be placed in an untenable political position. Burlingame was able to secure from British officials in London a commitment to pay for the vessels as soon as possible. Going on to Washington in November 1865, he had a reunion with Sir Frederick Bruce, whose government had transferred him to the American capital the previous year. Bruce agreed to help expedite the final financial settlement between London and Peking. Burlingame's timely assistance enabled the Tsungli Yamen to withstand the challenge of its conservative critics and helped ensure the continued existence of the fledgling Chinese foreign office. Once again Burlingame had salvaged the fragile cooperative policy.[39]

Shortly after Burlingame's return to China in 1866, two tragedies occurred in Korea that confronted the cooperative policy with another serious challenge. In one case, Koreans massacred several French missionaries and native converts. In the other incident, the American schooner *General Sherman* was wrecked on the Korean coast, and all aboard were murdered. The French responded to the attack on their missionaries with a punitive naval expedition of six ships and six-hundred men. Not receiving any satisfaction from Korean officials, however, the French admiral announced that he would return in the spring with a larger force. When Burlingame questioned Prince Kung about the *General Sherman*, the Chinese government's chief official denied any responsibility for the action of the Koreans. In Burlingame's opinion, this response removed the matter from his jurisdiction, but he wrote to Admiral H. H. Bell, commander of the American Asiatic Squadron, and suggested that a naval vessel be sent to Korea to investigate and report to Washington for instructions. Burlingame did not recommend forceful retaliation against the Koreans, and, in fact, his suggestion that the admiral consult with Washington may have been intended to dissuade the squadron commander from taking some precipitate action.[40]

Burlingame considered French officials in China since Jules Berthemy's departure in 1865 to be overly ambitious and hostile to the Chinese. Anticipating a second French expedition, he joined British minister Sir Rutherford Alcock and Russian minister George Vlangaly in plans to go to Korea at the same time as the French. They assumed that France intended to force open the Hermit Kingdom to foreign commerce, and the three men believed that they should be present to protect their countries' interests. Burlingame also hoped the three ministers could use their influence to prevent violence and promote friendship among the parties involved. He wrote Seward officially and privately, requesting permission to go to Korea to protect "the interests of civilization." The minister feared not only that the French might menace the Koreans but also that the chief United States naval officer in East Asia might be contemplating a military response to the sinking of the *General Sherman*. "Admiral Bell is a good and cautious officer," Burlingame observed, "but all naval officers know more about fighting than they do about making treaties."[41]

When Burlingame's request reached Seward, the secretary of state reacted very differently to the situation in Korea than had the minister. Thinking of the *General Sherman*, Seward proposed to join, not restrain, France in obtaining satisfaction in the form of a treaty with Korea. Furthermore, he told Berthemy, now French minister in Washington, that "it is expedient that the two countries [the United States and France] seek no foreign assistance in this circumstance and that, if there is need to resort to force of arms, no other flag fly next to theirs."[42] In contrast to Burlingame, Seward was perfectly willing to use force in Korea and also to exclude Britain from the affair. Berthemy, one of "the four Bs" who had initiated the cooperative policy, reported Seward's unwritten proposal to his government. Although the French minister made no recommendations, he implied in his dispatch that he disapproved of the secretary of state's suggestion. Paris concurred with Berthemy and rejected not only Seward's plans but also those of its own agents in China. The French government had no desire at that time to engage its forces in Korea, especially at the risk of antagonizing Great Britain.[43]

Seward finally wrote Burlingame denying him permission to go to Korea. The secretary explained only that he had "reason to believe" that France anticipated no further action there. After Burlingame left China in 1867, Secretary Seward revealed his continuing interest in Korea by approving a request by Consul General Seward in Shanghai to negotiate a treaty with some alleged Korean agents. The elder Seward instructed his nephew to avoid any threat of force in the discussions but permitted him to remind the Koreans that the "outrage" against the *General Sherman* could not remain permanently without redress. Because the supposed envoys turned out not to represent the Korean government, the negotiations never began, and Seoul remained unreceptive to any type of talks. This denouement saved Secretary Seward's reputation, because later information proved Burlingame's caution in the *General Sherman* case to have been correct. The American crew had precipitated its own fate by being in an unauthorized place and antagonizing the local officials. Seward automatically assumed the Koreans were guilty. Burlingame did not.[44]

Military force, or "gunboat diplomacy," competed with cooperation as the other policy alternative in Asia. The Opium War of 1839–42 and the Arrow War of 1856–58 had established among Westerners the efficacy of negotiation at gunpoint. Every foreigner in China believed that the Chinese could not possibly withstand the power of Western navies and armies whenever foreign governments chose to employ them. Consequently, many Western merchants, diplomats, military officers, and even missionaries constantly urged the application of this forceful approach to every question in China.

Not surprisingly, Burlingame, the long-time opponent of injustice, vigorously condemned this "tyrannic element which would treat the Chinese as *quasi* slaves."[45] His entire career in China testified to his opposition to the use of force for making demands on the Chinese. He recognized, however, that some Western military and naval units were needed in China for protection of foreigners. He became concerned, for example, that the Chinese government could not adequately protect foreigners when a Taiping army threatened Shanghai in 1861–63. At those times when antiforeign violence flared in China, Burlingame especially deplored the dependence of Americans on the British navy for protection. He complained to Seward that "it is very mortifying to an American to be told by an Englishman, 'You are indebted to the British for what protection you have on the coast of China.' "[46] Such comments, especially since they were true, not only rankled Burlingame's patriotic pride but also suggested grave diplomatic implications. He had warned the secretary of state at the inception of the cooperative policy that British and French power created a "great temptation to aggress" against China, and he had sought to make American participation in the cooperative policy a restraint on that temptation. He drew a parallel between some Englishmen in China and the hated overseers who had supervised the slaves on Southern plantations. Burlingame declared emphatically that his goal was "to end a system of overseerism on the part of those . . . British officers who look upon China as a kind of English preserve."[47]

Burlingame suggested to Seward that the United States could use one large ship and five smaller vessels in China. He also requested that the commanders be selected from among officers "who will at all times be regardful of the rights and feelings of the Chinese, and who will understand the co-operative policy which is a substitution of fair diplomatic action for force."[48] While the Civil War lasted, the United States occasionally had one naval vessel in Chinese waters but usually had none. After the war the small American Asiatic Squadron of five vessels finally appeared, under the command of Admiral Bell. Britain, on the other hand, had forty-five warships, including twenty-nine gunboats, in China in 1866.[49]

Although able and cautious, Bell and his officers simply did not possess the ideal qualifications that Burlingame had stipulated. For example, in 1865 when an American missionary tried to acquire a house at Tangchau near Chefoo (in Shantung province) and encountered strong opposition from the local population, Burlingame appealed to the Tsungli Yamen to enforce the treaty provisions ensuring foreign residence in China. Before his conversations with the government had produced any results, however, Burlingame left for the United States on his long-sought leave of absence. Following the minister's departure, Admiral Bell dispatched one of his ships, the USS *Wachusetts*, to Tangchau. Taking one hundred men into the town, Commander Townsend of the *Wachusetts* and the American consul at Chefoo threatened the Chinese prefect and demanded punishment of guilty parties, an indemnity, and security in the future for foreign residents. The admiral reported to Secretary of the Navy Gideon Wells that "Commander Townsend has performed the duty assigned to him with commendable zeal and decision."[50] Burlingame, on the other hand, reacted to the incident by reasserting his determined opposition to "gunboat propagandism."[51]

The greatest proof of Burlingame's consistently cooperative and conciliatory attitude toward the Chinese came in November 1867, when the imperial government appointed him its first diplomatic envoy to the Western nations. Prince Kung and his colleagues in the government expressed the same confidence in Burlingame as he had in them. They were registering their understandable approval of his cooperative approach over the coercive methods of other Westerners. Burlingame's acceptance of this unprecedented appointment terminated his diplomatic ministry in Peking and opened a new chapter in his life and in the history of the cooperative policy. What the future held for this man and his methods was not clearly discernible. Burlingame remained the perpetual optimist, but many others, including both Chinese and Westerners, were skeptical about his abilities to win adherents to his peaceful doctrines. Although the path ahead was uncertain, the impact of the New England reformer on American and Western policies in China was already apparent.[52]

As United States minister plenipotentiary to Peking from 1861 to 1867, Burlingame sought protection for the interests of the small number of American merchants and missionaries in China through international law and treaties rather than territorial acquisition and intimidation. Britain and other Western nations had their navies and their colonies, but the United States would secure its interests through moral and legal safeguards. Burlingame endeavored to make the cooperative policy an American "diplomatic equivalent for Hong Kong."[53] To Burlingame, cooperation was more than simply an expedient policy necessitated by limited American power and interests in Asia.[54] It was rather an expression of the liberal Western ideals of peace, freedom, justice, and self-government—principles that, in his opinion, the United States had championed since 1776. For Burlingame, American interests and ideals coincided. For example, in a report to Seward in 1867 on the increase in China's foreign trade, which he described as "so creditable to the Chinese and so advantageous to us," Burlingame declared that this growth in commerce was "an indication of the faith of those who believe in reason and kindness more than brute force."[55]

Burlingame himself was the essence of the cooperative policy. His personality and background, not the relative power and position of the United States in China, dictated its outlines. He spent his entire public career before going to China in crusades for individual liberties and freedom for oppressed peoples. In China he found another principle for which to fight. Although the practical questions such as trade and concessions were important to him, the basic objective of his policy was to change the way foreigners dealt with China and the Chinese. At the end of a long letter to Consul General Seward discussing American treaty rights and reviewing the cooperative policy, Burlingame singled out what to him formed the most important point of the entire subject. "You will perceive," he wrote, "that we are making an effort to substitute fair diplomatic action in China for force."[56] In Peking, Burlingame had played a leading role in this innovative policy for over half a decade. In 1867 he set out for America and Europe to pursue the realization of his ideals in the Western capitals.

CHAPTER THREE

"Determined Moral Pressure"

J. ROSS BROWNE AND
BURLINGAME'S POLICY

ANSON BURLINGAME'S DEPARTURE from China at the head of a Chinese diplomatic delegation marked the beginning of an often-heated debate over what direction Western policies in China should take. Burlingame conceived of his mission as an opportunity to gain official acknowledgment of the cooperative policy in foreign capitals, and he defended his efforts as the best hope for peaceful and mutually beneficial progress in Sino-Western relations. On the other hand, Burlingame's replacement at the United States legation in Peking, J. Ross Browne, concluded that the cooperative policy was too idealistic and hence impractical. Believing Burlingame's forbearance to be in fact detrimental to the improvement of East-West relations, Browne favored a forceful Western approach in China and became one of the most outspoken and bitter opponents of his predecessor's policy. Although this debate was not limited to Americans alone, the arguments of Burlingame and Browne became focal points in the examination of Western policies and especially in the delineation of American policy choices in China.

Motivated by "the interests of my country and civilization," Burlingame resigned as United States minister to China in November 1867 and accepted the Peking government's appointment as its envoy to the Western nations. His concept of his mission echoed the sentiments that he had expressed in 1862 in his first endorsement of the cooperative approach: his goal was to protect both "the rights of our citizens" and "the interests of civilization."[1] His preference for the peaceful and patient methods of diplomatic persuasion to achieve his purposes had been demonstrated repeatedly during his service in the Chinese capital. The *North China Herald*, an English-language newspaper in Shanghai that often advocated aggressive Western policies in Asia, acknowledged that Burlingame was one of the originators of a new situation in China: "It is hardly necessary to point out how greatly this policy [of force] has changed since the last war [1860]. Diplomacy has, in a great measure, superseded force, and arguments are used in preference to big guns."[2] Neither the newspaper nor Burlingame, however, equated these changes in Western methods with a change in Western purposes in China. "The object of all is the same," the paper editorialized, "—extension of intercourse, extension of our commercial relations. And the right mode of attaining these objects, is admitted to be argument and persuasion, rather than menace and violence."[3] The writer characterized the Burlingame Mission as an achievement of the cooperative policy and hoped that its Chinese members would send home accounts of "Western wealth, strength, and science" that would induce more foreign innovation in the Middle Kingdom. Burlingame harbored the same desire. In one of his first speeches following the mission's arrival in the United States in 1868, he declared that "the day would soon arrive when that great people [the Chinese] would stretch out its arms toward the shining banners of Western civilization," and, he announced, "that hour has struck; the day is here!"[4] Burlingame viewed his role as that of China's patron, protecting it from the blows of Western power, but also as that of China's tutor, leading it toward appreciation of the superiority of Western culture.

In authorizing this new and, from its point of view, experimental venture in international relations, the imperial Chinese government endorsed Burlingame's methods, but not necessarily his objectives. The members of the Tsungli Yamen considered Burlingame "honest and well intentioned," especially in comparison to other foreign officials. They did not repose complete trust in any "barbarian" but were confident that the American would make a sincere attempt to gain sympathy and understanding for China in the West, because, if for no other reason, "Burlingame intends to make a name for himself."[5] The mandarins responsible for "barbarian management" were also quite certain about what they wanted and expected the mission to accomplish. The Tsungli Yamen had polled high-ranking officials from throughout the empire and knew that a limited diplomatic initiative had general support but that sweeping innovations would be opposed. Specifically, the Burlingame Mission was to attempt to limit foreign demands on China for extensive treaty revisions. The foreign legations in Peking were pressuring the government for renegotiation of the Treaties of Tientsin, and Peking wanted Burlingame to communicate directly to the treaty powers specific Chinese objections to the proposed changes. The Tsungli Yamen also expected the members of the mission to report first-hand information on Western policies and material developments. This information, however, was not sought because China desired to emulate the West. It was requested more in the sense of political and military intelligence—a strategy of "know your enemy."[6]

In order to implement these objectives, the Tsungli Yamen prepared specific written instructions for Burlingame before his departure from China. Many of the American's later statements and actions in the United States and Europe, however, contradicted these instructions, which were dated November 26, 1867. Did Burlingame knowingly and purposefully disregard the wishes of the Chinese foreign office? There is no definitive evidence that the envoy actually received the formal instructions, and it is possible that the Tsungli Yamen wrote the carefully phrased directive only to diffuse conservative court opinion that opposed the mission.[7] On the other hand, Burlingame may have known the contents of the instructions and may have chosen to interpret their provisions very broadly in order to commit the Chinese government to more Western innovations than it desired. Was the Burlingame Mission a genuine effort by the imperial government to adopt Western-style diplomacy, or was it a token gesture to appease the powerful foreign barbarians without alienating the conservative mandarins who disdained Western methods and culture? The Tsungli Yamen was walking a tightrope between Western imperialist pressures for change in China and domestic Chinese resistance—both political and cultural—to that change. Prince Kung himself was sincere in his efforts to cooperate with the Westerners, but he also believed in the continued efficacy of the traditional Chinese tactic of balancing one powerful barbarian against another in order to protect China.[8] The prince and his colleagues in the Tsungli Yamen were attempting to find a middle ground in the Burlingame Mission.

Regardless of whether Burlingame was aware of the Tsungli Yamen's formal instructions, the envoy certainly knew the contents of two letters written by Prince Kung that spelled out the mission's purposes and powers. The two letters were very similar in content. One was addressed to Samuel Wells Williams on December 7, 1867, and the other was dated December 31, 1867 and was included in Burlingame's diplomatic credentials, which he presented to Secretary of State Seward in Washington on June 2, 1868.[9] These letters were consistent for the most part with the formal instructions that the Chinese foreign office had addressed to Burlingame on November 26. For example, all three documents clearly authorized Burlingame to represent officially the imperial government. Nowhere, however, was the American designated an official "of the first Chinese rank," as he identified himself in the United States. The official instructions authorized him "to deal with matters in exactly the same way as would a Chinese official."[10] The two letters by Prince Kung (and Burlingame's letters of credence from the emperor) carefully avoided any mention of rank in reference to Burlingame. Also, the two mandarins who traveled with Burlingame, Chih-kang and Sung Chia-ku, were designated coleaders of the mission in all of the documents, although Burlingame referred to them as "learners."[11] On the crucial matter of the extent of Burlingame's actual authority, however, the letters and the formal instructions diverged. According to Williams's translation of his letter from Prince Kung, "Everything . . . that relates to the duties of imperial commissioner in the United States will devolve alone on Mr. Burlingame, and his decisions will be final."[12] The translation of the letter that was handed to Secretary of State Seward similarly asserted that "on the arrival of the ministers in the United States and other countries, the government there will discuss and decide with Mr. Burlingame alone, all matters that may be dealt with."[13] Since Burlingame did not read Chinese himself, these two statements formed for him the basis of his authority. His formal instructions, however, which were written in Chinese and filed in the Ch'ing Dynasty archives, were more equivocal on the subject of Burlingame's powers. "Should matters arise which are altogether advantageous to both sides," the instructions read, the mission could make "a decision" and communicate it to the foreign office. On "matters of momentous importance," however, the facts should be sent to the Tsungli Yamen and the mission should "await its decision."[14]

Both Burlingame and Prince Kung had their own reasons for not being too specific about Burlingame's instructions. Both men were aware that many Chinese officials and Westerners in China opposed the idea of Sino-Western accommodation. The American envoy and his diplomatic superiors in the Tsungli Yamen were purposefully vague about the precise objectives of their cooperative endeavor, and hence the Burlingame Mission's charter left considerable room for interpretation and potential misunderstanding. Burlingame's efforts on behalf of China eventually became shrouded in controversy. Did he intentionally exploit his ambiguous instructions, or did his zeal for a reform effort cause him to lose sight of the tenuous nature of his mandate and prompt him to exaggerate the possibilities of his mission?

Burlingame and his colorful entourage of two Chinese coenvoys, a British and a French secretary, and almost thirty other Chinese orderlies, students, and servants traversed the United States and Europe during 1868 and 1869. As this curious group was hosted and feted in the various cities that it visited along its way, its leader revived his old talent for grandiloquent oratory that had first thrust him into national prominence before the Civil War. He painted flowery pictures of the merchant and missionary opportunities awaiting foreigners in China. In his most widely quoted and controversial speech during his American tour, Burlingame informed a New York audience on June 23, 1868 that China "is willing to trade with you. . . . She invites your merchants, she invites your missionaries. She tells the latter to plant the shining cross on every hill and in every valley."[15] Although not purposefully deceptive, his oratorical flourishes were misleading to eager American merchants and missionaries. The T'ung-chih Restoration then occurring in China had as its goal the reestablishment of Confucian orthodoxy. Its leaders had no intention of opening their arms to Western commerce and religion.

In keeping with his instructions from the Tsungli Yamen to appeal to the West for patience and forbearance, Burlingame pleaded with his

New York listeners: "Let her [China] alone; let her have her independence; let her develop herself in her own time, and in her own way."[16] His own enthusiasm for the possibilities of a peaceful and harmonious future for Sino-Western relations, however, obscured for most of his audience the fact that he was not speaking of the present. They heard his message clearly when he described the China market. Burlingame declared that China "says now: 'Send us your wheat, your lumber, your coal, your silver, your goods from everywhere—we will take as many of them as we can.'"[17] His auditors paid less heed, however, to his simultaneous plea: "Let her alone. . . . The imagination kindles at the future which may be, and which will be, if you will be fair and just to China."[18] Many Chinese officials in Peking and Westerners in China severely criticized Burlingame for his excessive rhetoric. The editor of the *North China Herald*, who originally applauded the Burlingame Mission, considered the New York "plant-the-shining-cross" speech an "absurd description of China." In the estimation of many observers who had considerable knowledge of affairs in China, Burlingame had misrepresented the deep distrust and misunderstanding that still underlay Sino-Western relations.[19]

Burlingame's mission was not just one long series of after-dinner addresses. In each capital that he visited, he attempted to gain from the government some official acknowledgment of the principles of cooperation to which the Western ministers in Peking had agreed in June of 1863. He had his greatest success in Washington in his conversations with his former chief and fellow Republican partisan Secretary of State William H. Seward. The result of the Burlingame-Seward meetings was the so-called Burlingame Treaty of 1868. The Tsungli Yamen had not granted Burlingame explicit treaty-making powers. His ambiguous instructions, however, allowed him to make decisions on matters "advantageous to both sides," and the Chinese government did ratify the treaty in 1869.

The treaty, which was a supplement to the American Treaty of Tientsin of 1858, was the primary diplomatic accomplishment of the Burlingame Mission. Burlingame and Seward signed these additional articles on July 28, 1868. The Burlingame Treaty explicitly stated that China retained dominion and authority over all territory and activities not specifically within the purview of existing treaties. It provided for free immigration between the two nations, the stationing of Chinese consuls in the United States, and protection of Americans and Chinese in each other's country. Most significant for the cooperative policy, the United States agreed not "to intervene in the domestic administration of China in regard to the construction of railroads, telegraphs, or other material internal improvements." China retained the right to decide when and where such Western innovations would be constructed. In return, China agreed to seek Western aid in such projects and to protect foreign persons and property involved in such service. The United States Senate quickly ratified the treaty in July 1868. Seward viewed the agreement as an expression of American friendship toward China; as additional protection for Americans, missionaries particularly, in China; and as a guarantee of an ample labor supply to develop the American West.[20]

For Burlingame, the treaty was the fruition of his long-time efforts to get formal recognition by a Western government of his cooperative principles.[21] It was simply a continuation of his efforts begun in June of 1863. In a speech at a dinner in Boston on August 21, 1868, Burlingame claimed that "this treaty recognizes China as an equal among the nations." He was especially proud, he told his fellow New Englanders, that the United States had asked nothing for itself and by this treaty had denounced

> the habit of the foreigners in China to lecture the Chinese and to say what they should do and what they should not do; in fact to . . . say when they should build railroads, when they should build telegraphs; . . . there has been an attempt to take entire possession of their affairs.[22]

In Burlingame's opinion, it was not only admirable but advantageous for the United States and other Western nations to allow the Chinese to manage their own affairs. He argued that

> by leaving China free in all these respects, she . . . will feel secure . . . that the railroad and the telegraph are not to be instruments by which she is to be disrupted or destroyed. Then she will come out of her seclusion and enter upon a course of trade, the importance of which and the amount of which no man can compute.[23]

Despite Burlingame's hyperbole—the treaty did not end the unequal treaty system, nor did it unlock the fabled riches of the China market—the Burlingame Treaty did recognize China as a sovereign nation able to assume and assert its responsibilities and rights in international relations. It was China's first equal treaty.

In September 1868, the Burlingame Mission sailed for Europe, where its diplomatic successes were much more modest than in the United States. In London, Burlingame found Lord Clarendon, the British foreign secretary, willing to give him a letter promising British forbearance in China. The statement did not bind Her Majesty's government to any particular policy, but it was a significant concession from a nation that had in the past found war expedient in China.[24] From London the mission traveled to Paris. Despite eight months of effort in the French capital, Burlingame was unable to elicit any form of statement from the French government. In Berlin, however, as the result of conversations with Count Otto von Bismarck, Burlingame received written assurances in January 1870 that Germany would respect "the well-being of China."[25] With some form of official acknowledgment of cooperation with China secured from the United States, Britain, and Germany, Burlingame and his entourage moved on to the Russian capital.[26]

Although Burlingame continued to conceive of his efforts as a means of promoting Sino-Western cooperation, his mission to the West ultimately came to demonstrate the tenuous, perhaps even visionary, nature of the cooperative policy. As the embassy moved through America and Europe, controversy dogged its heels in China as well as in the West. Burlingame succeeded in bringing the Chinese government and the treaty-port merchants together, not in cooperation but in a stream of protest. Both groups objected to what they considered to be Burlingame's exaggerated description of the Western commercial and missionary opportunities in China. The imperial court in Peking had no intention of adopting Western ways and had approved the mission only to limit, not increase, Western pressure on the Chinese empire. Burlingame's Western critics cited this hostility and resistance to foreigners in China as proof that Sino-Western cooperation was impossible as the means for advancing Western interests in the Middle Kingdom. The *North China Herald*, for example, termed the Burlingame Treaty "an unfortunate document" and asserted that "it was extremely unwise to expressly abandon pressure" when it could still be "usefully exerted to induce the Chinese authorities to open up the mineral resources of their country."[27]

Despite his adversaries, Burlingame remained the perpetual optimist. The obstacles in his path to peacefully reconciling China and the West loomed large, but he refused to believe that the task was impossible. He took hope from his early antislavery struggles and the ultimate success of that movement. He believed that the advocates of force in China were like Southerners whom he had heard say "that the only way to treat a 'nigger' was to enslave him and then, when slavery made him deceitful and lazy, would whip him to cure the sins resulting from their own false principles."[28] Emancipation had demanded the price of a bloody civil war. Burlingame believed change in China would be much less costly. In a letter to his old friend Samuel Wells Williams on January 23, 1870, he pleaded: *"Let us try once,* at least, to see what the Chinese will do if let alone by those who would Christianize them with gunpowder."[29] On February 23, 1870, one month after writing to Williams, Anson Burlingame died of pneumonia in St. Petersburg while negotiating with Russia in China's behalf. Perhaps his sudden death saved him from the bitter disillusionment of an impossible dream. On the other hand, the Russian winter may have silenced the one man who had enough magnanimity and audacity to attempt to bridge the gulf of misunderstanding between East and West. In the search for an American policy—with its inherent tension between ideals and interests—no other United States minister in Peking ever equaled Burlingame's idealism.

In January 1868, President Andrew Johnson selected John Ross Browne of California to succeed Burlingame as United States minister plenipotentiary in Peking. At the time of his nomination for the China post, Browne had no previous diplomatic experience, no special knowledge of China, nor any opinions about the cooperative policy. Burlingame had hoped that the appointment would go to Samuel Wells Williams, who not only was America's most qualified China expert but also shared the departing minister's faith in cooperation. With impeachment proceedings getting underway in Congress, Johnson did not wait to discuss his choice with Burlingame. The president nominated Browne for political, not diplomatic, reasons. Under attack from the Radical Republicans in Congress, the beleaguered chief executive viewed the appointment as an opportunity to gain support among West Coast political and commercial leaders. In addition, Browne himself was politically noncontroversial and was, in his own words, "the only

J. Ross Browne, author, satirist, and United States minister to China, 1868–1869. *Bancroft Library, University of California, Berkeley.*

kind of person likely to be confirmed by a Senate in bitter antagonism with the Executive."[30] In choosing Browne, Johnson could not have selected anyone whose personality was more the opposite of Burlingame's. In contrast to his optimistic and idealistic predecessor, Browne was a skeptic and pessimist, but like Burlingame, Browne was a man of firmly held convictions.[31]

Born in Ireland in 1821, young J. Ross Browne emigrated to Kentucky with his family in 1833 after his journalist father was exiled for writing anti-British satire. The son shared with his father a crusading temperament that throughout his life compelled Ross to speak his mind bluntly, without regard for personal consequences. In 1841 Browne went to Washington and worked briefly as a stenographic reporter in Congress. In the nation's capital he acquired what was to be a lasting contempt for the "big men" in Congress. After about a year, his yearning for travel and adventure prompted him to join the crew of a New Bedford whaling vessel. Although his experiences on the voyage further whetted his appetite for adventure, Browne developed no desire for a life at sea. Instead, he returned to Washington in 1844 and embarked upon two pursuits—writing and government service—that were to form the basis of his career. He became a clerk in the Treasury Department, and he wrote a book about his whaling journey. His work at the treasury attracted the attention, and eventual friendship, of Robert J. Walker, secretary of the treasury from 1845 to 1849, and led him into a career as a special government agent for the Treasury and Interior departments. From the 1840s through the 1860s he held various posts, primarily as an investigator of customs houses, Indian affairs, mining activities, and land dealings in the American West. During and in between his government assignments, Browne also developed into a first-class writer. Harper Brothers published his first book, *Etchings of a Whaling Cruise*, in 1846, and numerous other books followed—including *Yusef* (1853), *Crusoe's Island* (1864), and *Adventures in the Apache Country* (1869). These books and scores of magazine and newspaper articles made Browne a significant nineteenth-century American author, whose works influenced and compared favorably with those of Herman Melville and Mark Twain.[32]

Despite his literary successes and government assignments, Browne remained frustrated for many years because of his inability to secure a diplomatic appointment. In the 1840s he asked Walker for help in gaining a consular post. Instead the secretary of the treasury arranged for him to go to gold-rush California in 1849 to investigate the problem of merchant seamen's desertion to the gold fields. Browne himself was never tempted by gold fever, but he did become a permanent resident of California. For the next twenty years he accepted commissions from the federal government and the state of California but also continued to write in the hope that his literary accomplishments would lead to a diplomatic post. He uncovered inefficiency and corruption in the customs service and the Indian bureau, and in the 1860s, as federal mining commissioner for the area west of the Rockies, he prepared a report that established him as one of the nation's foremost mining authorities. As both an author and a government agent, Browne demonstrated a remarkable degree of candor and integrity. He has been labeled a "muckraker," and many of his books, articles, and government reports would certainly be classified as exposés. His writing style was humorous, satirical, and often sarcastic; but simultaneously it was honest and sensitive. Although well documented, his critical reporting often got him into trouble with powerful politicians back in Washington, and more than once he was removed or reassigned from an investigation. "He did exactly what he was instructed to do," he recalled, "which was exactly what he was not wanted to do."[33] When Browne finally received the nomination as minister to China, he had not anticipated it. Perhaps his confirmation by the Senate was aided by the desire of some senators to see this obstreperous critic shunted off to faraway Peking. Regardless, Browne was genuinely proud of the appointment. In April 1868, before his departure from the United States, he confided to an old friend, "The China Mission is the greatest triumph of my life."[34]

Before leaving the United States, Browne met Burlingame and was impressed by the former minister's generous disposition and "good sense." Browne described himself at that time as "permeated with the progressive spirit of the age." "The feeling was universal," he declared, "that the time had arrived when China was to be thrown open to American enterprise—to our commerce, our arts, sciences, and civilization."[35] Once in Peking, however, Browne discovered that he could not agree with his predecessor's assumptions about the prospects for progress in China. He found some of the specific provisions of the Burlingame Treaty, which was concluded just as he embarked for China, to be especially onerous. Browne quickly became one of the leading critics of Burlingame's cooperative policy.

Arriving in Peking in late September 1868, Browne immediately encountered a diplomatic situation involving the new Burlingame Treaty. Sir Rutherford B. Alcock, London's minister, was negotiating with the Tsungli Yamen for a revision of the British Treaty of Tientsin of 1858. Alcock's primary objective in these discussions was to expand foreign trade in China. Seward instructed the new American minister that the Burlingame Treaty represented all of the changes that the United States thought necessary at present. Browne was to take no part in initiating any modification of the commercial articles of the existing treaties. The secretary of state pointed out, however, that if Britain secured any changes, Browne was to insure that America's most-favored-nation status was respected. In addition, Browne could encourage the Chinese to make concessions to steam navigation and internal improvements, but the secretary remained faithful to the Burlingame Treaty and cautioned Browne that "these desirable changes are not to be pressed with such urgency as to endanger the stability of the present Government or the internal peace and tranquility of China."[36]

In the Burlingame Treaty, the Alcock negotiations, and Seward's instruction, Browne discerned a number of contradictions, which he thought placed him and the United States government in an embarrassing and untenable position. He reasoned that the Burlingame Treaty's provisions that recognized China's right to decide its own terms for trade and material improvements could not be reconciled with Alcock's efforts to expand the scope of foreign activity. Browne knew that he must adhere to the new American treaty but believed that it handicapped his participation with the other Western ministers in urging major concessions from the Chinese. Consequently, Browne viewed the Burlingame Treaty as inconsistent with the cooperative policy, which he obviously understood to be a system of consultation, agreement, and coordinated action on the part of the foreign representatives. He did not understand that cooperation as Burlingame conceived of it included the Chinese and that the treaty was therefore consistent with the original cooperative policy formalized in 1863.[37]

Because of his own concept of cooperation, Browne essentially disregarded Seward's caution and argued that he felt duty-bound "to use all friendly means" in aiding his British colleague. Ignoring the Burlingame Treaty, Browne asserted that all existing Sino-Western treaties were the result of force, not mutual regard. He maintained that China was so different from the West and so firm in her resistance to innovation that only by compulsion could and inevitably would a "forward step" be made. In his opinion, Americans deceived themselves in thinking that they were not included with other foreigners as objects of China's distrust and dislike. Since the United States could not avoid this association with the other Westerners, Browne contended, it would be foolhardy even to try. Only through cooperation with the other treaty nations could the United States protect its own and China's interests. Hence, Browne concluded that "it is extremely important that harmony of action be preserved." In other words, he believed that the Westerners, not the Chinese, would ultimately decide China's future, and he wanted to be sure that the United States remained in a position to influence the outcome.[38]

As Browne learned more details about his new job, he increasingly escalated his attacks on his predecessor's patient approach to improving East-West relations. The treaty-port merchants quickly convinced the new minister that Burlingame's optimism was unfounded. Conducting his own investigation of the United States legation records in Peking, Browne discovered numerous petitions from American merchants and missionaries complaining of treaty violations and maltreatment by the Chinese. Browne realized that current American policy obligated him to keep his discussions with the Tsungli Yamen "within the limits of friendly suggestion." He was not encouraged by the previous results of this policy, but for a while, at least, he gave the "system of fair dealing and frank discussion" a try.[39]

The new minister did not agree with Burlingame's claim that China was gradually accepting Westerners and their ways. After little more than three months in China, Browne asserted that he saw no evidence of "a more liberal or enlightened policy" on the part of the Chinese authorities. Too weak and timid to reform, the Ch'ing Dynasty procrastinated in the present and expected the future to take care of itself. Modern technology had changed the world, he noted, but China persisted in resisting all advances except those induced by force. Some people blamed dishonest Western merchants or missionaries, with their disturbing doctrines, for China's resistance to progress. On the contrary, Browne argued, foreign merchants were as moral as other men, and these courageous entrepreneurs and their evangelical counterparts risked life and property to carry Western civilization to the remote parts of the world. Browne concluded:

China is now [1869] in a state of demoralization and decay, whatever theorists may say to the contrary. I believe it to be the duty of Christian nations to lend their best efforts to its elevation and advancement. No exaggerated estimate of what has been done during the past eight years; no false conception of the difficulties in the way; no blind dependence upon an indigenous movement on the part of the rulers will tend to promote this great reform.[40]

This critique was Browne's assessment of Burlingame's efforts since 1861 to cooperate with the Chinese government.

When the official Chinese and English texts of the Burlingame Treaty arrived in Peking, Browne suddenly became very patient and willing to cooperate with the Tsungli Yamen. Prince Kung and his colleagues had not authorized Burlingame to negotiate any treaties, and when the time came to exchange ratifications in 1869, they hesitated. Their caution was understandable, considering China's unhappy experiences with other Western treaties. Not eager to see the treaty ratified, Browne generously declined to press the Chinese. When Burlingame heard of this delay, he immediately wrote from Europe to inform Hamilton Fish, secretary of state in the new Grant administration, that Peking planned to ratify the treaty. In addition, China's ambassador expressed disbelief at reports that Browne had repudiated the concept of cooperation with the Chinese. In reply, Fish reassured Burlingame that "the cooperative policy hitherto pursued by [America's] Diplomatic Agents in China in conjunction with those of the other Treaty Powers in the interests of peace, and solemnized by the pending Treaty, will be adhered to."[41]

Browne eventually developed a genuine loathing for the Burlingame Mission and for Burlingame's optimism. In June 1869, with Burlingame obviously in mind, Browne commented on the subject of Westerners' advising the Chinese government: "There is no real credit to be gained in the employ of a government so deficient in the attributes of a civilized power . . . and to be subordinated to Chinese rule would in my opinion be a degradation."[42] Browne agreed with the treaty-port press that Burlingame's diplomacy rendered impossible peaceful relations with the Middle Kingdom. He declared that both the Burlingame Treaty and the letter that Burlingame had solicited from Lord Clarendon yielded everything to the Chinese while requiring nothing in return. Eventually, he informed Washington, some antiforeign outrage or trade restriction would "compel a resort to more effective remedies than any hitherto applied" against the "isolation, ignorance, and superstition" of the Chinese. Browne acknowledged the "justness of the principles" inherent in the Burlingame Treaty but objected to them as difficult, if not completely impossible, to apply to China. He asserted, for example, that the treaty would create enormous legal complications, because it subverted the emperor's authority in cases where Chinese became citizens of the United States. The article to which he referred, however, clearly withheld naturalization from the Chinese. Browne did not reject the treaty because of the way he interpreted it. He interpreted it as he did because he already had rejected it.[43]

In Browne's opinion, what China needed was not treaties and

speeches about fair play. To this former federal mining commissioner, human progress meant railroads, telegraphs, and mines. These technological innovations would inevitably come to China, he assumed, and thus he urged their rapid introduction as the best means of elevating China toward the "more advanced civilization" of the West. Contrary to Burlingame's assertions, Browne contended that China's rulers could not be expected to invite the agents of these improvements into the Middle Kingdom. Browne singled out the scholar-general Tseng Kuo-fan as exemplifying the shallowness of Chinese official thinking. Tseng was a leader of the "self-strengthening" movement, an attempt by some Chinese officials to adopt Western methods while retaining traditional Chinese values. Browne noted that although Tseng appeared to make concessions to foreign innovations such as mining experiments and sending ministers abroad, the Chinese general also claimed that steamships and railroads would take away jobs and hence the livelihood of the people. The American minister attributed this view to Tseng's ignorance of the benefits of Western technology and to "the inherent prejudice of the Tartar race" against foreign ideas. Given the opportunity, the people would accept foreign technology, according to Browne, as a chance to improve their physical condition. In his opinion, the peasants were more enlightened than the literati, whose "retrogressive" education consisted mainly of memorizing ancient Confucian canons.[44]

Browne's recommendation to the State Department was that the irresistible force of commerce aided by "determined moral pressure" on Chinese officials by Western governments would hasten China's transformation. The present counsels of inaction, he warned in an obvious reference to Burlingame, would not achieve the desired objective of harmonious East-West relations. Railroads, telegraphs, and mines would improve the material condition of the people, remove prejudice, promote better understanding between the races, and cause essential political, civil, and religious reforms. The Chinese would learn quickly from "the superior races," Browne insisted, but the basic antagonisms between Eastern and Western civilizations must be honestly confronted. "Too sanguine a representation of the intelligence of the Chinese and their ability, statesmanship and desire to advance," he argued, "has a tendency to create exciting delusions, and can only result in disappointment to us and injury to them."[45] China had to reform or face further decay, demoralization, and eventually submission to stronger, more progressive nations.[46]

Burlingame and Browne agreed on the desirability of reform in China but not on the means of accomplishing it. Arbitrary and rapid introduction of Western technology into China would, in Burlingame's estimation, seriously undermine the social and political structure of the country—making China as vulnerable to collapse or outside domination as did the relative physical weakness of the empire. While in Peking, Burlingame never pressured the Chinese government to accept projects promoted by Western businessmen, nor did he encourage such schemes. When W. C. Ralston proposed to light the streets of China with gas, for example, Burlingame informed him that as minister he could not act either directly or indirectly in such a matter.[47]

While United States minister in Peking, Burlingame did take an active interest in a proposed international telegraph line between Europe and America through Russia and the Bering Straits. Most Westerners in the treaty ports and in the foreign legations had hoped that a branch of this line could be extended to China, and in 1867 Secretary of State Seward urged Burlingame to defend the interests of an American firm that was bidding for the contract. Although Burlingame's father-in-law, Isaac Livermore, was one of the directors of the American company, Burlingame did not press the government for an overland telegraph line. The Tsungli Yamen did give permission for an underwater cable with terminals at the ports, but Burlingame foresaw that strong and effective opposition faced any telegraph project in China. "I have persistently refused to advise the company or any one else, to risk money," he informed Seward, "and however much I should be pleased as a patriot to have Americans build the first line, I must still respectfully hold that position."[48]

In 1869, Browne seized upon the continuing delay in construction of the telegraph line as evidence of China's resistance to innovation and of Burlingame's misrepresentation of attitudes in the Celestial Empire. The hostility of the ruling class created, according to Browne, the chief obstacle to the line. "The stubborn fact may as well be confronted," he lectured Washington, "that there is nothing reconcilable between telegraphs and fung-shuey."[49] (*Feng-shui* was the harmony between man and nature that many Chinese believed would be dis-

turbed by telegraphs, railroads, and mines.) From reviewing Burlingame's correspondence with the Tsungli Yamen, Browne concluded
that the Chinese had made no concession to the telegraph project other
than to claim no dominion over the ocean. To Browne this negotiation
did not reveal a China ready to welcome foreign enterprise.

Actually, Browne took little real interest in the telegraph project,
because he believed that a railroad system should be the first improvement made in China. "A single mile of railway would do more
within ten years for the elevation and advancement of China," he
predicted, "than all the teachings of political theorists and rationalists
would be able to accomplish in a century."[50] The introduction of steam
navigation and coal mines might be used as preliminary steps, but only
a "progressive system of railways" could, according to Browne, peacefully and speedily open the way for the regeneration of China. Convinced of the inevitability of Western innovation in China, the American minister did not hesitate to urge such views upon the Chinese
government.[51]

Despite his disagreement with Burlingame's reliance on "fair diplomatic action," Browne in the beginning did not advocate gunboat diplomacy. He never discounted, however, the possibility of using Western
military and naval power in any given situation. He maintained that
American naval officers in both China and Japan should be careful
neither to display any weakness nor to misuse the force at their command. "It frequently happens in dealing with the Asiatic races,"
Browne instructed Washington, "that a vigorous manifestation of
power is the best way to ensure friendly relations in the future."[52]
Browne disapproved, however, when the fire-eating American consul
at Amoy, Charles W. LeGendre, supported a British decision to use
gunboats in settling a trade disagreement in Formosa. He counseled
LeGendre that Westerners in China should try to rise above the use of
brute force. While it was true that the Chinese authorities delayed and
evaded taking responsibility for resolving disputes, he cautioned the
consul that "we cannot strengthen their authority by bringing it into
contempt." Despite Browne's frequent criticisms of his predecessor's
policies, his advice to LeGendre in this case sounded reminiscent of
Burlingame.[53]

In mid-June 1869, the tone of Browne's dispatches to Washington
changed sharply. On June 5 he instructed LeGendre to give Burlin-

game's policy "a fair trial and a generous support." In language very similar to Burlingame's, he urged: "Let us endeavor . . . to elevate and enlighten the rulers of China by honorable conduct and Christian treatment than attempt in the plenitude of our strength to obtain by a hasty resort to force advantages over a pagan race. . . ."[54] Less than two weeks later, however, on June 16, he wrote that there was a limit to forbearance: "Reference of all important questions back to the home government before a single gunboat can be used . . . is simply to nullify and bring into contempt all diplomatic power in China."[55] Foreign interests, he asserted, could not be protected nor peaceful relations maintained with Peking by the present policy that allowed the Chinese unilaterally to restrict trade, that removed all coercive power from foreign representatives, and that condoned Chinese prejudices. China could accept reforms designed to help it enter the family of nations, he declared, or accept the risk of compulsion when it failed to meet its treaty obligations. Also in mid-June, Browne predicted that outrages would continue against Western merchants and missionaries until "force is interposed to arrest them." He announced that an "inevitable conflict . . . must before long grow out of such antagonistic civilizations."[56] He wrote these bluntly phrased dispatches at the same time that he also issued some of his most pointed criticisms of the Burlingame Treaty and Lord Clarendon's letter.[57]

Why did Browne suddenly shift from general disagreement but grudging acceptance of Burlingame's policy to open hostility? He probably heard in June from his friend Charles D. Poston that the new Grant administration had appointed its own minister to Peking. Writing to Browne from Paris on April 25, Poston described the new appointee, William A. Howard of Michigan, as a "former tutor of Anson Burlingame and formerly a M.C. of that ilk—very plain sailing Mr. B.—all in the family."[58] Although Howard had been one of Burlingame's professors at the University of Michigan, Burlingame had not played a role in his selection as minister. Howard eventually declined the post after initially having accepted it, but Browne assumed that he was about to be replaced by a Burlingame sympathizer and decided to put some of his unvarnished opinions on the record. Undoubtedly he expressed his most candid convictions when he wrote at this time that friendly relations with China in the future would require either "the withdrawal of all intercourse or prompt redress, extorted by force when peaceful means fail."[59] Insistence on redress constituted Browne's policy recommendation because he believed that the past thirty years of Sino-Western relations had made withdrawal impossible.[60]

Shortly after learning of Howard's appointment, Browne began to marshal all of his arguments against Burlingame's policies in preparation for submitting his resignation. In late June he addressed a number of questions to Robert Hart, the British inspector general of China's Imperial Maritime Customs Service. Hart had been closely associated with Burlingame since 1863, when Chinese officials had consulted the American minister about Hart's promotion to the chief customs post. Hart shared Burlingame's cooperative attitude toward the Chinese, and his honest and efficient management of the customs service earned him the trust of his superiors in the imperial government. Hence Browne assumed that Hart had knowledge of official Chinese thinking. Browne sought Hart's opinions on two subjects—the origins of the Burlingame Mission and the future of China's relations with the West. He asked if the mission was a spontaneous movement on the part of the Chinese, what the Tsungli Yamen considered its object to be, and if accounts in the foreign press accurately reflected that object. Browne also wanted to know if the Chinese were interested in making material improvements, if the Burlingame Treaty would induce progress in China, and specifically if the treaty would remove Chinese objections and prejudices against foreign innovations. Browne took excessive liberty in annotating Hart's reply and then forwarded the document to Secretary of State Fish without informing Hart. Although many of Browne's comments were petty and self-serving, his footnotes provided a detailed exposition of his thinking.[61]

In response to Browne's inquiries, Hart wrote that although he, the American missionary-educator W. A. P. Martin, and others had long urged the Chinese to send representatives abroad, the appointment of Burlingame originated strictly with the Chinese. In his footnotes Browne claimed, however, that the Chinese had never liked the idea of sending missions abroad, and he frankly doubted that the Burlingame Mission represented a new departure in Chinese diplomacy. Hart corroborated Burlingame's insistence that the purpose of the mission was to prevent pressure on China for concessions that Peking thought were premature. Browne footnoted this statement with a non sequitur:

"The object, therefore, was to prevent all progress inconsistent with Chinese isolation; to avoid the execution of treaties, and set aside the foreign ministers at Peking."[62]

Browne's comments on Hart's evaluation of the newspaper accounts of the Burlingame Mission further revealed how his assumptions contrasted with those of Hart and Burlingame. According to Hart, the press had led the Western public to expect China to agree "immediately" to the very things for which the mission was seeking more time. He suggested that Western ignorance of China had caused the misunderstanding, but Browne countered that the fault rested with China's emissary for not candidly describing the situation. Despite his criticisms of Burlingame, Browne conceded: "I have full confidence in the purity of his motives and the sincerity of his representations; but I believe he has been the dupe of his own enthusiasm and the cunning and duplicity of his employers." Hart emphasized that Burlingame's message was primarily a plea for the West to leave China alone. He maintained that the controversial "plant-the-shining-cross" speech had been intended to describe China not as it was then but as it would be in the future, if the West would follow "a policy of fair play and non-interference." "All experience is to be rejected," Browne rejoined, "the existing condition of affairs in China is to be disregarded; neither the past nor present is to be taken as a guide, but we are to build hopes for the future upon a policy not justified by any results obtained."[63] Hart shared Burlingame's preference for Western forbearance in China, and Browne did not.

Browne contended that the Chinese were wedded to their past—blindly imitating it and stubbornly resisting all reform. He asserted that in China, progress meant going backward. Hart thought, on the other hand, that the Chinese were already seeking the means for erasing their deficiencies and that they would continue to do so if left alone. Coercion, Hart argued, was not needed to move China in this direction, and could result only in distrust and jealousy, which would be harmful to Western as well as Chinese interests. In rebuttal, Browne contended that China had not taken a single step toward material improvement until foreigners forced open the ports, and since then the Chinese had welcomed only those innovations, such as Western gunboats and arsenals, that could be used to restrict further foreign intervention. He maintained that peaceful devices such as railroads and telegraphs were neither understood nor desired by the Chinese. Browne concluded his remarks on Hart's views with the emphatic, and in fact insolent, statement that "no personal abuse for opinions honestly entertained by the undersigned . . . will remove the prejudices of the Chinese against our civilization."[64]

On July 20, 1869, without any instructions or authorization from the State Department, Browne turned over the Peking legation to S. Wells Williams as chargé d'affaires ad interim. Browne had contemplated this decision to resign for over a month, because he considered the appointment of his replacement a disapproval of his actions. On June 15 he wrote Fish that "I am at a loss to know . . . how I am to be governed by opinions based upon statements which I do not believe to be true, and upon theories which are refuted by facts."[65] Browne was frustrated but assured Williams that he felt no personal enmity toward anyone: "If I have differed from Mr. Burlingame it has been an honest and outspoken difference. Nobody feels more kindly to him than I do personally; and I wish him all success. I even wish his policy success, but I do not believe it will succeed."[66]

In a departing statement to the American and British mercantile communities in Shanghai, Browne summed up his policy position. He recalled that the treaty system had been established by force against the will of the Chinese. Within that context, he termed Burlingame's policy of respecting Chinese prejudices and abstaining from interference in their affairs an "anomaly." Conceding that China should be given consideration and respect as a sovereign nation, he insisted that no pretense should be made about the empire's being the equal of a Western state in terms of power or effective government. Western nations should attempt instead to elevate China to their standard. They should recognize that by their very presence in Asia they had already interfered in Chinese affairs, and that they were not at this point going to seduce China into reforming by fair promises. The United States and the other Western nations had forced obligations on China and, Browne argued, must now either compel the Middle Kingdom to maintain those commitments or break off relations with it.[67]

Faced with these alternatives, Browne believed the second to be "impolitic" and "pernicious." To allow an "ignorant pagan nation" to do as it pleased was retrogressive and detrimental to all human progress. In the year since the negotiation of the Burlingame Treaty, Browne contended, the number of outrages committed against foreigners had increased, and redress was impossible unless backed up by force. Continued disregard of this situation would lead ultimately to war. He concluded that in the interest of peace, of China's independence, and of the future welfare of all nations, the United States must insist on the execution of the treaties.[68]

When Browne returned to San Francisco on August 19, he learned that Howard had resigned without assuming his duties as minister. By this time, however, the State Department had received the scathing dispatches that Browne wrote before leaving China, and Fish curtly declined the erstwhile minister's offer to return to Peking. Burlingame provided Williams with the following analysis of Browne's difficulties with Washington:

> The President is indignant at some of the despatches of our Chinese Minister and had determined to recall him—I had nothing to do with it. The reason given for it was his leaning against the Chinese and the policy of the United States. . . . I am sorry, for Mr. Brown [sic] was so much for my views when I saw him in the U.S. . . . Like those Northern men who travelled in the South and put their feet under the planters tables [and] came back *so in line with the South.* So men when they enter China cannot help falling into the old time notions about governing and directing the Chinese.[69]

The opinions of Burlingame and Browne indeed represented two distinct policy approaches, but the secretary of state was not necessarily making a policy determination when he decided to replace Browne. In the hectic atmosphere of his first months in office, Fish most likely concluded that the querulous holdover from the Johnson administration was one headache that he could do without. The Grant administration decided on a change in Peking because it owed no political obligation to the obstreperous Browne and it did not like his negative attitude toward the Chinese. Fish doubted the effectiveness of a diplomat who bluntly labeled his hosts "ignorant pagans." For Browne, his long-desired diplomatic assignment ended in bitterness and frustration. It took him some time to get over his personal disappointment, but he was back in high spirits and engaged in several business schemes and making plans for a novel when he died suddenly in December 1875.[70]

J. Ross Browne's criticisms of Burlingame's views dramatized the alternatives in America's search for a policy in China during the second half of the nineteenth century. Both Burlingame and Browne assumed the West to be culturally and physically superior to China. This assumption clashed with the belief of the Chinese in their own cultural superiority. Burlingame, who manifested idealism as a social and political reformer, argued that America should be patient with the Chinese and should seek a common understanding with them. Browne, who demonstrated realism in his career as an outspoken investigator and satirical author, argued that toleration was impractical, because accommodation was impossible. Browne's conflict with Burlingame was a confrontation over how best to pursue American interests. Could the American ideals of equality, fairness, and self-determination be preserved while the rights that Americans in China had gained under the unequal treaty system were simultaneously protected?

The two ministers also disagreed on timing. Burlingame emphasized the future and Browne the present. Browne agreed with the treaty-port residents' demands for immediate expansion of Western rights and influence in China. Burlingame acknowledged the interests of the merchants and missionaries but believed that more time would be required to achieve a lasting settlement of Sino-Western differences. Burlingame's patience reflected his basic optimism. Browne's urgency stemmed from his more pessimistic assessment of existing conditions in China.[71]

For those American diplomats who would follow Burlingame and Browne to Peking, the policy alternatives would be more complicated. Although Burlingame may have been overly enthusiastic about the prospects for China's acceptance of Westerners and their ideas, his policy of no coercion or interference made good sense. Why should the United States risk a war with China or with the other treaty nations over issues in Asia that had little impact on American security or overall interests? Conversely, Browne may have been right about the irresolvable antagonisms between East and West, but his advocacy of force posed a critical question: Were the specific points of conflict worth the cost and risk involved in resolving them? The successors of Burlingame and Browne would have to sort out interests from ideals and decide between force and forbearance.

CHAPTER FOUR

Disillusionment and Frustration

FREDERICK F. LOW AND BENJAMIN P. AVERY IN CHINA

FREDERICK FERDINAND LOW had been in Peking only two months as the new United States minister plenipotentiary when a Chinese mob at Tientsin killed the French consul, ten Roman Catholic nuns, and ten other foreigners. The Tientsin massacre of June 21, 1870 bared the reality of the mutual hostility between China and the West in its most antagonistic terms, and because of it some historians have labeled 1870 the end of an era of attempted reconciliation in Sino-Western relations.[1] Distinct turning points in history are difficult to discern, and in this case Low's cautious diplomacy revealed that Burlingame's counsels of forbearance did not die with those massacred at Tientsin. Low and his American successor in Peking, Benjamin Parke Avery, found it very difficult to sustain Burlingame's optimism, however, and eventually arrived at some of Browne's more foreboding conclusions about the prospects for the peaceful resolution of differences between China and the West.

From its beginning in June 1863, the cooperative policy reflected more the spirit than the letter of Western diplomacy in China. As the decade of the 1870s opened, that spirit seemed to have vanished. Its initiator, Burlingame, and its coauthor, Bruce, were both gone.

Browne and British minister Rutherford B. Alcock did not share their predecessors' faith in the possibility of harmonious Sino-Western relations. Browne's brief tenure in China coincided with Alcock's negotiations with Prince Kung and the Tsungli Yamen for revisions in the British Treaty of Tientsin of 1858. The negotiators for both sides were under considerable pressure from their more extreme countrymen. Many Chinese officials wanted treaty revisions that would curtail foreign privileges in China. Many British merchants and missionaries, on the other hand, demanded the creation of even broader privileges. Alcock and the Tsungli Yamen steered a middle course, and the convention to which they finally agreed in October 1869 represented concessions by both sides on tariff, transit, and other controversial legal questions. The agreement was the product of genuine bargaining. For this reason, and despite the Burlingame Treaty of the previous year, historian Mary Wright has labeled the convention China's "first equal treaty," and she has proclaimed Alcock the mainstay of the cooperative policy. Lobbying by British merchants prevented Parliament's ratification of the Alcock Convention, and, according to Wright, this setback was a fatal blow to the cooperative approach.[2]

American observers of Alcock's diplomacy recorded a somewhat different picture of the British minister's position on cooperation with the Chinese. Secretary of State Seward, his successor Hamilton Fish, and United States consul general George F. Seward in Shanghai grouped Alcock together with Browne and the treaty-port merchants, who argued that the Chinese were responsive only to coercion, not cooperation. During Alcock's negotiations, Secretary Seward warned Browne against joining the British minister in pressing demands upon the Chinese. Browne disregarded this caution, however, and supported Alcock in what Fish later described as a "vigorous policy" of treaty revision.[3]

Alcock's position may have been relatively moderate compared to that of some Englishmen, but Washington's doubts about his commitment to cooperation were not unfounded. On various occasions as both consul at Shanghai and minister at Peking, Alcock demonstrated his willingness to use gunboats to settle diplomatic questions. At times Alcock did cooperate with the Tsungli Yamen and allow it the opportunity to make decisions without interference. As Consul General Seward reported, however, the British minister argued that his "experience leads infallibly to a conviction that when treaties have been imposed by force upon an unwilling government, as all with China have been, they can only be upheld by the same means."[4] Alcock should not have been equated with J. Ross Browne, but the Americans knew that the British minister was certainly not a Burlingame.[5]

Although the British Parliament had yielded to pressure for an even more forceful approach than the Alcock Convention, and Browne had leveled scathing criticisms at Burlingame's policies, Secretary of State Fish made the Burlingame Treaty the basis of the Grant administration's China policy. In December 1869, Fish instructed the newly appointed Frederick Low to adhere to the 1868 treaty that recognized the sovereignty of China's imperial government and that, unlike previous treaties between China and the Western nations, was based upon friendship, not force. In ratifying the articles, China exercised on its own the right to grant or withhold commercial privileges and also accepted the duty of enforcing agreements already made, and thus, in the secretary's view, voluntarily entered the family of nations.[6]

Although Fish endorsed the Burlingame Treaty, he made a distinction between the treaty and the cooperative policy of 1863. Like Browne and most of the other American ministers who followed Burlingame to China, Fish overlooked the fact that Burlingame consistently included China when he referred to cooperation. The secretary of state assumed that the policy was one of joint consultation and united action on the part of the foreign representatives when dealing with the imperial government. As Browne had pointed out, a procedure such as this one could conflict with the Burlingame Treaty, which guaranteed American noninterference in China's handling of internal improvements. Fish was not, however, too concerned about how such a conflict would be resolved. If cooperation were used to coerce China into accepting what it did not want, the United States simply would not participate. The secretary of state applied this rule to Alcock's negotiations for revision of the British Treaty of Tientsin. He indicated that the State Department considered both Prince Kung's "dignified and moderate" conduct and London's patience with the Chinese as being wiser than Alcock's "vigorous policy." The Chinese leaders had demonstrated good faith and willingness to come to some accommodation in the negotiations, and under such conditions any consideration of forcing demands upon them was most inappropriate. In Fish's opinion, there was sufficient evidence to justify the basic premise of the Burlingame Treaty—the recognition of China's sovereignty.[7]

Fish also believed that the articles signed in 1868 would prove important in the future to the ever-increasing number of Chinese coming to America and Americans going to China. He seemed to have harbored no fear of Chinese immigration into the United States. As for foreigners going to China, he optimistically predicted that they would "cease to be an aggressive element in China." Despite his prediction of less foreign pressure, he hoped that "the advisers of his Majesty the Emperor may soon see their way clear to counsel the granting of some concessions similar to those asked for by Sir Rutherford Alcock and Mr. Ross Browne."[8] Insisting that these innovations would benefit the Chinese people, Fish declared that the United States still deferred to the Chinese as to when and how such changes would be introduced. In response to America's friendly attitude, the administration hoped that the "statesmen of China" would moderate "the restrictions which fetter the commerce of the great empire over whose destiny they preside." Fish wanted to use Burlingame's means to achieve Browne's ends.[9]

Shortly after forwarding this lengthy instruction to Low, Fish wrote to Burlingame, who was then in Berlin negotiating with Bismarck on China's behalf, and underscored the prospects for both friendship and expanded commerce that he believed the new treaty created. The secretary of state reassured China's envoy that the United States government did not share the doubts about the treaty that some foreigners in China had expressed. The administration did not expect the Chinese to use the agreement as grounds for a "narrow or exclusive policy," and Fish reasserted that Washington maintained the greatest respect for China's "ancient government and institutions." He did not miss the opportunity, however, to lecture Burlingame on the advantages of expanded commerce. He pointed out that Western experience "demonstrated the fact that those nations become most wealthy, powerful and happy which develop . . . markets for their surplus productions."[10] Improved transportation between China's interior and its seaports, Fish added, would facilitate trade and thus would increase U.S. profits and create additional employment for the laborers of both countries. These two goals—finding markets for America's surplus production and improving China's transportation systems—preoccupied many Americans in the post-Civil War decades and were beginning to affect United States policy in China.[11]

When President Ulysses S. Grant appointed Frederick F. Low as United States minister plenipotentiary to China in September 1869, the Californian had already distinguished himself as a businessman and political leader. Low was born in New England and as a teenager served a five-year apprenticeship with the Boston firm of Russell, Sturgis, and Company, one of the leading American commercial houses involved in the China trade. In 1849 the lure of gold in California prompted him to go West to seek his fortune. He arrived in San Francisco a few days before his twenty-first birthday. Like thousands of other forty-niners, he never had much luck as a miner, but he quickly realized the potential business opportunities in a booming place such as gold-rush California. After a brief partnership in a general merchandise store in San Francisco, he moved to Marysville. There, with his two brothers, he formed a successful mercantile and shipping business, and he later became a partner in the California Steam Navigation Company and in a Marysville bank.[12]

In 1861, as the nation was plunging into the Civil War, Low moved back to San Francisco as a prosperous entrepreneur, and to his surprise he received the Republican nomination for California's newly created third seat in Congress. Although he had not sought the position, in the fall of that year he was elected to the United States House of Representatives. He served one term in Washington but did not seek renomination. Low looked forward to returning to his business pursuits in 1863, but he found himself unable to refuse an appointment by President Abraham Lincoln as the collector of the Port of San Francisco. His loyal service to the Union cause both as collector and as a member of Congress made him a popular favorite among many of California's pro-Union politicians. In June 1863, his supporters successfully secured his nomination as Unionist (Republican) candidate for governor—defeating two better-known leaders, incumbent governor Leland Stanford and Congressman Aaron A. Sargent. In the general election, Low outdistanced John G. Downey, the Democratic nominee, by over twenty thousand votes.[13]

Inaugurated on December 10, 1863 as his state's first four-year governor, Low continued during his term in Sacramento to be a faithful

Frederick F. Low was a businessman and California's first four-year governor before becoming United States minister to China from 1869 to 1874. *Bancroft Library, University of California, Berkeley.*

supporter of the Northern war effort and the Republican party. Under his leadership, California supplied all of the volunteers and financial support for the war that Lincoln's government requested from the state. When the war ended, he endorsed the congressional plan of reconstruction. In December 1867, in one of his last official acts as governor, he recommended to the state legislature the ratification of the Fourteenth Amendment, which provided the constitutional authority for the congressional reconstruction program. Low remained outspoken in his support of the Republican majority in Congress and publicly expressed approval of the impeachment proceedings against President Andrew Johnson in 1868.[14]

Governor Low had proved to be an honest and even courageous chief executive. Not only did he unhesitatingly voice his own convictions on national issues, he even more fearlessly challenged the widespread anti-Chinese prejudice in California by criticizing state laws that discriminated against Orientals. In a January 1867 speech, he pleaded with his San Francisco audience: "We must learn to treat the Chinese who come to live among us decently, and not oppress them by unfriendly legislation, nor allow them to be abused, robbed, and murdered, without extending to them any adequate remedy."[15] His businessman's perception of a potential market in China for American goods undoubtedly colored his view of the Chinese, but still his sentiments were remarkably enlightened for his times. Indeed, in 1869, two years after he left the governor's office, Low's publicly expressed sympathy for the Chinese and his Republican loyalty made him Secretary of State Fish's choice for the post of United States minister to China.[16]

Low had not sought the position as J. Ross Browne's replacement in Peking. In fact, the former governor and congressman had always considered himself a businessman, not a politician. He was too independent and outspoken to feel comfortable in public life. It was precisely his frank defense of Chinese rights in California that made Washington believe that, despite his lack of diplomatic experience, he was the best man to continue Burlingame's cooperative policy. In October 1869, Low reluctantly put aside the management of his business interests in San Francisco and accepted his commission as the new United States minister plenipotentiary. He arrived at the small American legation building in Peking on April 19, 1870 and assumed the duties of his office the following day.[17]

The new minister's first impressions of the state of relations between Chinese and Westerners in China reconfirmed his earlier opinions, formed in California, that fairmindedness and friendship would be the most effective approach toward Orientals. In one of his first reports from Peking, Low advised Secretary of State Fish:

> It will require time and patience to work changes in the existing order of things by peaceful means. No one agency will be likely to do so much towards enlightenment, as a prelude to progress, as personal contacts, intercourse and discussion between the representatives of Western nations resident in China and the Chinese officials.[18]

The former governor, whom Robert Hart described as a man of "practical common sense," appeared to be a worthy heir to Burlingame's cooperative diplomacy.[19]

The Tientsin massacre of June 21, 1870 quickly tested Low's commitment to the principle of peaceful cooperation with the Chinese government. While other foreigners, particularly missionaries, panicked from fear of imminent antiforeign uprisings throughout the country, the new American minister viewed the situation more cautiously. He abhorred and condemned the carnage and destruction caused by the

Chinese mob but believed that the French officials and missionaries who were attacked in Tientsin had largely determined their own fate. The center of contention had been the Roman Catholic orphanage at Tientsin operated by the Sisters of Charity. Low felt "entirely certain that the people who brought children to the Sisters' Establishment were rewarded pecuniarily."[20] Such activities sparked rumors that the orphanage was buying children for diabolical purposes, such as the making of soap and medicines from their organs. The French consul in Tientsin had done nothing to allay popular suspicions and, in fact, had fired his pistol into a crowd of local officials and townspeople who had come to the mission demanding to know exactly what went on inside. The shot narrowly missed the district magistrate and killed one of his attendants. Instantly transformed into a mob, the Chinese delegation literally tore to pieces the consul and his assistant and then brutally killed and mutilated ten nuns, two French priests, and seven other foreigners. The enraged crowd also murdered several Chinese Christian converts and burned the mission property.[21]

Although no Americans were killed at Tientsin, Low took part in a joint foreign demand to the Tsungli Yamen for punishment of the murderers and for measures to prevent other such occurrences. He warily avoided, however, associating the United States with any of France's specific demands for redress. The American minister maintained a public facade of cooperation with his French colleague, but privately he sent Washington a stream of sharp criticisms of French diplomacy.[22]

Following the massacre, war between France and China appeared imminent, and it probably would have occurred if the Franco-Prussian War had not preempted the attention of Paris. Low placed total blame on Count Rochechouart, the French chargé d'affaires in Peking, for raising the specter of war in China. Initially Rochechouart simply joined with the other foreign representatives in their communications with the Tsungli Yamen. After going to Tientsin for a personal inspection, however, the chargé arbitrarily declared two local Chinese officials guilty and demanded their immediate decapitation. He threatened to turn the matter over to the admiral of the French fleet in the Pacific if the Chinese authorities did not comply.[23]

Low believed that Rochechouart had made a serious blunder. The Chinese refused to execute the officials; and the French admiral, uncertain of his country's strategy toward Prussia, would not commit his forces against the Chinese without orders from Paris. The French chargé had first impugned China's sovereignty and then had been unable to carry out his threat. According to Low, such conduct jeopardized the welfare of every foreigner in China. In the absence of French naval pressure, weeks passed without any action by the imperial government. The Chinese people would misinterpret Peking's inaction, Low feared, and think that their government condoned the massacre. The result would be more bloodshed, and the responsibility would rest squarely on Rochechouart. This dangerous situation could have been prevented, in Low's opinion, if the French chargé had remained united with his colleagues in addressing the Tsungli Yamen. The American thought that cooperation among the foreign representatives could have prompted the imperial Chinese government to settle the case. Low understood that cooperation could be both with and against the Chinese government and that "M. Rochechouart's isolated and infirm policy" had been neither.[24]

Although Low complained directly to the Tsungli Yamen about its dilatory and irresolute handling of the Tientsin affair, he sympathized with the government's difficult position. The foreign office had to satisfy both the Western representatives in Peking and the emperor's xenophobic advisors, who believed that the French had gotten what they deserved. Low was convinced that the disturbance at Tientsin had been a local affair, but the minister feared that Peking's silence would invite more antiforeign outbreaks. Low urged the Tsungli Yamen to deny officially the rumors that the nuns kidnapped children and committed other evil deeds. He also pointed out the need for prompt prosecution of those actually guilty of the attack. To Washington he reported that such action would not be easy. Low noted that since the English government, for example, could not ascertain and punish Irish rioters, it was not surprising that the feeble Chinese government was having difficulty in Tientsin.[25]

Although he understood the imperial government's limitations, Low did not hesitate to send a strong note to the Tsungli Yamen in September 1870, when fear of local hostility caused American missionaries to flee from their homes in Shantung province. He laid heavy blame on Peking for not taking forceful action. The imperial government's lack of "courage and resolution" following the Tientsin massacre contributed, in his opinion, to the unsettled situation throughout north China.[26]

The State Department generally approved Low's diplomacy, but Washington did make one noteworthy comment on his handling of the Shantung episode. Although the department endorsed the tone of Low's firm protest to the Tsungli Yamen, Secretary Fish indicated that Low gave "too strong an assurance of forbearance" by limiting his defense only to the rights of American citizens. Fish instructed the minister to make clear to Prince Kung "that any violation of the rights of our citizens and any flagrant violation of treaty stipulations of other powers" might endanger Sino-American relations.[27] Fish, like his predecessor Seward, appeared willing to commit the United States unreservedly to Western solidarity in China. Low, like Burlingame, was less quick to take sides.

In other instructions to Low, the department inserted observations that, although not policy directives, indicated another difference between Fish and Low. The State Department frequently stated that the United States' only interest in China was expanded trade under the treaty system, and in the midst of the Sino-French crisis, Fish wrote: "We seek the expansion of peaceful commercial relations with China and while every nation is justified in claiming ample redress for wrongs, due regard should be paid to all the interests involved in the relations of China with the maritime powers collectively."[28] Fish feared what a war in China would cost the United States in terms of trade. Low, too, believed in the importance of commerce but seldom mentioned trade either to Washington or in his correspondence with the Tsungli Yamen. Following the events at Tientsin, Low appeared more concerned about the cost in lives and property than any potential disruption of commerce.

The Tsungli Yamen's final settlement of the Tientsin massacre dissatisfied both Low and Rochechouart, but for different reasons. The Chinese government executed twenty people, exiled twenty-five, and only temporarily suspended the two local officials at Tientsin whom Rochechouart considered the leaders of the riot. In addition, China paid France a sizable indemnity and sent an imperial envoy to Paris to apologize to the French government. From the French representative's point of view, the Tsungli Yamen had not adequately punished all of the guilty parties, and the death and destruction had not been avenged. The outcome set a precedent, according to French historian Henri Cordier, that emasculated French policy in China for the rest of the century.[29] Low felt that it was the Chinese government, not the

French, that had been emasculated. He believed that the Tsungli Yamen had done too little too late and thereby had weakened its position relative to both its own subordinate officials and the foreign legations. Low described his own reaction to the Sino-French confrontation as one of "leniency" toward the Tsungli Yamen.[30]

In reporting to Washington on the Tientsin incident, Low characterized Rochechouart as "ambitious and unscrupulous, even for a Frenchman. His actions are controlled entirely by passion, prejudice, and personal ambition."[31] In Low's estimation, the French representative's conduct exhibited "in a clear light the petty jealousies which prevent the carrying out in good faith of what is popularly known as the cooperative policy."[32] He accused the chargé of attempting to dictate to the Chinese and to the other treaty powers and of trying to discredit American counsels of forbearance. Low believed that both he and his predecessor Burlingame had always tried to be just to everyone. In the case of damage claims, for instance, Low explained that he followed Burlingame's example of seeking payment equivalent to the value of the actual losses and of never allowing any money to pass through the American legation or consulates. Rochechouart, on the other hand, presented claims for 400 percent of the value of the losses at Tientsin and had this amount paid directly to him. Low did not know how much of this money actually went to the claimants, but the Roman Catholic bishop of Peking reported that "the Tientsin riot was a good financial operation for the representative of France. And what makes the matter worse the Chinese hear and repeat the same stories."[33] Recalling other incidents, Low contended that the French had always been so eager to get a pecuniary compensation when a missionary was murdered that the Chinese now considered such events a mere monetary transaction. From the Chinese point of view, it was money well spent. Low concluded that Rochechouart's actions simply represented the latest step in the long history of French "force and fraud" in China. Low proposed a different approach:

> Let foreigners conduct themselves properly towards this people. . . . Our progress may, and undoubtedly will be, slow; but it will be more sure and perhaps more advantageous to both foreigner and native than a greater nominal progress forced by wars and bloodshed.[34]

Although Low was not confident about the prospects for peace in China, he did not believe that force had to be used. He dismissed the conflicting-civilizations thesis of "irrepressible conflict," which Browne and the Western merchants in China advocated. Low classified the Chinese as a superior, although pagan, people who exhibited great "mental capacity, industry, and administrative power." He maintained that the Chinese were not like the African Negroes or American Indians, and he charged that foreigners were wrong to believe that "a Chinaman has no rights that a white man is bound to respect." The Chinese may have been ignorant of the West, Low observed, but Westerners were equally ignorant of China. Like Burlingame before him, Low concluded that foreign nations "should pursue a just and firm course, and at the same time be prepared to exercise patience and forbearance."[35] The Tientsin massacre had not convinced him of the need for abandoning peaceful cooperation in favor of a forceful policy in Asia.[36]

The Tientsin tragedy prompted Low to examine the general question of missionary activity in China. He believed that the Christian missions could be a source of enlightenment and education for the Chinese and promised to give them moral support and such legal support as the Western treaties with China allowed. After personally examining the treaties, Low determined that the missionaries had no treaty right to reside in the interior of China. Yet missionaries of all denominations persisted in moving inland and doing other things that intensified antiforeignism. Low considered this "misguided zeal" to be the source of many of the attacks on missionaries. Although during the Tientsin crisis he frequently cited the mistakes of the French Catholics, his indictment also included the American and English Protestant missionaries. Low regretted that these well-meaning men and women, who considered themselves diplomatic advisors to the legations as well as self-appointed spiritual mentors of the Chinese, had urgently advocated a war between France and China: "Their zeal . . . in invoking the vengeance of the God of War, seems greater than inculcating the divine precepts of the Prince of Peace, of whom they profess to be humble followers."[37]

Low observed, too, that many merchants favored force as the most direct and least difficult method of expanding their contacts with the Chinese. He conceded that there was truth in the merchants' contention that the treaties had been established by force, but he disagreed with the proposition that force was still necessary. Even if justice and morality were to be set aside, Low argued, war was an inexpedient policy for peace. Granting that Chinese recalcitrance and foreign impatience made war seem inevitable, he insisted that the "application of military force" would lead to only a temporary, not a permanent, resolution of Sino-Western differences.[38]

Privately, Low told Assistant Secretary of State Bancroft Davis: "You will find that I do not see things as my predecessor [Browne] did—all dark—nor so bright as the more enthusiastic people do."[39] Low placed himself between Browne and Burlingame, but actually at this time, January 1871, he came much closer to the latter. He reiterated his belief that a military solution to issues arising in China would be possible only if foreign governments maintained large military and naval forces in China to police the treaties. Neither the United States nor any European country would ever, in his opinion, make such a commitment of forces. Still, Low was not optimistic about the prospects for peace between the Middle Kingdom and the barbarians. Some incident would occur, he predicted grimly, "which will furnish the ground for a further forcible entry into the interior, and the further impoverishment of the Government and people by compelling them, after being whipped, to pay the expense of the whipping."[40] Burlingame was gone, but the American representative in Peking continued to express the New Englander's sentiments, if not his optimism.

Events soon proved that Low could not maintain Burlingame's level of tolerance and forbearance in the performance of his duties. The turning point in Low's diplomacy came in Korea in the spring of 1871. The Hermit Kingdom increasingly attracted the attention of Westerners after the late 1850s, because of the growing number of trading vessels in the waters between China and Japan. As more ships moved along the coast of the peninsula, frequent shipwrecks and the possibility of trade with Korea evoked the notice of Western officials. The Korean government, however, refused all contact with foreign governments. When Koreans presumably murdered the crew of the wrecked American ship *General Sherman* in 1866, Secretary of State Seward wanted the United States and France to mount a joint military expedition to force Korea both to allow trade and to protect foreign seamen. Paris rejected Seward's suggestion, but American officials continued to desire a settlement of the *General Sherman* case and to seek an opportunity to "open" Korea. With these objectives in mind, Secretary of State Fish included U.S. relations with Korea in Low's responsibilities as minister to China.[41]

On the day Low assumed his duties in Peking, Fish sent the new minister authorization and instructions to negotiate a treaty with Korea to secure "commercial advantages" and protection of shipwrecked Americans. Fish made arrangements with the Navy Department for Low to go to Korea with five warships under the command of Rear Admiral John Rodgers, commander-in-chief of the Asiatic Squadron. The secretary of state hoped that the Koreans, faced with a show of force, would negotiate as the Japanese had done in 1854 when Commodore Matthew Perry had steamed into Tokyo Bay with an American flotilla. Fish instructed Low to "exercise prudence and discretion" and to avoid using the warships as long as possible without "dishonor." The secretary knew that there were risks involved in the mission but never seemed to consider the possibility of failure and the effects of such a setback on America's limited and peaceful goals in Asia.[42]

After receiving his instructions, Low told Fish that he was "not sanguine of favorable results" in Korea but that he would make every effort to accomplish the mission. He noted that Germany and France had failed recently in similar efforts. Low reported that although Korea was a "tributary kingdom" of China (indicating a theoretical Chinese suzerainty), Peking had declared Seoul independent in its foreign relations. The Tsungli Yamen wanted no complications with foreign powers over Korea. Low knew very little about Korea, but he expected the Koreans to resist negotiations by "cunning and sophistry," and by force if necessary. He hoped for peaceful discussions but advised Washington: "It is a mistaken policy when dealing with oriental governments and peoples to allow insults and injuries to go unredressed. Such lenity leads them to believe that fear alone prevents retaliation, and adds to their arrogance, conceit, and hostility."[43] Although he knew that his mission exposed the United States to almost certain insult and injury, Low proceeded to Korea without protesting to Washington that the whole effort might backfire.[44]

Arriving on May 30, 1871 at the mouth of the river leading to Seoul, Low and Admiral Rodgers, whom Robert Hart called a "fire-eater," discovered that only their two smallest vessels could proceed up the shallow river. The two small gunboats, hardly an intimidating force, went forward to survey the channel and were fired upon by forts guarding the river. The Americans returned the fire and withdrew. Meanwhile, back on the admiral's flagship, Low had been able to contact only a few minor local officials. He also talked with some Koreans who claimed to be Christians and who told him that the crew of the *General Sherman* had definitely been murdered. These events convinced Low more than ever that the Korean government would resist all contacts, but he did not want the Chinese and Koreans to think that the United States and the West were weak. He and Rodgers therefore decided that they must respond to the "unprovoked" attack on the two gunboats. Low doubted that a counterattack by Rodgers's forces would induce the Koreans to negotiate, but he was no longer concerned about a treaty. He wanted only to salvage the honor of the United States that lack of American foresight had jeopardized. Thinking of the *General Sherman* and the gunboats, Low wondered "whether the statements of this semi-barbarous and hostile people shall be received without question in justification of their acts of robbery and murder, committed upon the property and people of the United States."[45] Low sounded like Rochechouart at Tientsin.[46]

Low and Rodgers gave the Korean government ten days either to apologize for opening hostilities or to offer to begin negotiations. When the Koreans refused to do either, Rodgers's forces completely destroyed five forts that had fired on the gunboats and killed about 250 Koreans in the battle. Twelve Americans were killed or wounded in the clash, which was the U.S. Navy's largest involvement in hostile action between the Civil War and the Spanish-American War. In attempting to justify the use of force, Low told Fish that Oriental governments did everything possible to maintain the fiction of their superiority over foreigners, such as refusing to negotiate or sending only minor officials to meet foreign envoys. "My own observation and experience, as well as the experience of others," he explained to the State Department, "convinced me that concession on these points would lower my position, lessen my influence, and thus render the task more difficult; I therefore determined to adopt a firm and dignified policy. . . ."[47] After the American attack, however, the local Korean officials refused to send any further American communications to Seoul. Low concluded that

the recent demonstration, which would have produced a profound impression upon any other government, has little or no effect, favorable or otherwise, upon this [government, which] . . . shows no sign . . . that there is any change in its attitude of defiance to all other nations.[48]

Low's frustration was readily apparent.[49]

The mission had proved to be a diplomatic disaster. Low and Rodgers had hoped that the Koreans, faced by an intimidating force, would negotiate, as the Japanese had done with Perry. Korea, however, was not Japan. When the Americans departed from the peninsula with several of their men and scores of Koreans dead, the United States had neither a treaty nor a settlement of the *General Sherman* case. In addition, the episode had a negative impact on Sino-American relations. The American failure reconfirmed the opinion of many Chinese officials that the United States was as blustering and inept as the other Western nations. Many of the mandarins became even more recalcitrant toward the foreigners. Low's frustrating experience greatly disillusioned him about the prospects for peaceful and cooperative Sino-Western relations in the future.[50]

In his final report to Washington on the Korean misadventure, Low admitted the complete failure of the expedition. He primarily blamed Korean recalcitrance for his lack of success. In defense of his decision to attack the Koreans, he argued that Peking had paid close attention to the entire operation and that any evidence of pusilanimity on the part of the United States would have strengthened antiforeign sentiment in the Middle Kingdom. Low predicted that China would never fully respect foreign governments as long as Korea successfully resisted Western advances. Low's recommendation following his Korean experience sounded quite different from his earlier views:

And every year that the Corean government is allowed to continue in its exclusiveness, increases the peril to the lives and property of foreign residents in China. If no adequate measures be taken to avert the impending storm in the East, the result will, I fear, be disastrous.[51]

Faced with a decision in Korea, Low underwent a transformation. He already believed in the need for firmness in diplomacy and had criticized Rochechouart for threatening and then doing nothing at Tientsin. When Low personally confronted Oriental obduracy in Korea, however, his previous counsels of patience and forbearance disappeared. He did not return to China as a gunboat diplomatist. He continued to act cautiously in administering his responsibilities, but he became much less hopeful of a peaceful resolution of East-West differences. Low went to China believing as Burlingame had that the two civilizations were compatible. After the Korean mission, Low increasingly adopted Browne's view of the great gulf between the cultures.

No single issue demonstrated more dramatically the differences between China and the West than did the Western diplomats' demand for an audience before the emperor. The Chinese had always viewed the world as a hierarchy, with the emperor at the top and the sovereigns of all other countries arranged below as subordinates. The Westerners maintained in accordance with their own tradition that the world consisted of equally sovereign nations. Although foreigners had frequently neglected to respect China as an equal, they had insisted that the emperor agree to receive the envoys from the West without the three kneelings and nine prostrations of the kowtow ceremony. The Chinese had just as stubbornly refused to abandon this ritual that symbolized the inferiority of all men to the emperor. Finally, on June 29, 1873, with Low representing the United States, the T'ung-chih emperor granted the first audience ever held by a Chinese emperor for Western diplomatic representatives. A few days earlier, the emperor also had received envoys from Korea, a tribute-paying state. The Koreans performed the kowtow and the Westerners did not, but the dynastic records termed all of them *shih-ch'en* (tributary envoys).[52]

The working out of the details of the audience had required long and arduous haggling between the Tsungli Yamen and the Western legations. Even after the emperor agreed to dispense with the kowtow ritual as a gesture of his benevolence, his advisors insisted that other symbolic indications of his superiority be observed. The diplomats, however, remained strongly opposed to any procedures that might suggest the vassalage or inferiority of their countries. The ceremony to which all parties finally agreed was very simple. Low and his colleagues from Russia, France, Britain, Holland, and Japan were escorted to the Imperial Palace shortly after 6:00 A.M. After a wait of about three hours, they were summoned to the imperial presence in the Pavilion of Imperial Light. Each minister bowed three times while placing his credentials on a table ten to twelve paces from the emperor's raised throne. With the foreigners standing, Prince Kung dropped to his knees before the throne and conversed briefly with the sovereign. The prince then rose and walked down the steps from the

The Palace of Heavenly Purity was one of the most elaborate of
the many audience halls in the Imperial Palace in Peking.

throne. He conveyed to the diplomats the emperor's greetings and his
acceptance of their letters of credence. The audience for the six foreign
representatives lasted a little more than five minutes.[53]

Although Low later termed the occasion a "new departure" in Sino-
Western relations, he had approached the diplomatic ceremony displaying the same disillusionment that had followed his Korean experience. He doubted that the audience concession would prove to be a
"panacea" for cultural accommodation but argued that failure to insist
on it would "confirm the high [Chinese] officials in their arrogance and
conceit which will be damaging to foreign interests and lead to inter-
ruption of friendly relations at no distant day."[54] Low understood that
the audience question assaulted the Chinese belief in the emperor as
the Son of Heaven, but he asserted that the ministers were duty-
bound to press the issue in the interests of peace as well as foreign
dignity. "Until the native mind can be freed from the belief that all
'outside states' are inferior," he concluded, "there can be no real relations of peace and amity between China and western nations."[55]

Immediately after the audience, Low returned to California on a

long-desired leave of absence. He had requested the leave almost a
year earlier, in order to return home to attend to his personal affairs,
which had suffered greatly while he was in China. After he was back in
San Francisco, he submitted his resignation from his diplomatic post.
Fish accepted his resignation on April 9, 1874, and thus ended the
government career of Frederick Low.[56]

Low had never intended to make government service his profession,
and he was happy to be back in the familiar surroundings of the California business community. He quickly accepted a managerial position
with the Anglo-California Bank and remained with that institution for
twenty years. Under his direction, the bank followed only the Bank of
California in the volume of its business within the state. Low was also
successfully involved in a street railway, Hawaiian sugar plantations,
lumber properties, and other enterprises. Although content to be out
of government, he maintained an interest in China. In 1880 he met
with James B. Angell, when Angell passed through San Francisco on
his way to Peking to negotiate the treaty that ultimately limited Chinese immigration to the United States. Recalling his own experiences,
Low advised Angell that the chances for a successful treaty mission in
China were doubtful.[57]

Low possessed the pragmatism and common sense that one would
expect to find in a successful businessman. Although not experienced
in diplomacy, he was practical enough to realize that a barrier of suspicion and hostility separated the Chinese and Westerners. The Tientsin
massacre graphically displayed this antagonism shortly after his arrival. The bloody events at Tientsin did not shake his own personal
belief that conciliatory means could be found to reconcile the differences between Orientals and Occidentals. His hopes for peaceful relations foundered, however, when the ill-conceived mission to Korea in
1871 ended in armed conflict. Even his unprecedented audience before
the emperor of China did not reassure him. Low was not a gunboat
diplomat who advocated the use of force as the basis of Western
policies in China, but his own experiences led him to predict accurately
that hostility and violence, not cooperation, would continue for some
time to plague relations between Chinese and Westerners.

Over a year elapsed between Low's departure from Peking and the
arrival of his replacement, Benjamin Parke Avery, at the legation on

October 28, 1874. Robert Hart described the new American minister as "a man of culture and ability; but poverty-stricken and showing it."[58] Avery may have seemed impoverished because of the totally inadequate funding that the United States government gave its Peking legation, and also because the new minister had suffered a severe illness enroute that had not only delayed his arrival but increased the expense of his trip. Avery's health had not been good for several years, and in Peking he remained a near-invalid most of the time. Despite his condition, Avery took an active role in renewal of the audience question and in negotiations with the Tsungli Yamen on the construction of telegraph lines. The failure of both efforts greatly disappointed him, for he had worked diligently to secure the cooperation of the other Western legations on both issues. He experienced additional frustration over the lack of harmony and patience among his Western colleagues when some Chinese in Yunnan province murdered a British consular official. Avery learned, as had Low, that Chinese recalcitrance and Western rivalries formed major obstacles to the vague altruism of Burlingame's cooperative policy.[59]

Like Browne and Low, who had preceded him in office, Avery was a Californian. In fact, all three men had trekked west to their adopted state in the gold-rush days of 1849. Avery was born in New York City in 1828, but at age twenty-one he left his widowed mother to the care of his brother and went in search of his fortune. Although he stayed with mining longer than did Low, Avery never struck it rich, and eventually he turned to other pursuits. In 1858 he purchased a small newspaper in Nevada County and began what was to be a successful career as a journalist. In 1860 he took over control of the *Marysville Appeal* and transformed that formerly Democratic and unsuccessful journal into one of the most important Republican party dailies in the state. The Republican landslide in the 1861 elections in California carried Avery into office as the state printer at the same time that Low won a seat in Congress. Although Avery managed his duties well for one term, he failed to gain renomination as state printer when Low's supporters defeated incumbent governor Leland Stanford's forces at the Republican state convention in 1863. Avery returned to journalism as an editorial writer for the *San Francisco Bulletin*. His favorable reporting on the controversial financing of Stanford's Central Pacific Railroad caused a rival newspaper to call Avery a "lick-spittle and

Benjamin P. Avery, journalist
and United States minister to
China, 1874–1875. *Bancroft
Library, University of California, Berkeley.*

toady to ex-Governor Stanford." In addition to his work on the *Bulletin*, Avery also became a leading promoter of art in California, and in
1871 he helped found the San Francisco Art Association. His writing,
especially on art, secured for him the editorship of the *Overland
Monthly* in November 1873. This excellent literary magazine, previously edited by Bret Harte, compared favorably with the best Eastern
journals. Avery's increasing prominence generated some consideration
of him as a candidate for the United States Senate, but instead his
return to public office led him to the other side of the world. When Low
resigned as minister to China, Senator Aaron Sargent of California
recommended to the Grant administration that Avery be appointed to
the post in Peking, because of both his ability and the fact that the
office had become a political perquisite of the state. After six months
as editor of the *Overland Monthly*, Avery formally became the new
United States minister plenipotentiary to China on May 7, 1874.[60]

Immediately upon his arrival in China in the fall of 1874, Avery
revealed that he was prepared to cooperate with his Western diplo-

matic colleagues in every way. This attitude contrasted with that of Low, who, following the Tientsin massacre, had joined the other foreign representatives in communications with the Tsungli Yamen but had attempted to maintain a middle position between the Chinese and the French. While still enroute to Peking, Avery declared that he sided with the Western legations on all questions. He stated this position in a meeting at Tientsin with Li Hung-chang, the powerful governor general of Chihli, China's northern coastal region. Beginning in the 1870s, Li's office at Tientsin began to preempt the functions of the Tsungli Yamen; and although the Western legations remained in Peking, Li in his capacity as superintendent of trade became China's virtual foreign minister for the last three decades of the nineteenth century.[61] Li had asked Avery for the good offices of the United States in settling a dispute between China and Japan over who should control the island of Taiwan (Formosa). The American minister informed the governor general that considerations of Western cooperation precluded his responding to Li's request.[62]

Avery had not even met any of the other Western ministers, and yet he was already expressing his willingness to defer all questions to joint consultation. He had no personal knowledge of the position of his colleagues on the Taiwan question, but he reported to the State Department:

> Bearing in mind how essential my government has for some years deemed it for its ministers at Peking to cooperate cordially with those of the other treaty powers, on all general questions, and believing it unwise to seek for any selfish advantage, or to do anything which might savor of disingenuousness or bad faith towards my colleagues, I . . . [suggested] that China could better obtain any counsel she might require if she would frankly communicate to the ministers, in a joint circular, a statement of the present condition of the controversy with Japan, inviting, if it was desired, their views on the subject.[63]

Li feared, however, that the English or the French, or both, might be in league with the Japanese. Avery finally agreed to ask Washington about good offices but told Li "that I should furnish copies to my colleagues and advise them of the nature of the reply."[64] Clearly Avery meant to cooperate with the Westerners, and not with the Chinese against the Westerners.

Shortly after Avery's arrival in Peking, the teenaged T'ung-chih emperor died, probably because of smallpox complicated by syphilis, and his death once again raised the audience question. Avery took the lead in attempting to organize an audience with the new, three-year-old Kuang-hsü emperor. Although his colleagues in the other legations took little interest in another audience at that time, Avery displayed his enthusiasm for cooperation by persistently urging a joint foreign approach on the subject. Avery argued that under standard international practice, new letters of credence should be delivered by the foreign envoys to the new emperor. He also noted that, although the sovereign reigned through a regency headed by Empress Dowager Tz'u-hsi, the infant Son of Heaven had received Chinese, Mongolian, and Korean officials. In the American minister's estimation, Western failure to push for another audience would nullify the precedent of 1873. Most of the other legations were more concerned with other issues or were in the process of changing personnel and gave Avery little encouragement. He disappointedly wrote to Fish that "while my own opinion is unchanged as to the desirability of securing a nearer conformity to international usage in this particular, I must admit that, failing cooperation, it is inexpedient for this Legation to move further."[65] Avery discovered that a policy of cooperation was not always easy to implement.[66]

Avery learned a similar lesson when he tried to promote Western technological innovations in China. More than any of his predecessors, he made an effort to aid specific foreign enterprises in China. Burlingame had treated business ventures with great caution. Although Browne argued for the rapid introduction of Western technology into China, he had had few opportunities to aid specific schemes. Low, though a businessman who spent over three years in China, never engaged in the promotion of commercial activities. Avery, however, spent a great deal of his brief time in Peking seeking "more avenues of labor and mercantile enterprise." He noted with approval the growth of foreign trade and the occasional remarks by Chinese officials favoring railroads or coal mines. He requested instructions from Washington concerning increased Chinese competition with the profitable American steamship business.[67]

Avery's greatest promotional effort came in behalf of telegraph construction. The Great Northern Telegraph Company, a Danish firm, had begun erecting lines in Fukien province. The provincial authorities had approved the construction for military reasons during the troubles with Japan over Taiwan. About twenty miles of line had been completed by October 1874, when local officials asked the company to stop. American consul M. M. DeLano at Foochow believed that Peking had ordered the work halted and that the Tsungli Yamen wanted to purchase the line. Avery speculated that the Chinese government's offer to buy might be a pretext for destroying the line. If, on the other hand, the mandarins intended to keep the telegraph system in operation, the American minister perceived a mutually advantageous arrangement for everyone involved. The imperial government would be making "a most important step in [technological] advance," and foreigners would still "have the profits of construction and management," since the Chinese would not be able to do the work alone for a long time to come. An additional bonus for foreigners, Avery noted, would be "the advantage to their commercial, financial, and political interests which rapid communication, even in Chinese hands, would insure."[68]

General Raasloff, Denmark's former minister to the United States, arrived in Peking in December 1874 to arrange for the protection of Danish telegraph interests in China. He requested the cooperation of his Western colleagues in his negotiations with the Tsungli Yamen. Raasloff proposed that the Westerners seek protection only for the Danish company's off-shore cable that was already in operation between Vladivostok and Hong Kong. Thinking that an agreement on the off-shore line would by implication cover land lines as well, the Danish minister did not want to risk the Tsungli Yamen's explicit disapproval of the controversial Fukien telegraph project, especially since construction of the line still continued, despite Peking's previous orders to the contrary.[69]

Although holding no specific instructions from Washington, Avery decided to cooperate fully with the other ministers in supporting Raasloff's plan. The American pointed out that he did so in the general interest of improving communications, and not to promote a specific scheme. He termed telegraphic facilities as essential as the postal service to all foreign commerce in China, including that of the United States. In his opinion, the Burlingame Treaty certainly did not prevent the United States from asking China to take a forward step when the general welfare required it. In terms reminiscent of J. Ross Browne, Avery argued:

> If we rest on the assertion that China will be left to advance in her own way, and fail to indicate when a good time and way are presented, we are simply allies of the native apathy and inertia which oppose progress now as they have opposed it heretofore.[70]

Avery drew up the plan of how the Western ministers would approach the imperial government on the telegraph issue. Raasloff wanted a "strenuous" collective note asking for protection of the cables. The others considered this tactic too extreme for the initial request. Avery's plan, which all his colleagues accepted, provided for the legations to address the Tsungli Yamen with notes identical in substance but not in language. If the Chinese answer proved to be unfavorable or unsatisfactory, identical notes and, if necessary, a collective note would be sent. Avery anticipated that "no satisfactory response will be elicited by the first note, and therefore the value of leaving the way open for two more, each more decided than the other, is apparent."[71] Obviously, Avery and his colleagues would not take no for an answer.[72]

In a masterful reply, Prince Kung conceded just enough to ease the foreign pressure without absolutely affirming the request. Reminding the ministers of popular opposition and other conditions inimical to the construction of telegraphs, the prince declared that Peking could not be responsible for any damage to the lines. He did, however, send instructions to the provincial authorities to protect the cables to the extent they thought feasible. Avery and his colleagues decided to interpret the reply positively and allow some time to judge the response of the local officials. By January 1875, thirty-five miles of line from Foochow to Amoy had been completed, despite continuing objections from the authorities there. Avery feared that the work would eventually be stopped but was willing to await the results of Prince Kung's action. The American believed that the Peking government's position made "a little progress possible under the prudent enterprise of individuals, and [prepared] the way for more liberal concessions hereafter."[73]

Events again disappointed Avery's hopes for innovation in China through Western cooperation. While the local officials looked the other way, a mob at Foochow forcibly halted construction of the telegraph line in February 1875. Neither the consuls nor the ministers of Britain and France took any action. Avery attributed the Europeans' conduct to jealousy and selfishness and concluded "that continued unity of action in favor of foreign telegraph enterprise cannot be expected." He predicted that Peking would not learn the value of the telegraph or promote its use as long as "foreign rivalries" persisted. It mattered not what nationality made the initial telegraph effort, he asserted, and he congratulated Consul DeLano at Foochow that "we may justly claim that American influence . . . has [been] given . . . in the interest solely, of commerce, civilization, and progress."[74] Raasloff accepted the Tsungli Yamen's offer to buy the line, and the Chinese later dismantled it, as Avery had feared they might. The imperial government appeared less than eager to acknowledge the value and usefulness of the telegraph as an agent of civilization and progress.[75]

At the same time in February 1875 that local hostility was blocking the Fukien telegraph project, a much more serious antiforeign incident occurred in remote southwest China. An armed band in Yunnan province murdered British consular official Augustus R. Margary and his Chinese attendants. The remainder of Margary's party, a British expedition exploring trade routes beween Burma and the Yangtze River through Yunnan, was forced back into Burma. As had been the case at Tientsin in 1870, the Margary massacre raised difficult questions about coercion, cooperation, and other Western policy alternatives in Asia.[76]

When news of the tragedy reached Peking in March 1875, Avery joined with the other legations in supporting British minister Sir Thomas Wade's request that the Tsungli Yamen allow British officers to go to Yunnan to investigate. This joint note avoided particulars, since the circumstances of the incident were complicated. The Chinese passports that Margary's party carried, for example, did not identify them as officials. A deadly feud existed between the Yunnanese and Burmese, and the former were expected to claim that they mistook the British-Chinese group for a hostile force. Although he condemned the attack as "premeditated, treacherous, and savage," Avery also blamed the British for pushing "rather rashly into a region which is infested by a wild race, strongly opposed to commercial intercourse with Europeans, and hardly more than nominally under the control of the Peking government."[77]

The Yunnan incident created, according to Avery, a grave situation in East-West relations because of two opposing factors. On the one hand, increasing foreign encroachments on China's neighbors had made the imperial government more stubborn than ever toward Western demands and proposals. With the British in Burma, the French in Cochin-China, the Russians in Manchuria, and the Japanese looking covetously at Korea, Peking feared the imminent demise of its traditional tributary system. On the other hand, the "vigorous" elements among the English continued to seek any pretext for the use of coercion in Asia. Avery acknowledged that a resort to force in the present case might lead to the opening of more ports and other commercial concessions. He predicted, however, that such a dictatorial course would, in the long run, increase Chinese fear and distrust and ultimately lead to retaliation and disaster for foreigners in China.[78]

As a true believer in Western cooperation, Avery criticized British minister Wade for keeping his colleagues in the dark about his negotiations. The American charged that Wade's reticence could eventually "break up the cooperative policy." Avery joined the other legations in warning both Wade and the Tsungli Yamen that "inconveniences" could result if the discussions were not broadened to include the other nations. Wade, who had replaced Alcock in 1870, responded bluntly that this case was not one for cooperation.[79]

Wade's isolated course concerned Avery and the other ministers, because Wade was attempting to use the threat of British retaliation to gain Chinese concessions on issues extraneous to the Margary massacre. These subjects—open ports, internal transit taxes, and diplomatic intercourse between consuls and provincial officials—concerned all foreigners in China. Avery agreed with many of Wade's objectives but thought that these other issues should be separated from the Yunnan affair. The United States could not, in Avery's opinion, seek changes "through an alliance with a coercive policy, adopted by a single Power under the irritation of a special grievance."[80] He believed that such a course would impair good relations between the United States and China and violate the spirit of the Burlingame Treaty, which made treaty reform a "matter of common action in a friendly temper." In

Avery's estimation, Wade would achieve nothing that could not be gained by a more conciliatory policy. Before the Yunnan question could be resolved, however, Avery died. His death came on November 8, 1875 in the United States legation in Peking, as a result of his chronic illness, a form of Bright's disease.[81]

Like their predecessors, both Avery and Low experienced the frustrations of attempting to reconcile Eastern and Western civilization using the limited means available to the United States. After the Tientsin massacre, Low advocated Burlingame's policy of Western patience and forbearance. Later in Korea, he tried both threatening the use of force and the actual application of naval pressure, but his tactics hurt rather than helped Sino-Western relations. In keeping with Browne's approach, Avery worked hard to introduce the leaven of Western technology into China's ancient culture, but his inability to achieve sustained foreign cooperation defeated his schemes. During the first half of the 1870s, the United States experimented with various types of cooperation, coercion, and conciliation in China as it searched for a policy that served both American interests and ideals. When William H. Seward visited China in 1870 during a world tour, the former secretary of state concluded that "a policy of justice, moderation, and friendship, is the only one that we have had a choice to pursue, and that it has been as wise as it has been unavoidable."[82] On a later occasion, however, Seward asserted: "Although China is far from being a barbarous state, yet every system and institution there is inferior to its corresponding one in the West. . . . Everything in China is effete."[83] Burlingame's idealism remained the touchstone of American diplomacy in the Middle Kingdom, but the imperialist urge to patronize the "sons of Confucius" was readily apparent.

CHAPTER FIVE

The Diplomacy of Expediency:

THE CHINA CAREER OF GEORGE F. SEWARD

THE SELECTION OF George Frederick Seward to succeed Benjamin P. Avery as minister plenipotentiary in Peking marked a new departure in post-1860 American China policy. Not only was Seward the only U.S. minister to China in the nineteenth century who had previous diplomatic experience or knowledge of China, but he also was the first to practice a policy based primarily on expediency without some restraining principle. In many ways expediency had shaped Browne's thinking, but Browne had few opportunities to put his views into effect. Burlingame, Low, and Avery were not always consistent, but they had some definite policy standards and limitations. Seward claimed to be an adherent of Burlingame's cooperative approach, but in several instances he explicitly rejected cooperation. On some occasions he advocated enforcement and at other times evasion of the treaties. Neither the treaty system, the cooperative policy, nor even morality formed an absolute standard for Seward's diplomacy.

A member of the prominent Seward family, George F. Seward was born in Florida (Orange County), New York on November 8, 1840, in the same house as his uncle William Henry Seward. Young George Frederick received his early education at Seward Institute, founded

George F. Seward was the first United States consul general at Shanghai, 1863–1876, and served a controversial term as United States minister to China from 1876 to 1880. *Bancroft Library, University of California, Berkeley.*

by his grandfather. At age fifteen he entered Union College in Schenectady, New York, but left without graduating in order to take charge of his family's affairs. In 1861 he received the appointment as United States consul at Shanghai from his uncle William, the new secretary of state. Shortly after assuming his duties, young Seward threatened to resign, because he found his salary and budget to be totally inadequate for the expenses and responsibilities of the Shanghai post. The new consul's complaints, supported by Burlingame's reports of the importance of the Shanghai office and of the need for "young men of character" in the U.S. consular service in China, prompted the secretary of state to elevate the post to a consulate general in 1863.[1]

During his thirteen years as consul general in Shanghai, Seward witnessed or participated in Burlingame's cooperative policy, the Burgevine affair, Alcock's negotiations, the Tientsin massacre, Low's mission to Korea, and other key events. He saw the number and activity of foreigners in China greatly increase. While four ministers occupied the legation in Peking, Seward remained, along with S. Wells Williams, as one of the few fixtures in America's official presence in China.

Stationed in the bustling port of Shanghai, the consul general developed an obvious interest in the future of American commerce. "China is the most important field for Western enterprise," he reported to his uncle William H. Seward in 1863, and "indeed the policy of other nations is such that if our merchants are not sustained they cannot maintain the unequal contest."[2] When Burlingame initiated the cooperative policy, young Seward termed the approach "wise in conception" and the basis of "peaceful and mutually advantageous" Sino-Western relations. He assured the Shanghai merchants of his desire for such things as customs reform, railroads, telegraphs, and mines but argued that these changes would come about only gradually. Consequently, following the signing of the Burlingame Treaty, he refuted J. Ross Browne's charges that the treaty was retrogressive. The consul general contended that America's best strategy in the emerging Western rivalry in Asia was a slow and calculated cultivation of Sino-American friendship such as the treaty expressed. He explained to Browne:

> We do not wish to lose the confidence of the Chinese. It would be better to go more slowly than to do so. Difficulties of one sort and another will come up, not so much with our people as with . . . the French, and with the missionaries and traders of Great Britain. By standing well with the Chinese we may sometime avert serious complications, and so conserve our position and the Empire for our benefit in the long and intimate intercourse which I hope is in store for America and China. We want to see no part of this coast subject to European domination.[3]

Seward shared Browne's concerns for American commerce, but he had high hopes for Burlingame's conciliatory approach to the Chinese. His objective as a diplomat was "to instill in China an idea that a development of intercourse is most desirable in the interests of China and not that there is a perfect clash and opposition between her interests and those of our traders."[4]

Seward's own policy recommendations were derived from his personal experiences in Shanghai and his observations of the diplomatic efforts of Burlingame, Browne, Alcock, and other Western envoys in Peking. In April 1870, while home on leave from his consular post, he detailed his views in a lengthy treatise for Secretary of State Fish. He began with a defense of the Western commercial community in China.

He conceded that self-interest motivated the merchants' advocacy of railroads and other projects, but in keeping with classic American dogma, Seward argued that the pursuit of profit through the introduction of Western technology into China did not conflict with the businessmen's sincere belief that technological innovation equaled progress. Burlingame had once referred disparagingly to the merchants as "opium dealers," but Seward attributed this remark to the minister's isolation in Peking from the Western commercial center of Shanghai. In Seward's opinion, the foreign merchant was an honorable individual who "would be unworthy of the Anglo-Saxon blood which runs in his veins if he should teach himself the Chinese habit of thought, and sit down to believe with the immobile mass around him, that what ever is is best."[5] Seward agreed with Browne that the Westerner as a friend of China must abhor the poor roads, unsanitary conditions, and other material deficiencies in the Middle Kingdom.[6]

On the controversial issue of predicting China's response to Western efforts toward change, Seward shared neither Browne's foreboding pessimism nor Burlingame's unrestrained optimism. He believed that the Chinese had carried out fairly well what they considered to be the "strange" and "irksome" provisions of the Treaties of Tientsin. Eventually "free intercourse" would be established with the West, he contended, and railroads and other innovations would appear, enabling China to lift itself out of its lethargy. In contrast to Browne, Seward insisted that the changes would occur peacefully. The foreign communities in the treaty ports had exposed the Chinese to the miracles of modern progess: new fabrics, sailing craft, new houses, municipal administration, Western courts of law, vessels of war, and the customs service. The unseen forces that produced these advances and improved life in Europe and America would do the same in Asia—there was no staying them. Since the "Chinaman" was sober, industrious, and peaceful, and his leaders were men of ability, Seward saw no reason why China could not easily accept these innovations. The young diplomat's strong faith in the appeal of material progress and Western ideas characterized his diplomacy until he left China in 1880. He sought to educate the Chinese by example.[7]

Until the Chinese learned to appreciate the superiority of Western ideas, Seward recognized that many disputes would occur throughout China between natives and foreigners. In these clashes, what protection could and should Western envoys give their countrymen? The American knew that many foreigners agreed with British minister Rutherford Alcock that diplomacy in China could mean only "armed reason"—a treaty system imposed by force and upheld the same way. Furthermore, the general consensus among treaty-port Westerners was that using gunboat persuasion on local officials was a more effective way to achieve quick results than the standard diplomatic practice of seeking remedies through the imperial authorities in Peking. Seward disagreed with prevailing treaty-port opinion, and explained to Secretary Fish that it was premised on the impotence of Peking during the Taiping Rebellion. Under the new T'ung-chih leadership, according to the consul general, the dynasty could and would maintain China's treaty obligations. He admitted that the Ch'ing bureaucracy still contained many independent-minded, antiforeign mandarins, but he believed that the central government had the means (the power to remove lower officials) and the motive (the desire to avoid another war that experience proved China could not win) to ensure enforcement of the treaties. Since the American objective was "a free field" for future trade, Seward hoped that the United States would never give its representatives the power to make war for such a limited goal. He reasoned that "the Chinese government, weak as it is, with everything to lose and nothing to gain by a foreign war, will never fail to find a way to do justice when the demand is made with the statement, 'Do this or we shall find a way to right ourselves.'"[8] Seward's recommendation for a successful Western policy in China, then, was a middle position between Burlingame's avoidance of the use or even suggestion of force and Browne's anticipation of an unavoidable East-West clash. The consul general opposed the localized use of force but would keep an implied threat of war behind all foreign demands on the Peking government.[9]

After Avery's death in November 1875, Secretary of State Fish named Seward minister in Peking, although Low and some others were hoping to see S. Wells Williams receive the nomination.[10] The consul general had coveted a top diplomatic post for a long time. In 1870 he actively sought the honor of initiating diplomatic relations with Korea, but his ambitions were frustrated when Fish chose Low to head the expedition to the Hermit Kingdom. The departure of the American minister from Tokyo in 1871 prompted Seward to offer himself as either chargé d'affaires or minister, but Washington again disappointed him. After hearing of Avery's nomination as Low's replacement, Seward wrote the State Department that he had "certainly looked forward to the possibility of receiving this promotion."[11] He also suggested that he would like to be considered for the minister's office in some other country. Before Avery's coffin even left China, Seward telegraphed Washington: "If appointed minister or instructed take charge can proceed immediately. Appointment respectfully solicited."[12] Upon receipt of the telegram, Fish suggested to President Grant that Seward's experience made the consul general the best choice for the vacant China post. The president's initial reaction was negative: "I do not think I will appoint Secretary Seward's nephew. He is not much of a Republican, and I don't like any of the family."[13] Fish persisted, however, and Grant eventually relented. The Senate confirmed Seward's nomination on January 10, 1876.[14]

After waiting for the weather to warm enough to allow sea passage northward from Shanghai, Seward arrived in Peking in the spring of 1876 and found that British minister Sir Thomas Wade was still pressuring the Chinese for treaty concessions because of the murder of British consular official Augustus R. Margary the previous year. In contrast to Avery, Seward believed that Wade should proceed alone with his forceful approach. The new American minister's experience in China had taught him that joint action was difficult to secure in cases that immediately affected the citizens or interests of only one nation, such as the tragic incident in Yunnan. He argued that by acting alone, Wade "may accomplish a great deal for his nationals, and incidentally, for all others in China." If the British minister succeeded in gaining more open ports or modifications in the internal transit taxes, Seward reasoned, "we will share in the advantage derived, which may be of a substantial sort," without jeopardizing America's own friendly relations with the Chinese.[15] Even when Wade finally asked his Western colleagues to unite with him, the American refused. Seward advocated jackal diplomacy: the United States would wait on the side lines and then share the spoils of Britain's success. Seward made no attempt to influence Wade in the direction of forbearance but instead opportunistically sought to advance American interests without the United States itself receiving opprobrium for an imperialist act.[16]

Secretary of State Fish approved Seward's decision not to cooperate with Wade. Fish's instructions in this case distorted beyond recognition the American policy initiated by Burlingame, criticized by Browne, and attempted by Low and Avery. The secretary wrote that the United States government had no desire to abandon the cooperative policy and asked Seward to explain to the other Western ministers "that it is only in order that such cooperation may be made more effective that you urge the adoption of the course decided upon."[17] Cooperation had always been a vague concept, but Fish raised it to a new height of obfuscation. The secretary claimed, in effect, that the United States planned to preserve cooperation by not cooperating. Preoccupied with the campaign and contested outcome of the Rutherford B. Hayes-Samuel J. Tilden presidential election of 1876, Fish gave Seward almost no other policy guidance.[18]

As Wade's negotiations moved into the summer of 1876, Seward continued to stay out of the discussions but still made his opinions known. He told Robert Hart, the inspector general of the Chinese customs service who was advising the Chinese negotiators, that he hoped the transit tax and other commercial questions would be referred to the entire diplomatic body. Seward acknowledged that perhaps Wade's "strong language" had gone too far in irritating the Chinese. Basically, however, the American minister condoned Wade's conduct, because "after making liberal allowances for the obstinacy which he may have aroused, it is evident that [the Chinese] Government does not come up to Western standards of duty."[19]

Finally, after months of haggling, Hart managed to bring Wade together with Li Hung-chang to settle the Margary affair and the other questions raised by the British envoy. They met in Chefoo, the coastal city in Shantung province where foreigners often went during the summer to escape the oppressive heat of Peking. Wade and Li signed the Chefoo Convention on September 13, 1876. Like most international agreements, the document represented a compromise that satisfied neither side. Section one covered the Yunnan incident and provided for an indemnity, an apology, and the protection of trade and exploration in Yunnan. The Chinese had conceded these points from the beginning. Section two dealt with official intercourse and judicial questions and represented a defeat for Wade. The British minister had hoped to establish rules of diplomatic etiquette and legal procedure but managed only to get an agreement from the Tsungli Yamen to consider these subjects with the legations. Section three on commercial questions opened some additional ports and revised the regulations governing *likin*, the complicated system of local taxes levied on goods in transit from the ports to the interior. Because many foreigners wanted *likin* abolished rather than reformed, the other Western ministers jointly refused to recognize the new rules pending further discussions.[20]

Seward believed that the convention improved in some ways "the condition of foreigners in China," but he considered the *likin* provisions "unfortunate." He had feared that some Western officials, angered by Wade's independent action, would attempt to block a Sino-British settlement. After returning from Chefoo to Peking in October, Seward wrote:

> I am really in hope that now a new departure may be taken here, among the foreign representatives. There has been nothing like harmonious working for the last eighteen months. This has been partly due to natural national prejudices and partly to the idiosyncracies of the British, French, and German Ministers.[21]

Seward did not mention that he too had contributed to the absence of harmony by favoring Wade's independent course.[22]

Because the American minister had intentionally maintained a discreet noninvolvement in the Chefoo negotiations, he failed to perceive accurately Robert Hart's role in the settlement. The inspector general told Seward that he had urged Wade to accept the Chinese proposals, but Seward suspected that the two "Irishmen"—Wade and Hart—had a "perfect understanding" between themselves to promote British interests. When Hart had warned the Chinese of grave consequences if they did not come to terms, Seward had interpreted the inspector general's advice as a threat rather than a caution. Actually, Hart served as a true intermediary. He used strong language to Li Hung-chang but also threatened to go over Wade's head to London if the British envoy did not negotiate in good faith. Contrary to Seward's impression, Hart's diplomacy severely strained relations between the two "Irishmen" and enabled China, not Britain, to get a better settlement than otherwise possible.[23]

In the weeks and months immediately after the signing of the Chefoo Convention, Seward took a more active and important role in discussions of treaty revision. The Western ministers met together several times to consider the complicated legal and diplomatic questions that the Wade-Li agreement had explicitly designated for later negotiations. Because Seward's long consular experience made him something of an expert on extraterritoriality and judicial proceedings under the treaties, he usually chaired the sessions and drafted the memoranda on many of the unresolved Sino-Western issues.[24]

Of all the complex legal entanglements created by the unequal treaty system, those involving mixed cases, i.e., the plaintiff and defendant not of the same nationality, created the most difficulty. Seward argued that the treaties clearly provided for trial in the court of the defendant's nationality in mixed cases. Although some legal experts disagreed with this interpretation, most Westerners and Chinese agreed with its practicality. Even with the judge and defendant of the same nationality, however, the question remained as to whether Chinese or Western law applied. What constituted a crime in one society was not necessarily a legal offense in the other. Under certain circumstances in China, for example, a father could legally kill his child or be punished himself for the crime of his child.[25] In Seward's opinion, consular courts could not be required to enforce Chinese law, nor could Chinese courts be expected to uphold Western law. Seward recognized, however, that extraterritoriality obligated the two sides to respect and sustain each other's judicial responsibilities as far as possible under their own laws. Although Seward never concluded a legal convention while he was minister, some of his recommendations eventually appeared in the supplemental treaty between China and the United States signed in November 1880. Treaty reform did not remove the problem of conflicting cultures, and extraterritoriality with the United States remained in effect until 1943.[26]

Seward came to believe that Sino-Western differences could be better resolved by stricter application, rather than reform, of the treaties. The British Treaty of Nanking and other Western conventions with China contained specific provisions against *likin* taxes, for example, but local authorities persisted in collecting these internal tariffs. Alcock and Wade had attempted in their negotiations to limit these extra duties, but most foreigners wanted the domestic levies revoked, not revised. From his own study of treaty problems, Seward concluded that both judicial and commercial questions were so complicated that strict enforcement of existing treaty stipulations had to be attempted before new provisions could be written. He explained:

> We meet many evils under the extraterritorial system and many under the system of treaty tariffs, but both were imposed because of the necessities of the case, and both are of measurable advantage. We must make the most of them until the days of better administration arrive, and those days will arrive the sooner if we stand firmly for the rights accorded us by treaty.[27]

He pointed out that extraterritoriality and treaty tariffs had never been logically consistent with the sovereignty of China and that attempts to revise them would only create greater confusion. He concluded, therefore, that only Western insistence on Chinese compliance with the treaties could begin to reconcile East-West differences. In other words, he would not consider compromising with the Chinese until China's sovereignty had been completely decimated.[28]

Seward's experiences in China made him a crafty diplomat with decided objectives and indirect methods. As a young consular official he had been influenced by both Burlingame and the Shanghai merchants. By the 1870s he claimed to follow Burlingame's cautious policy while seeking the innovations and changes sought by the merchants and most other Westerners. While Seward lacked the forthrightness of Burlingame and Browne, he was more adept than Low and Avery. Seward was a practiced politician who professed to believe in a cooperative approach but who chose carefully when and with whom to cooperate. He maintained a cordial, usually conciliatory, and never coercive attitude toward the Tsungli Yamen. He was perfectly willing, however, to let other Westerners pressure the imperial government while the United States waited to reap the most-favored-nation benefits.

In 1878, after seventeen years of seemingly able diplomatic service in China, Seward became the target of a nearly successful impeachment effort. John C. Myers, Seward's successor as consul general at Shanghai, charged his predecessor with irregularities in office. Seward responded by suspending Myers—allegedly for misconduct, although Myers termed the action an attempted cover-up. The House of Representatives Committee on Expenditures in the State Department, chaired by Congressman William M. Springer, spent more than a year investigating the charges and countercharges of the two officials. Finally, in March 1879 the Democratic majority of the committee voted in favor of an impeachment resolution. In a move to delay or prevent any formal action, the Republican minority offered a counterresolution to send the matter to the Judiciary Committee for further hearings on the legal complexities of the case.

The majority report charged Seward with (1) violating the treaties by using his official influence to promote a railroad from Shanghai to Woosung; (2) being an accomplice to fraud in the railroad scheme; (3) committing crimes of "injustice, tyranny, extortion, and bribery" while judge of the Shanghai consular court; (4) appropriating to his own use fees due to the marshal of the consulate general and portions of the Seaman's Relief Fund; (5) manipulating the rate of exchange between United States currency and silver coin in order to defraud the United States government of consular and postal receipts; (6) receiving pay as both consul general and minister for the first quarter of 1876; (7) releasing Oliver B. Bradford, vice-consul general at Shanghai, from confinement knowing Bradford to be guilty of embezzlement; (8) unlawfully suspending Myers in an attempt "to secrete and conceal" crimes; and (9) falsifying, destroying, and failing to provide records of consular business.[29]

The minority report refuted some of the charges, questioned whether others were impeachable offenses, and cited extenuating circumstances for the remainder. The committee's Republicans argued that the articles involving the marshal's fees, the Seaman's Relief Fund, and the consular court lacked sufficient proof or were disproved by testimony. State Department records exonerated Seward, in their opinion, of the charges involving his pay and the exchange rate. The rebuttal of the other allegations, however, was less convincing. On the accusations connected with Myers's suspension, Bradford's incarceration, and the missing and damaged records, i.e., the alleged cover-up, the Republicans noted that the State Department had approved Seward's conduct and never questioned his accounts. They did not mention that the State Department (in which Seward's cousin Frederick W. Seward was assistant secretary) accepted the minister's explanations despite the possession of conflicting information. Since reasonable suspicion of Seward's conduct could not be eliminated in all cases, the minority also cited the difficulties of administering the Shanghai consulate general. The Republican congressmen emphasized that the office received grossly inadequate funds and instructions from Washington to handle the tremendous volume of routine consular work plus the additional responsibilities of an extraterritorial judicial system.[30]

When John Myers first arrived in Shanghai in 1876 and began to report his suspicions of his predecessor's conduct, Seward made a concerted effort to discredit his accuser. The new minister in Peking and Vice-Consul General Bradford—Seward's protégé and right-hand man in Shanghai—both sent long dispatches to Washington describing Myers's irresponsibility and drunkenness and questioning his sanity. They reported that Myers had no Western friends in China. Seward, in fact, offered the following item as proof of Myers's unfitness for office: "That his course with the Chinese authorities has indicated unbounded confidence in them. . . ."[31] By such a standard, Seward also would have considered Burlingame unfit to serve in China. Without instructions from Washington, the minister suspended Myers and put Bradford in charge of the consulate general. Seward removed Myers on the grounds that the consul general had given the press a slanderous story about Seward's accepting a bribe.[32]

Apparently Myers did originate the newspaper article about the bribe, but Seward himself had indulged in similar tactics to criticize Low's handling of the Korean mission. Although not a very able public official, Myers was not the bête noire Seward attempted to make him. After Myers had been in Shanghai less than a year, the other Western consuls expressed their confidence in him by electing him chairman of the consular body. A loyal Republican, Myers held no partisan feeling against Seward, such as characterized the Democrat-controlled investigating committee. Although Myers tended to exaggerate and contradict himself at times, his motives were sincere from his first suspicions of Seward through his testimony before the Springer committee.[33]

During the committee's hearings, Seward returned from China to defend himself and managed to prevent the congressional investigators from determining many of the details of his activities in Shanghai, including the exact amount of his income and his means of obtaining it. One of Myers's first complaints had been that the account books in the consulate general were concealed from his inspection.

Vice-Consul General Bradford had even refused to give Myers a key to the safe. G. Wiley Wells, whom Washington had sent to Shanghai as consul general to investigate Myers's and Seward's charges against each other, corroborated Myers's description. Wells reported that Bradford kept all records of public monies and had removed them from the consulate as his private property. Wells found no accounts or vouchers in the building dated prior to June 24, 1876. Court records, correspondence, and other files were disorganized and in some cases had been mutilated. Seward's docket book for the consular court looked, according to Wells, like "a butcher's book."[34]

The Springer committee attempted to subpoena the missing records from Seward and charged him with contempt of Congress for refusing to give the committee the documents or to testify as to their contents. The minister appeared before the bar of the House and defended his right under the Fifth Amendment of the Constitution not to testify against himself. The House Judiciary Committee ruled: if the records were public, the subpoena should be directed toward the executive branch through the courts, and if the records were private, Seward could claim Fifth Amendment protection. The committee did not decide whether the records were public or private, but nevertheless the financial information had been kept out of the hands of the prosecution.[35]

The most serious of the impeachment charges against Seward in diplomatic terms were those involving the Woosung railroad. While Seward was still consul general, his deputy Bradford took the initiative in 1872–1873 to construct a twelve-mile railway from Shanghai to Woosung, the anchorage at the confluence of the Yangtze and Wangpoo rivers. Seward reported to Washington that "such a railway is needed, and its construction would be of special service by familiarizing the Chinese with the use of railways, and the wisdom of introducing them throughout the Empire."[36] Acknowledging that some government opposition could be expected, he contended that the Chinese were beginning to accept Western methods and that no serious political difficulties were anticipated. The original promoters encountered problems raising enough capital, because American investors simply were not sufficiently interested in China in the 1870s. An English company finally took over the project, but Seward and Bradford retained a strong interest in the scheme.[37]

After becoming minister, Seward instructed Bradford, who was temporarily in charge of the Shanghai consulate general, on how to deal with any Chinese objections to the railway construction. Still sympathetic with the didactic objective of the project, Seward wanted Bradford to give the company and the British authorities full cooperation. He advised Bradford to avoid arguments based on treaty rights and instead to point out the advantages of the system to the Chinese. Seward's letter to Bradford, a copy of which went to Washington, revealed that "the ground was bought ostensibly for a maloo, (or horse road,)."[38] Undoubtedly this original deception was well known in the Shanghai foreign community, but Seward's letter marked its first appearance in official American correspondence.[39]

The revelation shocked Fish. He did not assume that Seward or Bradford had been party to the misrepresentation, but he wanted them to keep a respectable distance from the project. Long desirous of Western technological innovation in China, Fish had favored the Woosung railroad ever since Avery had informed him of it in 1874. Even after this new intelligence, Fish hoped that the line would be completed but cautioned Seward that, if the right-of-way had been obtained dishonestly, "it would not comport with our sense of justice and morality for us . . . to insist upon the right of men . . . to profit by their own wrong."[40] Fish did not mention that Seward's and Bradford's promotion of the scheme also violated the Burlingame Treaty, which assured the Chinese that the United States would not intervene in China's domestic administration of railroads.[41]

In response, Seward claimed that he had given only general support to the introduction of railroads and that he had not condoned the particular methods in this case. Contending that he had never affirmed the promoters' right to undertake the venture, the minister asserted that he only had brought forward the argument of "expediency." In other words, he believed that the railway represented such an important advance in China that it transcended the limits of the treaties. Seward insisted for the sake of progress that the Chinese adhere to the letter and spirit of the treaties, but he excused Western noncompliance for the same reason.[42]

From the inception of the project through the impeachment hearings, Seward maintained that his only interest in the railroad had been to promote technological innovation. He insisted, and it was never proven otherwise, that he had no financial stake in the company or in the right-of-way sold to the company. Bradford, however, definitely owned stock in the corporation. Seward's long-time assistant was the kind of government official whose conduct made civil service reform a pressing issue in the 1870s. Whether their motives were public or private or both, the two men clearly pushed promotion of the railroad beyond the bounds of propriety as defined by the treaties. The Chinese government eventually bought the line, dismantled it, and shipped the track, locomotive, and cars to Taiwan. Seward's overzealousness had completely backfired. A later State Department investigation of the episode concluded that the fraud and deceit associated with the scheme had increased the suspicions and ire of the Chinese officials and delayed the introduction of railroads by several years.[43]

The impeachment inquiry revealed that Seward shared with many other Westerners in China the view that laws and treaties could be enforced or ignored as the situation required. The Woosung scheme had been one example of how this treaty-port "game" worked. Another example involved the United States statute that required ships of American registry to be officered by American citizens. As consul general, Seward had always overlooked this regulation, but Myers insisted on enforcing it. When American merchants in Shanghai complained of Myers's action, Seward sent to Washington one of their letters, which contained the following extraordinary paragraph:

> The strict letter of the law is, no doubt, as laid down by Mr. Myers, but I would humbly submit that the United States Government impliedly authorize its representatives abroad to exercise, whenever it may be found in their wise discretion expedient so to do, some latitude in the interpretation of acts of Congress which were never framed with the view of a strictly literal observance of their various clauses being enforced in places situated as Shanghai.[44]

By forwarding this letter, Seward charged in effect that Myers had refused to play the treaty-port game and that Americans in Shanghai should not be expected to obey inconvenient laws.[45]

Congress never decided whether Seward had committed an impeachable offense with regard to the Woosung case or any of the other articles presented by the Committee on Expenditures in the State Department. Committee chairman Springer introduced the impeachment resolution in the House of Representatives on March 3, 1879, the closing day of the tumultuous Forty-fifth Congress. Ever since the controversy over the Hayes-Tilden presidential election, partisan wrangling and bitterness had been at a peak in Washington. As the clock in the House chamber moved ever closer to the hour of adjournment with much unfinished business remaining, Democrat Springer stubbornly held the floor, seeking a vote on the Seward resolution. Just as stubbornly, the Republicans refused to vote, thus preventing a quorum on the question. Without this parliamentary tactic, the resolution would have passed by one vote. After the labor of a year of hearings and investigation, Springer dejectedly yielded the floor.[46]

Seward had probably committed some, although not all, of the alleged offenses. Three different federal officers on three separate occasions reported irregularities and improprieties in the Shanghai consulate general involving Seward. Many of their charges claimed that Seward collected excessive and unauthorized "unofficial fees" and in other ways used his position for personal gain. Government funds for the consulate general certainly were insufficient for salaries, rent, and other expenses, and thus Seward had to create ways to bring in more money. On the other hand, Seward went to China in 1862 with no assets other than his name, and by the time he became minister in 1876, he had substantial holdings of both money and land.[47]

After the defeat of the impeachment effort, Seward returned to China as minister. He served in the post for another year and during that time proved to be a more cautious and perhaps better diplomat than at any other time in his career. As the facts and circumstances behind the impeachment attempt revealed, however, personal advantage sometimes determined Seward's policies. In addition, in his efforts to expand all foreign privileges in China, he showed much less restraint than did Burlingame, Low, and Avery. Even during his final year in Peking, he continued to follow the dictates of expediency as he turned his attention to the mounting concern in the United States over Chinese immigration.

"The Chinese must go!" This angry cry, heard in anti-Chinese riots all along the Pacific Coast of the United States in the 1870s, heralded potential danger for Seward's efforts to promote American interests in China.[48] Although fueled by domestic grievances, this anti-Chinese movement—whose avowed goal was total exclusion of the Chinese from the United States—had serious implications for American China policy. The Burlingame Treaty had guaranteed free immigration and legal protection to the Chinese in America. The burgeoning domestic movement to exclude Oriental immigrants violated both the letter and the spirit of the Burlingame policy of respect for the Chinese government and people. Could the United States evade its treaty commitments and still expect American businessmen and missionaries to continue to enjoy previously won treaty rights in the Middle Kingdom?

When Seward first became minister, he did not consider the domestic anti-Chinese movement a serious problem. The number of Chinese immigrating into the United States would never be very large, he predicted in 1876, because Orientals did not want to live in America. They were deterred in part by their hostile reception, but the primary reason, according to Seward, was that they "shrink from contact with our restless, energetic civilization." In the minister's view, only the lure of money had prompted them to relocate, and "when the call for labor ceases to be an urgent one, the Chinaman will stop his migration in that direction."[49]

The Chinese who traveled to the United States with Burlingame in 1868 were somewhat of a curiosity, but by the 1870s the Chinese in America, particularly in the western states, were viewed as the "yellow peril." Their numbers increased from 35,000 in 1860 to over 105,000 by 1880, with 99 percent of these immigrants concentrated in the Pacific Coast region.[50] Originally, capitalist entrepreneurs had welcomed these newcomers as a cheap labor source, but by the mid-1870s the completion of the transcontinental railroad, growth of the white labor force along the coast, and nationwide economic depression had encouraged white workingmen to turn against Oriental workers. White Californians deeply resented competing with what they considered Chinese "slave" labor. Although these immigrants were not slaves, most did come to the United States as contract laborers who worked for extremely low wages. "Chinamen" were also unacceptable because they were not Caucasian. Many Californians viewed the filth, crime, opium smoking, and crowded conditions of local Chinatowns as racial stereotypes rather than manifestations of poverty. Economic and racial hysteria led to demands for exclusion backed by threats, intimidation, and violence.[51]

The growing number of anti-Chinese incidents in the United States in early 1876 prompted the Tsungli Yamen to address Seward on the subject. Copying the language and arguments used innumerable times by Western diplomats, the mandarins reminded Seward of his nation's treaty obligations. They cited the fifth and sixth articles of the Burlingame Treaty, which guaranteed free immigration and protection to Chinese in America, and requested that Seward communicate their views to Washington. The minister's reply read like those written by the Tsungli Yamen when faced with protests of treaty violations in China. Seward pointed out the difficulties of the situation in California, assured the officials that his government was anxiously seeking a solution to the problem, and promised to convey the foreign office's concerns to Washington.[52]

The increasingly violent agitation for exclusion posed a grave threat to America's diplomatic position in China. Any unilateral restriction of Chinese treaty rights in the United States, which was essentially what exclusionists demanded, could lead to retaliation by Peking. All of the legal rights and privileges held by Americans and Europeans in the Middle Kingdom rested on the system of unequal treaties, which insulted and undermined the sovereignty of the emperor's government. Geographically and culturally isolated, the Chinese had agreed to these one-sided treaties not only because of military pressure but also out of ignorance of Western international law and practices. As imperial officials learned how foreign diplomats had used the tenets of international law to justify demands for ever-increasing rights and privileges, the mandarins became more cautious and also began to turn Western methods to their own use. If the United States prevented Chinese immigration into California, Peking might move to exclude American and European merchants and missionaries.

Under the pressures of a political campaign, both the Democratic and Republican parties included a plank on "Mongolian immigration" in their national platforms of 1876. The politicians were courting California's votes in the upcoming presidential election, which they expected to be a close race. The Democrats forthrightly recommended exclusion, and the Republicans proposed that Congress investigate the effects of Chinese immigration. The Republican candidate, Rutherford B. Hayes, avoided the issue throughout the campaign, however, because his party was split on the question. Many northern and eastern Republicans, such as Hannibal Hamlin, Lincoln's first vice-president, opposed exclusion as racially prejudiced and contrary to America's liberal traditions. Republicans from the western states such as California senator Aaron Sargent, on the other hand, led the fight for restrictive immigration laws. Although proexclusion sentiment prevailed on the West Coast, one prominent California Republican, former minister Frederick Low, cautioned a committee of his state's senate: "It is highly desirable not to offend the Chinese Government. They are a numerous people and we have a good trade with them."[53] Privately, Low expressed misgivings that the "great hullabaloo" over Chinese immigration could mean "goodbye to American influence in China."[54]

While candidate Hayes equivocated, Senator Sargent tried to prompt congressional action limiting the influx of Chinese. The Senate and House refused to move quickly but did set up a joint committee to investigate the question. Because of the illness and eventual death of the committee chairman, Oliver P. Morton of Indiana, Sargent headed the investigation. After extensive testimony, more than half of which was favorable to the Chinese and immigration, Sargent submitted a report for the committee that unequivocally recommended exclusion. Senator Morton's notes, published posthumously and based upon the same testimony, concluded that the investigation had failed to prove that California had suffered either morally or economically from the presence of the Chinese. In fact, Morton argued, the state had benefited measurably from its Chinese population.[55]

Despite the political rumblings over "Mongolian immigration," Seward at his post in Peking did not become overly concerned about the effect of the exclusion effort on Sino-American relations until 1878. Serious anti-Chinese rioting occurred in San Francisco in the summer of 1877, and petitions from the California legislature buttressed the joint congressional committee's findings in favor of exclusion. Under this pressure, both houses of Congress passed resolutions in 1878 urging President Hayes to seek changes in the existing treaties. At this same time, China sent its first permanent envoys to the United States, and Seward feared that the Chinese ministers would send home "some very unpleasant reports in regard to the treatment of Chinese in California." As a result, Peking might "deal in a very cavalier way with all our efforts to secure redress for wrongs suffered by our countrymen here."[56]

Seward expressed further concern that an anti-Chinese law passed in Washington might threaten the entire Western treaty system in China. Although some congressmen believed that they could abrogate through legislation those portions of the Burlingame Treaty that guaranteed free immigration and protection to the Chinese, the minister contended that such unilateral action would set a dangerous precedent. The Chinese did not like the existing treaties, he reminded the new secretary of state, William M. Evarts, and they would welcome justification for declaring null and void all the provisions that they found to be objectionable.[57]

Seward believed, though, that Washington could convince the Tsungli Yamen to revise the treaty provisions on immigration. The minister reasoned that despite the incidents in California, Chinese in the United States enjoyed substantially more rights than did Americans in China. Although there was an element of sophistry in his failure to acknowledge the unequal treaties, technically he was correct in his assessment. Using this "lack of reciprocity" as a bargaining point, Seward continued, the United States could demand that China either extend more privileges to Americans or approve the desired changes in the treaty. The minister predicted: "It is very certain that China would not consent to the extension of the privileges enjoyed by foreigners in this country, and it is possible that, rather than do this, she would agree to such a revision of our treaties as I have indicated."[58]

Seward's fears of unilateral congressional action were realized in January 1879, when the House passed a bill permitting only fifteen Chinese to enter the United States on any one ship docking on the West Coast. The Senate concurred and added an amendment authorizing the president to abrogate the fifth and sixth articles of the Burlingame Treaty.[59] The western congressmen had finally managed to force action on exclusion.

Many other Americans began to push for a presidential veto. Most eastern newspaper editors and politicians contended that the fifteen-passenger bill violated the sanctity of treaties and reversed America's traditional open-door immigration policy. The *New York Times*, for example, argued that "the enactment of this bill into a law would violate all the principles upon which our government is founded."[60] Religious and commercial groups complained that the bill invited "the danger of retaliatory action" against American missionaries and businessmen in China.[61]

Not surprisingly, President Hayes vetoed the bill. His concern was not with the substance of the legislation but with the method of limitation. Hayes indicated privately that he considered the Chinese "labor invasion" to be "pernicious," classifying the Chinese as one of the "weaker races," along with Negroes and Indians, who would be oppressed in the United States and would make their oppressors "hoodlums or vagabonds." Hayes therefore favored the limitation of Chinese immigration—but by some means consistent with the treaties and with recognized international practices. In reaching this decision, Hayes may have conferred with Seward, who was in Washington in February 1879 defending himself in the impeachment proceedings. Several of the minister's views appeared in the president's public and private statements on the exclusion issue. While preparing to veto the bill, Hayes recorded in his diary:

> We have accepted the advantages which the treaty gives us. Our traders, missionaries and travelers are domiciled in China. Important interests have grown up under the treaty, and rest upon faith in its observance. One of the parties to a treaty cannot rightfully by legislation violate it.[62]

In his veto message to Congress, the president noted that if the United States abrogated part of the treaty, the Chinese would be free to renounce the Treaty of Tientsin of 1858, upon which rested all American rights in China.[63]

After successfully blocking unilateral congressional action, Hayes began his own diplomatic steps to limit Chinese immigration. "It should be made certain *by proper methods*," he wrote in his diary, "that such an invasion [of Chinese workers] can not permanently override our people. It cannot safely be admitted into the bosom of our American society."[64] Accordingly, Hayes's secretary of state Evarts instructed Seward to enter into preparatory discussions with the Chinese government on the subject of immigration and to allay Peking's concern about the growing exclusion movement. Evarts also requested facts on the contract labor system and on the number of criminals and other undesirables who emigrated from China. His instructions did not authorize Seward to make any specific treaty proposals, because Hayes and Evarts themselves hoped to draft some revisions acceptable to Americans both at home and in China.[65]

Seward welcomed the opportunity to discuss the immigration question with the Chinese, but he bent his instructions to conform to his own views. Considering massive immigration unlikely, he therefore deemed exclusion an unnecessary complication. From the perspective of the legation in Peking, antagonizing the Chinese with restrictive legislation would stupidly exacerbate the chronic Oriental hostility and suspicion toward the West. Meeting with the Tsungli Yamen, Seward boldly expressed the hope that the imperial government would voluntarily limit the emigration of paupers, criminals, and prostitutes to the United States, and thereby he violated his instructions to make no specific proposals. He also refused to raise the question of contract labor, despite Evarts's request for information on this point. In Seward's estimation, the Chinese were sensitive to criticism on contract emigration (the so-called "coolie trade"), and broaching the subject would only further irritate an already difficult situation. Instead he chose to be almost apologetic about the anti-Chinese incidents in California and to assure the mandarins of America's devotion to "liberal government and humanity."[66] Although Seward had frequently ignored the Chinese foreign office when he found its objections to Western activity troublesome, in this case he exceeded his instructions by assuring the imperial officials that he sympathized with their grievances. Following his meeting with the Tsungli Yamen, Seward informed Washington in July 1879 that

> the sooner we rise to the idea of dealing with this Government as being actuated by very much the same motives of dignity, patriotism and public policy which actuates other governments, the sooner we shall be able to place our relations upon an enduring basis of good will and common interests.[67]

Seward may have echoed the Burlingame Treaty's doctrine of respect for the Chinese, but he spoke from expediency, not principle. As consul general in Shanghai, Seward had consistently promoted Western commercial interests. By both inclination and instinct, he thought in terms of what would best serve the needs of Westerners in China, not justice for the Chinese. "Our people in this part of the world, merchants and missionaries," he reiterated in August, "would be much reassured if they could know even that the disruption of our relations with China may be averted."[68]

Seward's diplomatic career and his official efforts to resolve the immigration issue came to an abrupt halt in 1880. With national elections approaching in the United States, the Hayes administration identified Seward as a political liability. The minister's refusal to pursue vigorously the immigration issue with the Tsungli Yamen began costing the Republicans potential votes in Pacific Coast states. Moreover, the concerted, although unsuccessful, effort the preceding year in the House of Representatives to impeach Seward had also made him a political detriment to his party. Accordingly, Evarts asked Seward for his resignation. When the minister stubbornly refused, Hayes formally recalled Seward from his post. Before leaving China, Seward made a parting attempt to thwart the exclusion movement. In a farewell meeting, he tried to prejudice the powerful governor general Li Hung-chang against revision of the Burlingame Treaty by telling him that only the "Irish rabble" in the United States favored exclusion. Further, the exiting minister predicted that future American proposals on Chinese immigration would insult the dignity of the imperial government.[69]

Upon his return home, Seward wrote a book refuting the proexclusion arguments. In *Chinese Immigration* (1881), he contended that there was no basis for America's fears of a massive influx of Chinese, that the Chinese had been of great service on the West Coast, and that lawful remedies already existed for such problems as crime in Chinatowns. Seward's book made him seem more liberal and enlightened than he actually was. Although he wrote, for example, that "all men under the sun are worthy in the measure of their intelligence and moral excellence, and not according to their grade in life or the hue of their skin,"[70] a few years earlier he had also written that "the darker races fall successively before the Caucasian" and that "in the long run the Chinese cannot prove the exception."[71] Seward's main consideration, then, was the promotion of foreign interests in China.[72]

As J. Ross Browne had done, Seward left China maintaining that Washington did not understand or appreciate his efforts. Browne's pessimistic assumptions about the future of Sino-Western relations led him to believe that the State Department was too considerate of the Chinese point of view. Seward remained optimistic about improved East-West relations but thought that Washington was not considering Peking's reaction at all. Despite their differing assessments, both ministers were convinced that their diplomatic careers had been terminated for no good reason. Before departing, Seward pronounced the following bitter valedictory:

> The field of labor is so distant and so obscure that [his] effort cannot be expected to win for the given officer adequate compensation. . . . It may . . . bring him into collision with his own Government . . . [and] the given Government may unwittingly sacrifice its best interests, overruling and condemning its Minister to its own damage.[73]

Seward eventually joined the Fidelity and Casualty Company of New York and became president of the firm in 1892. He probably would have been president of the New York Chamber of Commerce if his health had not failed in 1910.[74]

By the end of Seward's career in China, the United States in its search for a policy had moved a long way from Burlingame's views. Under domestic political pressure for exclusion, Washington was working to dismantle part of Burlingame's greatest achievement—a Sino-Western treaty negotiated upon a basis of mutual respect for the interests of both parties. Seward disagreed with this particular treaty revision, not because it violated the original principle and purpose of the treaty but because, in his opinion, it hurt American interests in China. On exclusion as on other issues, Seward thought always of the most expedient way to improve the privileges and conditions of Americans in China. For this reason he had practiced jackal diplomacy during Wade's negotiations. Similarly, he had insisted that the Chinese abide by the letter of the treaties but had excused the treaty violations of the Woosung railroad promoters. With Seward's ministry, Burlingame's magnanimous policy toward China became a means, not an end. Seward and his successors continued to claim adherence to Burlingame's ideals, but American China policy would never regain the presumed innocence of its youth. As international rivalry mounted in East Asia in the last quarter of the nineteenth century, America's self-proclaimed friendship for China was altruistic but also advantageous. By appearing less grasping and less antagonistic than other nations toward the Middle Kingdom, the United States could opportunistically use this goodwill with the Chinese authorities to gain benefits for itself alone. For American diplomats, the competing motives of idealism and imperialism could also be complementary.

CHAPTER SIX

Attempts at an Independent Policy

JAMES B. ANGELL AND JOHN RUSSELL YOUNG IN PEKING

THE UNITED STATES sent James Burrill Angell to Peking in 1880 with instructions to seek modifications in the Burlingame Treaty of 1868. George Seward had broken with the spirit of Burlingame's policies, and now Seward's successor would endeavor to change the substance. Specifically, Secretary of State William M. Evarts wanted to amend the free-immigration provisions of the treaty. Appointed both minister and treaty commissioner, Angell quickly negotiated the desired treaty, as well as a commercial and judicial convention.

John Russell Young, who followed Angell as minister, arrived in China during 1882, as a new wave of antiforeign sentiment swept the Middle Kingdom. Although numerous manifestations of hostility toward Westerners appeared during the nineteenth century, the early eighties were a period of particularly intense xenophobia throughout the empire. This hostility led to war between France and China in 1884–1885 and to numerous other incidents during the decade, as both imperial and provincial authorities suddenly chose to defy all foreigners. Young repeatedly became involved in these confrontations—both in defense of American interests and in attempts to mediate between the Chinese and other foreign representatives.

The period 1880–1885 marked a continuing transition in American

China policy away from the orderly cooperative endeavors of Burlingame toward the attempted U.S. mediation of tumultuous international rivalries, which would eventually threaten China's independence by the 1890s. The Angell Treaty, which was another nail in the coffin of Burlingame's magnanimity, and Young's attempts to act as both referee and participant in Sino-Western clashes revealed the underlying dilemma between idealism and imperialism in America's approach to China.

Careful consideration went into Secretary of State Evarts's choice of James Burrill Angell as the new American minister plenipotentiary to China. Evarts believed that Angell, a Midwesterner, would be more acceptable to the Chinese than a representative of either the West Coast exclusionists or the East Coast merchants. Angell was president of the University of Michigan, a background that the secretary thought would appeal to the Chinese, who so highly esteemed education and scholarly achievement. Although Angell had no practical diplomatic experience, he knew a great deal about international law, or what President Hayes referred to as "proper methods." In addition, his personal qualities were ideally suited to his delicate assignment. The man who would ask the Chinese government to allow its subjects to be discriminated against by American immigration laws was a sensitive, intelligent, and urbane gentleman. Although Angell occasionally employed racial stereotypes in his speech, his private as well as public writings were singularly lacking in racial aspersions, especially as compared with Seward.[1]

An eighth-generation descendant of one of the original settlers of Providence, Rhode Island, Angell was born in 1829 in Scituate, Rhode Island. His father, Andrew, was the proprietor of the Angell Tavern, which had been operated by the family since 1710 and had once been the center of Scituate politics and society. Temperance reform in New England led to a decline in the status of innkeeping as a profession, and after a fire destroyed the tavern, Andrew Angell determined that James's inheritance would be not the family business but a college education. At age sixteen, James entered Brown University, and he graduated first in his class in 1849. After a period of travel in Europe, Angell joined the faculty of his alma mater as a professor of modern languages. He taught at Brown from 1853 to 1860, and two of his

James B. Angell, United States minister and treaty commissioner to China, 1880–1881, and president of the University of Michigan, 1871–1909. *Michigan Historical Collections, Bentley Historical Library, University of Michigan.*

students there later became secretaries of state—Richard Olney and John Hay. Angell and Hay developed an especially close relationship and remained friends throughout their lives.[2]

Angell left Brown in 1860 to become editor of the influential *Providence Daily Journal.* The young professor had written articles and editorials for the newspaper for several years and had earned the confidence of the *Journal's* owner, Henry B. Anthony. Anthony entered the United States Senate in 1859 and asked Angell to assume full editorial control of the newspaper. Angell's eagerness to participate directly in the political drama unfolding in America in 1860 and his discouragement with the lack of intellectual challenge in drilling freshmen in French and German prompted him to make a complete, but temporary, departure from academic life. Under his direction, the *Journal* was a strong Republican voice in support of Abraham Lincoln and the Union cause. Concerned that the heavy workload of editing a daily newspaper was damaging his health, and attracted by a new challenge, Angell accepted the post of president of the University of Vermont in 1866. His personal vigor and prompt success in revitalizing that languishing university attracted the attention of the regents of the University of Michigan. After two years of discussions with the regents, he agreed to become president of the University of Michigan in 1871. By making this move, Angell received a considerable increase in his personal income, but he also found himself embroiled in serious campus conflicts. During the 1870s, the University of Michigan reeled under public controversies over such issues as the role of religion in the university and the alleged misappropriation of laboratory fees. The fact that the institution grew and strengthened despite these upheavals demonstrated Angell's abilities as an administrator, but his first years in Ann Arbor were difficult ones.[3]

His nomination in 1880 to be minister to China came unexpectedly to Angell. It was not until he met with Evarts in Washington to discuss the appointment that he learned that an old friend from his days in Vermont, Senator George F. Edmunds, had suggested his name to the secretary of state. Angell was cautious and did not immediately accept the offer of the China post. Although he was receptive to the prospect of a brief respite from the turmoil on campus, he sought assurances from Evarts that his appointment as minister and treaty commissioner would be only temporary, because he wanted to return quickly to the university. He also expressed serious doubts about the merits of the effort to limit Chinese immigration. He considered the current movement to exclude Orientals to be a reversal of America's traditional policy of welcoming all newcomers. Angell feared, however, that Congress would eventually pass restrictive legislation despite the Burlingame Treaty and that such unilateral action might cause Chinese retaliation against American treaty rights in China. Some kind of treaty revision permitting congressional regulation was therefore necessary. He informed Evarts that he would accept the position, but only if his instructions did not require him to seek absolute prohibition of Chinese immigration.[4]

One major factor in Angell's final decision was his own and his wife's interest in Christian missions. The Angells were devout and faithful members of the Congregational Church of Ann Arbor. Both were very "missionary-minded," and Mrs. Angell took an active role in several missionary societies. The prospect of being able to make some direct contribution to missionary efforts in China appealed overwhelmingly to the couple. While in China, Angell had few opportunities to do anything officially for the missionaries, but he did meet with them frequently. He attended services regularly, usually more than once a week, and only rarely and with great reluctance conducted any official business on Sunday.[5]

To assist Angell, the State Department appointed two other commissioners plenipotentiary to participate in the treaty negotiations. John F. Swift, who was a San Francisco assemblyman, advocated total exclusion of Chinese immigrants from the United States; William H. Trescot of South Carolina, on the other hand, viewed exclusion with professional caution reflecting his considerable diplomatic experience in the service of both the United States and Confederate States of America. All three commissioners were Republicans. Chester Holcombe, who had succeeded S. Wells Williams as secretary of the legation and also acted as interpreter during the treaty negotiations, later termed the composition of the commission a political masterstroke. The Democrats in Congress grumbled about how this move stole their thunder on the exclusion issue, which they had long supported, but they did not dare oppose it.[6]

In May 1880, Secretary Evarts met several times with Angell and Trescot in Washington to discuss the mission. Since the secretary gave them no specific instructions, apparently he established the commission primarily to relieve exclusionist political pressure on the administration rather than to implement any considered policy. The three men agreed that the immigrants' lack of interest in assimilation created a social problem, but that the United States wanted to be "just and generous" to the Chinese government. Although the meetings dealt with a broad range of potential treaty questions, the three men reached no conclusions. In fact, Angell and Trescot learned from Evarts only that the Burlingame Treaty must be revised, that the State Department had no specific changes in mind, that it was the commissioners' job to make some revisions, and that in doing so they must seek to ease concern on both sides of the Pacific.[7]

Evarts's only unequivocal remarks during his discussions with Angell and Trescot came in reference to Britain. Angell recorded in his diary that the secretary of state "emphatically does not wish to be tied to England—especially in treating oriental natives with less fairness and consideration than others, but have an Amn. policy—just, dignified and frank."[8] Although many Chinese entered California via the British possessions of Hong Kong and Singapore, no one suggested bringing the British into the treaty discussions. Similarly, Evarts contemplated a separate American treaty that would allow Peking to set its own tariff rates if the Chinese government would agree to abolish *likin* and guarantee that Americans would continue to pay no higher tariff than any other nation. The secretary of state left no doubt in Angell's mind "that we should have an independent policy, not simply be attached to England."[9]

Evarts's written instructions to Angell and his colleagues consisted only of a series of general points to be considered during the treaty negotiations. The secretary of state's failure to frame any specific guidelines was characteristic of Washington's vague direction to its ministers in Peking in the nineteenth century. Evarts did not even provide the commissioners with any draft treaty provisions. On commercial questions, the commission was to insure continuance of the most-favored-nation principle and to heed the interests of both China and the other powers. On the all-important immigration question, the secretary told the commissioners to take into account sentiment on the Pacific Coast, United States commercial relations with China, American traditions of liberal admission of foreigners, and the opposition of certain religious groups to exclusion. Evarts did not mention how these diverse factors were to be reconciled. The secretary suggested that George Seward's argument about the inequality of rights enjoyed by Chinese in America and Americans in China might be raised. To offer a final guide, Evarts sent the commissioners copies of the Democratic and Republican party platform planks on Chinese immigration.[10]

Enroute to Peking, Angell stopped for several days in San Francisco and talked with former minister Frederick Low and several other local spokesmen. He also visited Chinatown and met the leaders of San Francisco's Chinese community. Angell determined that although most men in California favored some limitation of immigration because of the problem of nonassimilation, Californians thought that the Chinese should be treated well. The new minister also found neither deplorable conditions in Chinatown nor widespread white unemployment in California, and he concluded that most of the exclusion agitation had been politically motivated and created by the press. In his opinion, a few demagogues had exploited the white agricultural "tramps" who poured into San Francisco after the harvest to become "bummers and sand lot politicians."[11]

When Angell, Swift, and Trescot arrived in Peking, one minor, yet significant, problem required attention before the commission could set about its work. Where was everyone going to stay? Angell moved his family into the modest United States legation, which barely had room to accommodate them. Since Peking had no Western-style hotel for the others, Swift and Trescot and their families found quarters in the spacious British legation. This arrangement greatly concerned the commissioners, who had explicit instructions to keep their distance from the English. Trescot wrote Washington:

> It does seem unfit that the U.S. should depend upon the hospitality of a foreign legation with whose policy it may not always be in accord and the over-shadowing influence of which even now in Eastern affairs stands directly in the way of the course that it may be our interest in the future to pursue. . . . [Furthermore, the situation may] produce here the impression of inferiority.[12]

Despite this somewhat inauspicious beginning, the commissioners quickly set to work preparing for the treaty deliberations. Before making their initial proposals to the Chinese, the three Americans held their own caucus. Swift, the Californian, wanted a treaty that absolutely prohibited Chinese immigration into the United States. Angell and Trescot disagreed and argued that the treaty should only give Congress the discretion to regulate immigration as it deemed necessary. Although Swift continued to advocate his position vigorously in this meeting and in later sessions, the majority ruled. Trescot accordingly drafted a memorandum to the Chinese asking that Washington be allowed the authority to regulate Chinese immigration whenever the United States "feels that its social or industrial interests require a limitation or prohibition of such immigration."[13]

At the first negotiating session with the Chinese, on October 1, 1880, the emperor's two treaty commissioners proposed leaving the Burlingame Treaty unchanged. Pao-yün and Li Hung-tsao, the Chinese negotiators, both served in the Tsungli Yamen. Pao was a member of Prince Kung's progressive faction in Peking, and Li was a leader of the antiforeign and reactionary mandarins. Pao and Li wanted to make Seward's proposals concerning the limiting of certain classes of people, such as paupers and prostitutes, the basis for discussion. Trescot countered that Seward's suggestions were made without official authorization and that the present commission had come specifically to revise the Burlingame Treaty. The Chinese agreed to give further consideration to the issues and indicated that they thought a settlement was feasible. Trescot believed that the Chinese were stalling. Angell and Swift left the meeting thinking that the emperor's representatives would negotiate on a basis of limitation of immigration but not prohibition. Although the Americans were prepared to waive prohibition, they decided to wait a while longer before revealing their hand.[14]

Several days later, the Chinese called a meeting and presented the Americans with a full draft for a treaty. Their projet applied immigration restrictions only to California, exempted "artisans" from the excluded class of "laborers," and proposed what amounted to an imperial veto over any regulations that Congress might adopt. The Americans expressed their objections to the draft articles, but the conference adjourned on a cordial note. After this meeting the Americans decided to play their trump and resubmit their own projet, asking only for limitation, not prohibition.[15]

The decisive session took place on November 5, slightly more than a month after the first official meeting. With both projets before them, the Chinese and American commissioners turned to the first article, which dealt with regulating immigration. The two drafts were at such variance that Swift and Trescot were ready to abandon the entire effort, but Angell believed that the Chinese were prepared to negotiate in earnest and counseled patience. "Let us leave this Article," he suggested, "and take up the last. Let the fish chew the bait awhile." Proceeding to other provisions, the two sides quickly came to agreement on several minor points. Returning to the first article and "having now gotten into the mood of agreeing," the commissioners succeeded in "dove-tailing" together the two drafts, and the work was done.[16]

The commissioners agreed to the final wording of the treaty on November 8 and signed the document on November 17, 1880. Genuine bargaining had taken place between the American commissioners and their Chinese counterparts, and the rapidity of the settlement must have set a record for Sino-Western diplomatic dealings under conditions other than duress. A simultaneous border controversy with Russia may have prompted the Peking government to come to quick agreement, but more likely the Chinese simply were not concerned enough about emigration to quibble.[17]

Article I of the Treaty of 1880 allowed the United States to "regulate, limit, or suspend" but "not absolutely prohibit" the immigration of Chinese laborers. The other three articles provided specifically for the entrance of students, merchants, and tourists into the United States; for protection of Chinese already in America; and for communication to the Chinese government of any laws passed in accordance with the treaty.[18]

Angell, Swift, and Trescot believed that the Chinese had agreed to these terms only because of the mandarins' faith in America's friendship for their country. In their summary report to Washington, the three commissioners concluded that once the Chinese had granted that the United States should have discretionary power over immigration, they assumed that America would "exercise that discretion with justice, and in a spirit of friendship." "We were fortunate enough," continued the report, "to satisfy the Chinese commissioners not only of the justice of our views, but of the entire good faith in which they were advanced."[19] The Chinese apparently trusted that future American restrictions and behavior would be reasonable, and Angell considered the immigration treaty a good solution of the "Chinese question," as it was called in the United States.[20]

With the immigration agreement concluded, the Chinese treaty commissioners raised the possibility of also negotiating some commercial articles. Specifically, the Chinese desired the outlawing of the opium trade and the granting of a most-favored-nation tariff for their country's goods in the United States. Angell and his associates found no objection to these proposals and readily agreed. The Americans then gained Chinese approval of two additional articles. One established judicial procedures for mixed cases in accordance with George Seward's earlier proposal that such cases be tried in a court of the defendant's nationality. The other article provided for mutual consideration of expanded commercial intercourse between the United States and China. The only one of these four provisions with any real diplomatic significance was the opium article. The Chinese wanted such an agreement from the United States in order "to isolate the British Government on this question from the other Christian Powers, and to compel that Government to take the odium of forcing this wicked and demoralizing traffic for the avowed purpose of financial advantage."[21] The three Americans were eager to disassociate their policies from those of the British. This motive and their personal aversion to the evils of the opium trade prompted them to accept willingly the "absolute prohibition" of the import, transport, purchase, or sale of opium by U.S. citizens in the open ports of China.[22]

Although Angell stayed in Peking until the autumn of 1881, the treaty negotiations remained his primary contribution to American China policy. On later occasions he consulted with his colleagues in the other legations, but his initial diplomacy revealed that American envoys would deal independently with the Chinese on issues concerning only the United States. As the opium provision demonstrated, Angell would twist the tail of the British lion when the opportunity presented itself—a development that did not go unnoticed by London.[23] Angell resumed his duties at the University of Michigan in 1882 and served as president of that institution until his retirement in 1909. He returned to government service three additional times: twice under President Grover Cleveland, to serve briefly on international commissions, and also as United States minister to Turkey in 1897–1898. He enjoyed the role of diplomat but preferred the security of academic tenure to the political vagaries of government service.[24]

Angell's expectation that the United States would find hardly "any need of availing itself of the power conceded it" by the immigration treaty proved sadly inaccurate.[25] The ink was barely dry on the treaty's signatures when Congress began debate on seven different exclusion bills. The goals of politics and diplomacy continued to contravene each other. Congress tended to view the Angell Treaty not as a mutual international accommodation on a sensitive issue but rather as carte blanche for luring constituents' votes at the expense of Chinese immigrants. Congressional debate centered not on whether to suspend Chinese immigration but rather on how long the suspension should be. The negotiated treaty, purposefully vague, allowed the United States to close immigration for a "reasonable" period, but even the American treaty commissioners did not agree on the timetable. Angell contended that five years was a reasonable period, but Swift maintained that forty years was not excessive.[26]

The first exclusion bill approved by Congress in 1882 under the aegis of the new treaty provided for a twenty-year suspension of immigration of Chinese laborers. It also created an elaborate system of regulations that would have effectively impeded the immigration of merchants, students, and other Chinese whom the treaty had specifically exempted from such restrictions. During the debate on this bill, which was authored by Senator John F. Miller of California, Senator Joseph Hawley of Connecticut perceptively summarized the ironic history of Sino-Western relations: "We are asked to deny to the Chinaman the right [of immigration and residence which] he was bombarded into accepting" for foreigners in his own country.[27]

President Chester A. Arthur vetoed this twenty-year suspension bill for much the same reason that President Hayes had vetoed the earlier fifteen-passenger-limit bill. The new president agreed with the purpose of the bill but thought that the twenty-year period and onerous regulations were unreasonable and hence indefensible under both the new Angell Treaty and accepted international practice. Unsuccessful at overriding the veto, Congress quickly passed a second bill establishing a ten-year exclusion period and modifying but not removing the provisions affecting the supposedly exempted classes. Arthur thought that this substitute bill also went beyond the suspension period and regulations permitted by the Angell Treaty, but he yielded to political pressure for some type of exclusion and signed it into law.[28]

Confronted with these quick moves to restrict all Chinese immigration to America, Peking was incapable of responding with anything more than formal remonstrances. Plagued by difficulties much more serious than the treatment of its emigrants in America, the Ch'ing Dynasty faced increasing pressures from other countries for economic and territorial concessions, as well as insurmountable internal problems ranging from pervasive poverty to political upheaval. Because China's government, economy, and entire way of life were collapsing under the weight of these burdens, the Chinese were thus unable to retaliate by restricting the rights of foreigners, as Seward and Angell had feared they might.[29]

America's decision to exclude immigrants revealed one of the most unsavory and unequal aspects of Western policy toward China in the nineteenth century: namely, the invocation of treaties and international law to give legitimacy to arbitrary actions against the weak Chinese government. Earlier in the century, using international conventions and practices as justification, Western nations had penetrated Chinese society. The American Treaty of 1880, however, led to an ironic reapplication of diplomatic principles. Again using the sanctimonious shroud of a treaty, the United States in 1882 blocked the entry of the Chinese into American society. Exclusion was an issue on which U.S. ideals of justice and equality proved incompatible with overriding perceptions of political, if not commercial, self-interest.

John Russell Young, a well-known journalist with the *New York Herald,* followed Angell as minister to China in 1882. Former president Ulysses S. Grant used his influence to secure the appointment. Young and Grant first became friends when the newspaperman wrote a series of editorials commending the impeachment and criticizing the acquittal of Andrew Johnson. Young later aided in Grant's presidential campaigns and was the only member of the press to accompany Grant on his around-the-world trip in 1877–1879. Some newspapers termed the selection of Young for the China post blatant patronage and characterized the new minister as a sycophantic reporter with no diplomatic ability.[30]

Born in northern Ireland on November 20, 1840, Young was less than a year old when his family emigrated to the United States and settled near Philadelphia. Following an apprenticeship in a printing office, he went to work at age seventeen as a copy boy for Colonel John W. Forney's *Philadelphia Press.* He rose rapidly on the newspaper staff as a reporter and editor, and in 1862 he became managing editor of both the *Philadelphia Press* and the *Washington Chronicle.* Clashes with Forney and other staff members caused Young to resign from the two papers in 1865. Joining the staff of the *New York Tribune,* he was managing editor of that influential Republican paper by 1866. As an editorial writer, he attracted much attention with his attacks on President Johnson and with his appeals for justice to former slaves. His views on controversial issues were often too radical even for his liberal editor-in-chief, Horace Greeley, and in 1869 Young left the *Tribune* because his support of Grant for president conflicted with Greeley's preference for Salmon P. Chase. Young had achieved recognition as a talented journalist but had not yet found a paper that allowed him full independence in his editorial opinions. His search for a journalistic home finally ended in 1872, when he teamed up with James G. Bennett and the *New York Herald.* Bennett shared Young's

John Russell Young, journalist, United States minister to China from 1882 to 1885, and Librarian of Congress from 1897 to 1899. *Library of Congress.*

admiration for Grant, and the *Herald* supported Grant throughout his presidency. Grant reciprocated this loyalty by helping secure Young's appointment as minister to China in March 1882.[31]

Despite criticism of Young's appointment as political spoils, he proved to be an able representative of the United States in Peking. His journalistic background made him an acute observer, and his dispatches were thorough and informative. His political experience enabled him to detect and decipher many of China's internal intrigues. During his previous visit to China and Japan with Grant in 1879, he had acquired not only knowledge of the current issues in East Asia but also a personal acquaintanceship with several high-ranking officials. Young's particularly amicable and intimate relationship with Li Hung-chang influenced the diplomacy of both men on several occasions.[32]

Young's tenure in China coincided with a sudden increase in tension between Chinese and foreigners. Settlement of a long-standing border dispute with Russia in 1881 gave the conservative, antiforeign element among the mandarins new incentive to resist foreign activity. In 1871, Russian troops had occupied the Ili Valley in northern Sinkiang province, and finally, after ten years of almost continuous negotiations, the

Russians agreed to withdraw from part of the disputed territory. Although Peking had to pay an indemnity and make other concessions to gain this limited success, the conservatives, who had repeatedly insisted that Ili be retained at all costs, felt vindicated. They did not realize that St. Petersburg had consented to a compromise settlement only because the czar was beset by more pressing foreign and domestic difficulties. Despite cautions against overconfidence by Tseng Chi-tse, who negotiated the agreement, many Chinese officials believed that Russia had been awed by Chinese determination and on that assumption prepared to deal forcibly with other foreign governments.[33]

Also in 1881, Empress Dowager Tz'u-an died. She and Empress Dowager Tz'u-hsi had ruled China as coregents since 1875, because of the minority of Emperor Kuang-hsü. Tz'u-an generally supported Prince Kung and his moderate policies toward foreigners. Tz'u-hsi, on the other hand, was intensely antiforeign and disliked the prince, not only for his handling of the barbarians but also because his power kept her from absolute control of the imperial government. After years of feuding with the prince, Tz'u-hsi may have murdered Tz'u-an in a move to gain a monopoly of power. With Tz'u-an's death, Prince Kung's influence dwindled, enabling the antiforeign faction of Tz'u-hsi increasingly to determine imperial policy.[34]

These political developments manifested themselves in an attempt by Chinese authorities to close down foreign factories in the treaty ports. One of the first targets of the suppression was W. S. Wetmore's American cotton-yarn operation in Shanghai. On instructions from higher officials, the chief Chinese official in the city, the *taotai*, declared the factory illegal because it violated an imperial monopoly. Young immediately protested to Prince Kung, who was still head of the Tsungli Yamen. The new minister pointed out that the French Treaty of 1858 clearly permitted foreign "industry" in the open ports and that the United States enjoyed this right under the most-favored-nation clause of the American treaties. Although the Chinese government recently had insisted that the treaties did not provide for foreign manufacturing, Young hoped that the Tsungli Yamen would receive his protest in a friendly and accommodating spirit. If the mandarins proved to be stubborn, however, the American envoy believed that the other Western ministers would join with him in his protest, because the basic issue in this case far transcended the fate of Wetmore's company alone. At stake, according to Young, was the need for the

Chinese to recognize that their exclusion of Western manufacturing was "a violation of the modern laws of practical economy." Reflecting the convergence of self-interest and altruism that often permeated American opinion, he argued that the Chinese damaged their own interests when they stifled the efforts of Western citizens "whose capital, enterprise, industry and genius have done so much to give China the benefits of an advanced and enlightened civilization."[35]

Subsequent developments in Shanghai soon revealed that, despite Young's appeal to Prince Kung, this case would not be settled easily. Tso Tsung-t'ang, the highest-ranking imperial official in central China, issued a secret warrant for the arrest of Wetmore's comprador on the charge that he had aided the Taipings seventeen years earlier. During the Ili crisis, Tso had established Chinese control over Sinkiang and had made possible the settlement with Russia. He was the conservatives' champion, and as governor general of Kiangnan and Kiangsi, he equaled Li Hung-chang in rank and power. Foreign diplomats referred to Li and Tso as viceroys in recognition of their broad-ranging authority. Tso's action against Wetmore's comprador represented a serious menace to the American's business. The Chinese comprador was essential to any foreign enterprise as its interpreter, agent, and key link to the Chinese economy. In addition, the comprador and his Chinese associates usually invested heavily in the foreign firm. Hence the arrest warrant threatened not only to cripple Wetmore's enterprise but also to intimidate rich Chinese from providing capital for foreign concerns.[36]

Young could not ignore what he considered a "violent" attack on the interests of an American citizen, but he recognized as well the extreme delicacy of the situation. Although the charge against the comprador appeared to be fabricated, the minister acknowledged that the viceroy had every right to deal with one of his own subjects in accordance with Chinese law. Young decided to permit the comprador to remain temporarily within the sanctuary of the foreign concession area in Shanghai until more could be learned about Tso's intent in issuing the warrant.[37]

Meanwhile, F. D. Cheshire, the American vice-consul general at Shanghai, complicated the affair by visiting Tso in Nanking without informing Young. In his zeal to protect Wetmore's immediate interests, Cheshire suggested to the viceroy that the comprador's case be submitted to the mixed court in Shanghai. Although the orderly procedures of this tribunal would practically assure a dismissal of charges arising from a seventeen-year-old offense, the offer severely weakened Young's diplomatic position. In the minister's opinion, Wetmore's case involved grave diplomatic questions concerning interpretation of the Sino-Western treaties—issues that could be settled only between the Tsungli Yamen and the legations. Once the threat to the comprador had been removed, it would be difficult for Young to prove to the Tsungli Yamen that the United States still had a grievance. A resolution of the case without any reference to the treaties would also leave Tso's ability to intimidate other foreign factories undiminished.[38]

Despite this tactical setback, Young decided to resist the governor general's antiforeign action. Wetmore informed the minister that the imperial authorities had offered him a compromise: if he would dissolve his company, the warrant would be withdrawn. This intelligence convinced the minister that Tso was using Chinese law to "blackmail" Wetmore. Unwilling to permit American interests to be destroyed in this fashion, Young sent to the Tsungli Yamen a note of protest signed by all the foreign envoys in Peking. At the same time, he reassured Washington that he sought only to protect American interests and that he would duly regard "the rights and susceptibilities of the central government."[39]

While Young walked the tightrope between protecting American treaty privileges and respecting China's sovereign rights, Tso Tsungt'ang continued to issue decrees against foreign businesses. As an advocate of "self-strengthening" in the 1860s, Tso had planned a Western-style shipyard at Foochow and had engaged French advisors for the project; but by the 1880s he was, in the opinion of Westerners, intensely antiforeign, as well as arrogant, intolerant, and cruel. The old mandarin outlawed electric light in Shanghai and requested that the American firm of Russell and Company stop manufacturing silk filatures. Young considered these decrees "the expression of a general policy of antiforeignism towards all foreign industries in the open ports."[40] It was clear to the American minister that this case was not like previous amicable debates over commas and characters in the treaties but was one of open Chinese hostility toward foreigners.[41]

Young, in fact, considered the situation serious enough to communicate with Admiral Pierce Crosby, commander of the American Asiatic Squadron. While not specifically requesting that a vessel be sent to

Shanghai, the minister informed Admiral Crosby, who was in Japan, that "the presence of an American man-of-war during the complications, would serve our interests, and strengthen the Legation in its discussions with the Foreign Office." Young asked the admiral to use the utmost discretion and to make no appearance of threatening the Chinese. If a vessel was dispatched to Shanghai, the diplomat suggested that its commander should treat "the visit as only an ordinary incident in a winter cruise along the Chinese coast."[42]

Young never questioned China's right to deal with its own subjects in its own way and insisted that the Western governments sought only to help the Middle Kingdom develop its resources and improve its public administration. He recognized that China, like all preindustrial nations, feared technological innovation, because of the belief that machines would destroy the livelihood derived from manual labor. Despite his sympathy for China's rulers as they faced the difficult task of modernization, he could not overlook their interference with treaty rights. He deemed the actions against Wetmore retrogressive and unfriendly and hoped that Peking would overrule the viceroy. To leave Tso's conduct unchecked would, in Young's opinion, cause the treaties to have "no more value . . . than so many ropes of sand." He informed Washington that to avoid such an outcome, "the foreign Governments should resist, by every species of argument and persuasion, the reactionary tendencies now in force."[43]

While Young was protesting affairs in Shanghai, local Chinese authorities ordered closed the German iron foundries in Amoy and Swatow. When the Tsungli Yamen failed to give prompt assurances of protection, German minister von Brandt had marines with fixed bayonets landed to guard the factories. Peking then quickly instructed the mandarins at the two ports to cease interference with German subjects. These events profoundly affected Young, who had consistently deplored force or the show of force and had maintained that diplomacy alone should settle such cases. Von Brandt's course caused the American to reexamine the options that had repeatedly faced United States envoys in China. Young conceded that the Tsungli Yamen's prompt action under threat of force tended "to confirm the opinion of all who advocate the policy of repression and severity in Asia," but he countered that such tactics were "so repugnant to all American traditions and habits" and so personally distasteful that he could not accept them.

Despite this reaffirmation of American ideals, Young could not help but betray a wavering ambivalence. He pointed out to Washington that while Wetmore's "right to manufacture is in abeyance without much hope of satisfactory settlement," the German show of force had "brought immediate redress."[44]

The Amoy incident was not finished, however, because the local *taotai* refused to obey the Tsungli Yamen's instructions. The inability of the Chinese foreign office to enforce its order created what the American minister termed a "serious complication." Young advised the American admiral to send a vessel to Amoy, because there was no guarantee that the Chinese government would or could protect foreigners, but the landing of additional German marines ended the incident. Young regretted the whole affair and felt "a natural repugnance towards doing with China what we would not do with Germany or England." On the other hand, he believed that Peking's "weakness" and the *taotai*'s "ignorance and caprice" had left von Brandt little choice.[45]

The discussions with the Tsungli Yamen disappointed Young as much as did the German resort to naval action. The warrant against Wetmore's comprador had been withdrawn, and as he had expected, Young's argument thus lost much of its impact with the government. After much delay, Prince Kung sent an identical response to all the foreign representatives. Maintaining that the treaties had never been intended to allow foreign competition with native industry, he implied that Western factories were dangerous to China. Consequently, the prince refused to overrule local Shanghai officials, whose intimidation had paralyzed foreign industry. Young dejectedly informed Washington that, despite his arguments and the German marines, absolutely no progress had been made toward a satisfactory understanding and that the treaties as they applied to manufacturing had practically been abrogated.[46]

In addition to the joint note to all the foreign legations, Prince Kung sent Young a separate request that penetrated to the core of American China policy. Beset by both foreign and domestic critics, the old prince appealed to the United States not to join with the other powers in forcing his government to allow foreign manufacturing. Although Young sympathized with the prince's difficult position, the American assumed that an affirmative response would mean abandoning the cooperative policy. Unlike Burlingame, but like his other predecessors, Young defined cooperation as acting "in harmony with the other powers," not with China. In his opinion, the policy had served the United States well to the extent that it helped "to maintain treaty privileges" and aided in the protection of Americans against "a vast, impulsive, suspicious population." Characterizing cooperation in these terms, Young admitted that "we have had as much to gain by it as any other power."[47]

In many respects, though, Young believed that the United States had little in common with the other treaty nations. He observed that, since its successful war against France in 1870, Germany had ventured into an ambitious and aggressive policy in China with which America could not identify. Angell's commercial treaty broke with England on opium. Young doubted that the English really wanted to see foreign manufacturing in China that would compete with their trade in finished products. As for France and Russia, the American thought that the former cared only about the church, and the latter only about aggrandizement. Finally, he noted that neighboring Japan was China's natural rival and antagonist.[48]

According to Young, the United States had two options: to (1) demand "scrupulous" Chinese compliance with the treaty provisions that protected foreign manufacturing or (2) take heed of Peking's "hopes and fears" and agree to a new convention suppressing foreign industry. In other words, the United States could cooperate with China or with the Western nations, but not with both. This choice had been the persistent problem in American China policy. Burlingame had usually been able to cooperate with all parties, but his successors had generally sided with the Westerners. Young was aware that the treaty system contravened Chinese sovereignty, and for him this fact created a diplomatic dilemma. He continued to hope that Prince Kung would leave the way open for some accommodation between Chinese and Western manufacturing interests but meanwhile concluded that the challenge to American treaty rights in the Wetmore case required a firm and united Western stand.[49]

Because the issues were of such fundamental importance to the treaty system, Young wanted the State Department to choose between the options he had outlined. As was typical of Washington's instructions to its nineteenth-century envoys in China, Secretary of

State Frederick T. Frelinghuysen gave Young little specific guidance. The department opposed force and "preferred to trust to frank and friendly argument." Washington would not assent to a return by the Chinese to their "ancient exclusive system" but was "loath to believe" that any departure from the traditional policy of friendship would be required to insure American interests. Frelinghuysen did not, however, rule out the use of force, as long as it created no complications with the other legations. The secretary of state advised Young that, in the event he needed more help from the navy than "moral support," he was first to confer with his "colleagues of the Diplomatic Body, that the harmony and concert of action so long maintained . . . may not be impaired."[50]

Left on his own to determine American policy, Young finally decided to reject coercion, because in his opinion the United States did not have sufficient interests at stake to justify the use of force. From the beginning, he had realized that the amount of American manufacturing in China was too small to be of practical importance. For a while he worried about the precedent that would be established if the Chinese succeeded in suppressing Wetmore's firm. "If we concede [in this case]," he wrote at one point in the negotiations, "other concessions will be asked and won in the same way, and China will once more become a hidden nation, her ports closed to our ships and her markets sealed to our capital and enterprise."[51] On further reflection, Young determined that not even America's future manufacturing interests merited recourse to von Brandt's "strenuous policy." He realized that Americans in China sought trade in items, such as silk, tea, and kerosene, in which they could gain a quick profit and go home. They did not usually establish factories or other businesses that required a long time to realize a profit. Hence Young acquiesced in the face of Prince Kung's strong resistance and let the treaty question on manufacturing end. He concluded that the United States government could "wait patiently the march of events."[52]

Young was well aware of the contrast between how he and von Brandt handled the manufacturing question. Although he never used the word *imperialism* and he tended to idealize the American policy record in China, his analysis of the Western impact on the Middle Kingdom was very perceptive:

In many aspects our interests in Asia are not in sympathy with those of the Western powers. Our prestige in China depends upon the fact that we have always treated her with patience, firmness & kindness, never overlooking her sovereign rights, recognizing the embarrassments attending the government of a vast population, the peculiar, conservative character of her institutions and her people, and the fact that even with best intentions, the advance of Western civilization is an aggression, disturbing institutions that have existed for ages, and customs that have remained unchanged since a period long antecedent to the Christian era.[53]

He was not exactly sure whether he or the German minister had made the right choice, but he knew that he had taken the only course consistent with America's limited interests. Young was wrestling with the basic dilemma in American policy: whether to attempt the costly and perhaps impossible task of pressuring China into becoming a Western-type nation or to accept China as it was and seek some accommodation between Chinese sovereignty and foreign ambitions.

Sensitive to the mutual antagonisms between East and West, Young spent much of his time as minister trying to mediate the dispute between China and France over control of Vietnam. Motivated by national pride, particularly after its defeat by Germany, and by its self-proclaimed mission to protect Catholic missionaries, France in the 1860s and 1870s increasingly extended its control over Vietnam. Although the Chinese claimed the states of Indochina as part of their tributary empire, Peking at first made no attempt to challenge French expansion. Following the Ili settlement, however, China considered itself prepared to deal with the French interlopers to the south and sent troops to Tongking, the northern area of Vietnam. The result was a series of military clashes and unsuccessful negotiations that culminated in the Sino-French War of 1884–1885.[54]

From the beginning of these troubles, Governor General Li Hung-chang conducted most of China's negotiations with France. Li and French minister Frederic A. Bourée reached an agreement in November 1882, whereby China would withdraw its troops from Vietnam and allow French trade on the Red River. In return, France would recognize the independence of Annam (central Vietnam) and not conquer Tongking. This eminently practical compromise did not satisfy the truculent mood in either Paris or Peking. France recalled Bourée and sent Arthur Tricou, French minister in Tokyo, to Shanghai. Li met with Tricou, but their discussions resolved nothing. Tricou demanded that China recognize France's 1874 treaty with Vietnam establishing a French protectorate. Because Peking would not allow him to make any concessions, Li broke off negotiations and returned to Tientsin. [55]

During the talks between Li and Tricou, Young had several frank discussions with his friend the governor general about the probable results of a war with France. Young forecast a disastrous defeat for China that would lead to French demands for a large indemnity and more territory. Li undoubtedly realized the dangers that his country faced, but the old general had to satisfy a war party in Peking that had never heard a shot fired in battle. Young reported to Washington: "All that mass of thieving, treacherous, cowardly, cunning adventurers which surround the throne and live an insectivorous, parasitic existence on this venerable and august monarchy, were all for war." [56]

Li and Young sought ways in which the United States could demonstrate its friendship for China in the present crisis. But when Li asked about the American army and navy, Young changed the subject. Young suggested that China would not be so weak if it would build railroads and make other improvements with American help. Li proposed that China might send a Burlingame-type embassy to the West, with Young and himself at its head, to seek support for China. There was not enough time, though, to employ any of these ideas. [57]

When Li broke off his discussions with Tricou, the viceroy asked Young if Washington would arbitrate the dispute. The American minister had been the only foreign representative to demonstrate any sympathy for Li's efforts. Young cautioned his friend that the United States would do nothing to affect its friendly relations with France, but he telegraphed Li's request to Washington. The State Department informally raised the question of arbitration through the U.S. legation in Paris. The French government considered this alternative briefly but finally rejected it, claiming to be "ignorant of differences to be referred." [58]

Although a sincere desire for peace motivated Young's mediation efforts, he was not neutral in the dispute. He privately considered French actions "ignominious" and French claims of ignorance of differences with China "disingenuous." The American minister labeled

French policy "aggression, having no regard either for the rights or the susceptibilities of the Chinese." Even if there was some justification for the French position, Young argued that the benefits in trade and prestige that France might gain were not worth the risks involved in war. In December 1883 he predicted that war would create such chaos that no nation would be able to anticipate or control the final outcome.[59]

The year 1883 was sad for John Russell Young. Not only was he distressed over the Sino-French hostilities, which he considered tragic and avoidable, but he also suffered the loss of his wife, Julia, on October 22. She had accompanied him to China but had traveled to Paris in April 1883. There she gave birth to a son in August and developed her fatal illness shortly afterward. They were married only seventeen months and lived together only seven months. After receiving the news of her death from Paris, the minister recorded in his diary: "She was the most accomplished & beautiful woman I have ever known."[60] Julia Young was only twenty-four years old, and her death left her husband feeling very lonely. He began to think of leaving China after the 1884 elections, regardless of which party won. The elections were still a year away, though, and Young gave no thought to resigning in the winter of 1883–1884. "China is now in a most critical position," he wrote to a friend, "and I cannot abandon my post."[61]

Throughout 1884, China and France alternately fought and negotiated. After France won several victories in Tongking, Li again attempted to extricate China from the conflict diplomatically. In May 1884 Li signed a convention with French navy captain Francois E. Fournier that essentially repeated the Bourée agreement. The imperial government again disavowed Li's efforts, and the fighting resumed. Paris then demanded a large indemnity from China—an item that the Li-Fournier convention had omitted. In August, France moved its campaign into China itself and won several victories over Chinese naval and land forces on Taiwan and at Foochow. Following an attack on Foochow that devastated China's modern shipyard there, Peking formally declared war.

Faced with these reverses and French demands, Chinese officials once again looked to the United States. At the beginning of the conflict, the Chinese had thought that Britain and Germany might aid China in order to prevent their rival France from gaining some advantage in East Asia. Germany lacked sufficient naval power in the region in the 1880s to risk intervention. British opinion was divided between those Englishmen who were suspicious of France and others who desired to see China pressured for more commercial concessions that could be exploited by the most-favored-nation provisions of the treaties. America appeared to be China's best hope for an honest broker. Young was pessimistic about achieving an agreement without further fighting, but he telegraphed the Chinese request for good offices to Washington. France at first rebuffed American inquiries but in September 1884 approached the United States on its own about mediation. The prolonged skirmishing had begun to strain the French economy and public mood. Consequently, Paris indicated that it would settle with China along the lines of the Li-Fournier convention, provided some nominal indemnity was included. American and French representatives haggled over the amount, which was finally set at five million francs after Paris originally demanded eighty million. Peking, however, stubbornly resisted paying any indemnity at all and continued to fight. In March 1885, General Feng Tzu-ts'ai managed to inflict a major defeat on French forces at Langson on the Kwangsi-Tongking border. Shortly afterward, Robert Hart concluded arrangements through his personal agent in London for a Sino-French peace settlement based upon the Li-Fournier convention, and the belligerents signed a formal treaty on June 9, 1885. China paid no indemnity, but it suffered economic losses from the war far in excess of any payments demanded by France.[62]

Throughout the conflict, Young confessed to Washington that he could not understand why the Chinese so adamantly refused to accept the French terms. The American did not fully comprehend the strength and determination of the recalcitrant conservatives in Peking. With each Chinese reversal, their demands for even greater resistance to France gained additional weight with Empress Dowager Tz'u-hsi. Their ascendancy finally made possible the removal of the moderate Prince Kung—a move that Tz'u-hsi had long desired. Although these political developments largely determined the court's response to the French, Young had his own theory to explain Peking's actions. Despite his failure to discern the extent of the xenophobic faction's power, he did detect Western imperialistic designs in the Sino-French imbroglio.[63]

Young contended that most foreigners in China desired a war and that the other legations had for this reason encouraged Peking to resist the French. According to Young, the Europeans shared the following vision: "War means revolution, dissolution, Russia coming to the Yangtze, France pressing on from the South, England seeing that whatever befalls, her interests are safe."[64] The American predicted grimly that England and Russia would let France do the "dirty work" and then demand territorial compensation to preserve the "balance of power" in Asia. Young expected Russia to claim Quelpart Island in the Korean Strait and England to take Port Hamilton, another island off the southern coast of Korea. He reasoned further that a French war with China also served English interests in Egypt and eased German concerns about the Rhine by preoccupying Paris elsewhere in the world. Similarly, the American contended that "Russia with ever-extending boundaries to rectify, is always served by complications in Asia."[65]

The United States could not share European desires for war and domination in Asia, Young argued. He declared that America's first consideration was the independence and well-being of China, because "whatever menaces that independence affects our influence in the East." In a masterful blending of American ideals and self-interest, he explained that the United States

> must look to the East for an imperial trade, and if, without a protest, we accept any political or commercial policy here, which paralyzes that trade we do ourselves a wrong. . . . [We see] in peace the welfare of China, and the strengthening of American influence in Asia.[66]

These ideas would eventually be reaffirmed in John Hay's Open Door Notes of 1899 and 1900. Significantly, the man who would later be Hay's chief advisor on Chinese affairs, William W. Rockhill, joined the Peking legation as second secretary during Young's ministry.[67]

Foreigners in China criticized Young for "peddling mediation." They claimed that the American had sided with China against France— assuming that if Young was not with his colleagues, he must be against them. While not denying that he thought France had acted unjustly and ignobly, the American minister contended that he had behaved honorably toward France. In addition, he admitted privately that beyond diplomatic efforts, the United States would never intervene in behalf of China.[68]

Doubtless Young viewed his own actions as unbiased toward either belligerent and as premised only on how best to protect United States interests. For example, he received particularly sharp criticism from French officials for engineering the transfer of the steamers of the China Merchants Steam Navigation Company to the American firm of Russell and Company. The French had anticipated confiscating the fleet as an act of war and thus considered the American purchase an unfriendly act. Well aware of French intentions, the Chinese preferred to sell the vessels rather than lose them. Young did not hesitate to take advantage of the Chinese offer at French expense and, in fact, purposefully "departed from the old policy of cooperative action" among the Western nations. He explained that in China, the British had established the principle "that when matters went to please Great Britain there was joint action. Otherwise, there was no action until Great Britain was pleased." Consequently, Young decided that during the Sino-French hostilities, "it was deemed best for the American interests that the [U.S.] Legation should act alone, and, like its British associate, unite in 'joint action' when such a course served the United States."[69] In his opinion, this independent policy enabled the United States to pursue its own interests while also strengthening Chinese-American relations.[70]

Former minister George F. Seward disagreed and charged that since 1880 the United States had abdicated its former position of "friendly arbitrator of differences" between China and the foreign powers. In an article published in the *North China Herald* in December 1884, Seward alleged that the immigration treaty and its implementing legislation had been "unfairly procured and unfairly made" and had "destroyed the old faith which the Chinese reposed in us." In other words, while European critics were characterizing American policy as pro-Chinese, the erstwhile U.S. minister was labeling his nation's conduct as anti-Chinese. Although Seward's comments were clearly intended to vindicate his own opposition to exclusion, his article also demonstrated the ambiguous nature of America's relationship with the Middle Kingdom. He recalled that the United States had created the cooperative policy, which had assured both China and the treaty powers of "a peaceful solution to all difficulties." Americans had assumed the role of arbitrator, he claimed, because "we do not wish to see the great Empire broken up or subjected to humiliation." In rhetoric reminiscent of Burlingame's "plant-the-shining-cross" speech, Seward proclaimed that the Chinese wanted railways, telegraphs, mines, and other forms of "peaceful progress," and thus he lamented that "it should have been our mission—and in better days it appeared to be our mission—to sustain and support them in their efforts to work out their proper destiny."[71] Respect for China's sovereignty and independence was vital, Young agreed, if America's limited interests were to be secure against the imperialist ambitions of other nations. In forwarding a copy of Seward's article to Washington, however, Young dismissed his "distinguished" predecessor's charges and debunked the notion that immigration restriction had destroyed China's faith in the United States. In rebuttal, Young contended that "our Government is stronger today in China, . . . not in arms and ships, but in the confidence and respect of the Authorities and People, than it has ever been."[72]

Young's ministry in China came to an end early in 1885, with the change in presidential administrations. The inauguration of Grover Cleveland brought the first Democrat to the White House since the Civil War. Because Young owed his own appointment to political patronage, he was keenly aware that the new administration would expect to place a Democrat in the China post. Consequently, he voluntarily submitted his resignation as soon as news of Cleveland's election victory reached Peking, and upon his return to the United States, he rejoined the editorial staff of the *New York Herald*. In June 1897 the new Republican president, William McKinley, named Young the Librarian of Congress, and Young still held that post at the time of his death on January 17, 1899.[73]

The old cooperative era of Anson Burlingame had been gone a long time when Young left China in 1885. American policy had changed, but not only because of the immigration treaty, as George Seward alleged. Seward and other Western diplomats had steadily eclipsed "friendly cooperation" by their pursuit of selfish interests in China. Young operated under conditions very different from those that had faced Burlingame. Through most of the 1860s, there were only four legations in Peking. The number of foreigners in China and the extent of their activities had been nothing like that of the 1880s. Young could not sit down over tea with two or three European colleagues and settle the issues of the day.

Young attempted to mediate complex international rivalries involving not only affairs in China but conditions totally extraneous to Asia. He also had to contend with the Chinese government's own struggle to protect itself and its territory. At the same time, Young tried to protect America's limited interests in China from being crushed by these competing forces. The international and indigenous pressures in China forced the United States into some difficult policy choices. Should the American minister join his Western colleagues in their diplomatic and military efforts to protect and expand foreign privileges? Should he seek security for American interests by actively defending the integrity of the imperial government? Was it possible for the United States to pursue an independent policy—limiting its commitment to both the treaty system and Chinese sovereignty?

These questions had confronted every American minister since 1861. Through a combination of fortuitous circumstances and his own personal commitment to cultural accommodation, Burlingame frequently was able to reconcile Sino-Western differences peacefully. His cooperative policy respected the interests of all nations, including China. Browne had argued, on the other hand, that East and West were ultimately irreconcilable and that only united foreign pressure for change in China could bring the civilizations together. The policies of Burlingame and Browne represented the two extremes in the American options—cooperation or coercion. Their diplomacy also established two contrasting precedents: Burlingame's leadership among the foreigners in forging an innovative approach to the Chinese, and Browne's tactic of following the other Westerners in their old domineering attitude toward Orientals. Low and Avery tried variations of both Burlingame's "fair diplomatic action" and Browne's "determined moral pressure," but they became disillusioned and frustrated by the lack of success with either course. Finally, George Seward completely abandoned abstract policy principles and simply sought the most expedient way to protect and promote American interests. Angell and Young moved beyond Seward's policy of convenience and attempted to establish an independent American position in China. The question remained whether the United States could successfully maintain some unity with the treaty nations and simultaneously give some support to China without making a total commitment to either side. Could the United States achieve and sustain a position that neither jeopardized the benefits of Chinese goodwill nor abandoned the protection of the treaty system? If such a policy could be devised, it would reconcile the altruistic American ideals of fairness and justice with the nation's pursuit of economic and other self-interests.

CHAPTER SEVEN

Two China Policies

CHARLES DENBY VERSUS THE STATE DEPARTMENT

CHARLES DENBY OCCUPIED the American minister's chair in Peking longer than any other U.S. envoy. He served from 1885 to 1898—a critical period in China's foreign relations. Throughout China in the 1890s, serious antiforeign riots threatened a return to active gunboat diplomacy by the Western powers, and China's humiliating defeat in the Sino-Japanese War of 1894–1895 fully exposed the Peking government as weak and helpless before the world. Largely as a result of the war, the Western nations began to lease large portions of Chinese territory in 1898, and the partition and disappearance of a sovereign China appeared imminent. These increasingly ominous developments placed great pressure on Denby and the State Department to resolve the existing ambiguities in the American approach to China and to create, if possible, an effective policy consistent with both abstract ideals and tangible interests.

The minister and his superiors could not agree on which policy option to pursue. Denby usually, although not consistently, advocated that the United States join the other Western nations in a forceful, interventionist role. The State Department, on the other hand, generally forbade the minister's active participation with the other treaty powers, especially in matters not directly involving the United States.

TO CHINA
5 TO 1898

MEMBER OF THE PHILIPPI
COMMISSION 1899

Charles Denby served for thirteen years as United States minister
to China, 1885–1898. A cigar was later named for Denby, and this
portrait appeared on the cigar boxes. *Willard Library, Evansville,
Indiana.*

Better telegraphic communications and improved staff work in the
department enabled Washington to give Denby more timely policy
guidance than that received by his predecessors. Preferring a limited
and independent policy in China, the State Department frequently
clashed with its activist minister, who sometimes transcended the department's wishes. As a result, American policy during the several
years immediately prior to the Open Door Notes was the product of a
continuous tug of war between Washington and the legation in Peking.

Charles Denby's background and beliefs defy simple labels, and his
life reflected many of the competing forces and influences in
nineteenth-century America. Born in Virginia in 1830, he traveled as a
teenager to France with his father, a ship owner who had been appointed naval agent at Marseilles (a position similar to consul). While
abroad, young Charles became fluent in French, the diplomatic language, but did not retain much of this ability by the time he became a

diplomat. He returned to the United States to pursue his education at Virginia Military Institute and graduated with high honors in 1850. After teaching school for a short time in Alabama, he traveled northward to Evansville, Indiana in 1853. There he became a lawyer, and in 1856–1857 he served as a Democratic member of the state legislature. When the Civil War came, he forsook his Southern origins and joined the Union army. He commanded an Indiana regiment until he was seriously wounded at the Battle of Perryville in 1862; he received a medical discharge the following year. For the rest of his life, he proudly retained the title of colonel. As a railroad lawyer and director for twenty years after the war, Colonel Denby took an active role in the nation's dramatic economic growth. His double connection with railroad interests and the Democratic party produced his appointment as minister to China in 1885. He was a long-time supporter of Thomas A. Hendricks of Indiana, Grover Cleveland's first vice-president. Secretary of State Thomas F. Bayard's interest in building railroads in China further assured Denby's nomination. Railroad promoters, including James H. Wilson, who traveled to China in 1886, heartily approved the selection of Denby.[1]

When Republican Benjamin Harrison defeated Cleveland in 1888, the new president decided to leave his fellow Hoosier in the China post after the emperor's government opposed Harrison's original choice, Senator Henry W. Blair, who had supported Chinese exclusion legislation. Upon his return to the White House in 1893, Cleveland saw no reason to make a change in Peking, especially since his new secretary of state, Walter Q. Gresham of Indiana, expressed great confidence in his close friend Denby. Hence, the Indiana Democrat remained U.S. envoy in Peking thirteen years, through three presidential administrations and part of a fourth—a remarkable record for a period of bitter partisan politics.[2]

When Denby first arrived in Peking, in September 1885, he knew practically nothing about China, but he was fortunate to have the able assistance of William W. Rockhill. Although Rockhill had been in China only since the previous year, the young secretary of the legation was a serious student of Chinese language and culture. During Denby's first three years as minister, he relied heavily on Rockhill's expertise and even allowed the secretary to draft, not just transcribe, dispatches to the State Department. Denby had no patience for the scholarly Rockhill's preoccupation with esoteric Orientalia, however, and similarly, Rockhill became frustrated working under Denby, who tended to be vain and imperious. Because of their personality clash, Rockhill resigned from his post in 1888. The minister immediately secured the appointment of a more compatible legation secretary, his son Charles, Jr.[3]

Some of the attitudes and values that Colonel Denby carried to China in 1885 became even more pronounced during his years of exposure to East Asian culture. In his opinion, Western civilization was clearly superior to that of the East, and China was profiting from such Western innovations as railroads, steamships, and telegraphs. While admitting that the opium trade was "the blackest stain" on the history of Sino-Western relations, he pointed with pride to the antiopium convention that James B. Angell had negotiated with the Chinese. Denby boasted that Americans had treated Asians according to the Golden Rule and that his own nation's record in China was especially beneficent. Sharing the belief in Social Darwinism and Anglo-Saxon superiority that was popular in late-nineteenth-century America, he expressed paternalistic satisfaction in "the labour of bearing 'the white man's burden.'" Between 1885 and 1895, John Fiske, Josiah Strong, John W. Burgess, and Benjamin Kidd published influential works that purported to explain how nature and providence sanctioned white superiority over "native" and "backward peoples" and obligated the superior race to bestow the benefits of its progress on the less fortunate. In vogue with current literature, Denby assured readers of his memoirs that "you will respect your race more than ever, because you will contemplate it engaged in building up among peoples, whose complexions are darker than yours, institutions pointing toward the elevation of all races and conditions of men."[4] Denby assumed that the West had a great deal to teach China.[5]

While viewing the treaty system as the vehicle of Western progress in the Middle Kingdom, the former railroad lawyer also recognized the legal inconsistencies in Sino-Western relations. Quoting an old adage that "when two men ride a horse one must ride behind," Denby confessed that he preferred his race to "ride in front." He admitted that "it may be brutal to adopt this theory which rests on force, and not on international law," but he argued that "its existence rests on the supreme necessity of self-defense." Aware of Chinese antipathy toward foreigners, the diplomat maintained that "we are in China by their consent expressed in several treaties, . . . [and] we must force her to do what she promised to do."⁶ Despite his acknowledgment that Westerners did not always follow accepted international practices, he declared that the rule of law must prevail. To Denby, international law was both a justification for and a limitation on the use of force:

> Treaties are to international intercourse what the constitution is to domestic intercourse, and China can do no act which contravenes them. It is the business of the diplomatists, backed by the armies and navies of the world, to hold her to her written contracts. . . . In order to do so we must dictate the internal policy of China so far as foreigners are concerned. So far we may justly go and no farther.⁷

In spite of his coercive prescription for the treatment of China, Denby drew the line at seizure of territory, indemnities without just foundation, and "unjust and useless wars against the Chinese for purely selfish purposes."⁸ Like his diplomatic predecessors in Peking, Denby experienced the paradoxes inherent in America's approach to China: a blend of imperialistic assertiveness and idealistic restraint.

One area in which Denby was most conspicuously aggressive as United States minister was the promotion of American commercial interests in China. The State Department warned him against using his official influence, but he still exerted great personal effort both helping businessmen in China and publicizing the details and potential of the China trade back home. Although Denby resented helping those whom he considered merely "promoters," he believed that he had a duty "to endeavor to secure grants, franchises, and concessions" for "any and all schemes." Despite his aversion to "promoters," he insisted that more bona fide American "resident representatives," i.e., consuls and private agents of legitimate companies, were needed in China. The U.S. envoy knew that other nations were employing such commercial representatives to good advantage. During an inspection trip to Taiwan, Denby observed the success of British agents and consuls on the island and reported to the State Department: "It is impossible that the American abroad, should not desire to see his own flag floating in every port and on every sea."⁹

Although he aided any American capitalist, it was not surprising that Denby's principal commercial efforts involved railroads. Like

J. Ross Browne and George Seward, he predicted that an extensive railway system would destroy antiforeignism and hence open China to more foreign trade and manufacturing. Railroads would also "bind the distant parts of the Empire together," according to the minister, and thereby strengthen China politically. Denby was encouraged by the interest that Governor General Li Hung-chang and members of the imperial family showed in working models of American railroads, and he believed that progressive elements around the emperor would overcome the conservative mandarins' opposition to this marvelous gift of modern technology. Denby unofficially aided American James H. Wilson's bidding on the contract for a line between Tientsin and Taku in 1886. Wilson's scheme failed, as did that of another American railroad group that the minister also attempted to help. These setbacks disappointed but did not discourage Denby. To Secretary of State Bayard, who was himself eager to see railroad development in China, the minister wrote: "To the world at large it must be said that it little matters who builds the roads. The main thing is to open up China to foreign trade."[10]

Denby also sought to aid businessmen by warning Washington that continued exclusion of Chinese immigrants would adversely affect trade. He complained, as had George Seward, that exclusion created friction between the two countries that hurt American trading prospects and enabled other nations to benefit commercially at U.S. expense. Despite the Angell Treaty and 1882 exclusion law, open hostility toward Orientals had not ended in the American West, and the Cleveland administration wanted to satisfy that region's demands for more immigration restrictions. A month before the presidential election of 1888, President Cleveland yielded to the desire to woo West Coast voters and signed the hastily prepared Scott Act. This illiberal law denied readmission to any Chinese who left the United States— even those already abroad holding valid reentry permits or owning land in the United States. Clearly violating the Angell Treaty's guarantee of free exit and reentry, the legislation caused Denby to fear reprisals against American business interests in China. Moreover, Cleveland had antagonized the Chinese unnecessarily, because he lost all four western states and the election to Republican Benjamin Harrison.[11]

Denby's concern for the continuation of friendly and profitable Sino-

American relations increased, because the Harrison administration displayed no interest whatsoever in pursuing a diplomatic solution to the exclusion question. In contrast to Bayard, Secretary of State James G. Blaine declined even to answer protests about discrimination and treaty violations from the Chinese legation in Washington. In Peking, Denby attempted to reassure the Tsungli Yamen of America's goodwill toward the Middle Kingdom, but Washington persisted in viewing exclusion as a domestic political issue. In 1892, with the original ten-year ban on immigration about to expire and another presidential election imminent, Harrison signed the Geary Act, which extended exclusion for another ten years. The law also allowed trials without juries, arrests without warrants, and other extremely harsh measures affecting Chinese in America. George Seward condemned the Geary Act as shameful and part of "a continued chapter of wrong doings, of violations of Treaties, and of National perfidy."[12] Finally, after Cleveland's return to the White House, the United States and China concluded a new treaty in Washington that essentially sanctioned the Geary Act but granted the Chinese some face-saving concessions by reversing the Scott Act's restrictions on reentry. This 1894 convention eased the diplomatic tension enough to calm Minister Denby's apprehensions about the threat of exclusion to American commercial privileges in China.[13]

Amelioration of the exclusion friction could not have come at a more opportune time from Denby's perspective, because by the mid-1890s he believed that the expansion of United States trade with China was more important than ever. He shared the common assumption among American business leaders that overproduction, especially of manufactured goods, had caused the serious economic depression that hit the United States in 1893. According to this theory, American manufacturing output was daily exceeding home consumption, and the obvious solution was to find export outlets for the surplus. From Denby's vantage point in Peking, China's teeming population of four hundred million potential customers seemed to be a promising market for "our superabundance of manufactured goods." Although the minister labeled predictions of the China trade's reaching billions of dollars "roseate dreams," he forecast that future commerce would be astonishing. He noted, for example, the growing importance of American kerosene sales in China, which at forty million gallons in 1894 were almost four times higher than in 1888.[14]

Despite Denby's probusiness efforts and his estimates of the great potential of the China market, total U.S. exports to the Middle Kingdom had dropped after 1891, when Russell and Company closed its Canton office and left no American commercial house remaining to promote trade. Denby attempted to reverse this downward trend by taking advantage of the commercial bargaining opportunities that emerged from the Sino-Japanese War of 1894–1895. The American envoy saw an excellent chance for his country's capitalists to buy business franchises, because the humbled Chinese government needed money to pay the huge war indemnity demanded by victorious Japan. Not leaving anything to chance, Denby suggested to the State Department that the United States insist upon franchises as payment for helping to end the war through the exercise of its good offices. Cool to the idea, Secretary of State Walter Q. Gresham warned the minister in April 1895 to be more discreet about such suggestions. Committed to a laissez faire philosophy, the Cleveland administration was reluctant to sanction any overt role by its minister in the promotion of commercial enterprises. Richard Olney, who became secretary of state in June 1895 after Gresham's sudden death, repeated his predecessor's instruction to the envoy in Peking: "You should carefully abstain from using your diplomatic position to promote financial or business enterprises."[15] In spite of these reprimands from Gresham and Olney, Denby did not cease his efforts in behalf of American business.[16]

Finally, in December 1896, following the presidential election victory of probusiness Republican William McKinley over agrarian Democrat William Jennings Bryan, the lame-duck Olney yielded to Denby's repeated urgings and authorized him to assist officially American concerns in China. After cautioning Denby not to assume any responsibility for any American business, Olney wrote that "you should use your personal and official influence . . . to secure to reputable representatives of such concerns the same facilities . . . as are enjoyed by any other foreign commercial enterprise in the country." This instruction allowed Denby to exercise his own judgment in accordance with the following rule: "Broadly speaking, you shall employ all proper methods for the extension of American commercial interests in China, while refraining from advocating the projects of any one firm to the exclusion of others."[17] Although Denby had gained Washington's endorsement of his promotional activities, the more significant fact was the length of time that the State Department resisted. For years Denby had assisted American enterprises, and Olney was simply acknowledging what the minister had been doing on his own all along. While the secretary of state's formal sanction was important, it did not change Denby's de facto policies, nor did it necessarily reveal a carefully conceived decision by Washington. In the same instruction that granted Denby permission to aid American firms, Olney actually admitted his own ignorance of what specific projects the minister intended to support and requested more information.[18]

Numerous Americans had plans for "constructing railroads, establishing banks, and developing mines," Denby explained to Olney, but the most persistent firm was the American China Development Company, which was currently seeking a contract with the imperial government to build a railway from Peking to Hankow. Declaring that "my duty [is] to see that the rights of my compatriots should be protected as well in the matter of contracts as in other matters," the minister took up the company's case with the Tsungli Yamen. His intervention resulted in the foreign office's ordering the mandarin responsible for railroads to make a preliminary agreement with the Americans. Despite this apparent diplomatic success for Denby's new authority to promote American business, the American China Development Company never built the line. In May 1897, Peking awarded the actual contract to a European syndicate composed primarily of French financiers. Two factors led to this setback for Denby and the American company: the new Republican secretary of state, John Sherman, dogmatically opposed official "endorsement" of the enterprise, and China's final contract terms were unacceptable to the American investors. In April 1898, the American China Development Company finally secured imperial permission to construct a Hankow-to-Canton railway; but when Denby left China in July 1898, Americans had not laid a single mile of track there and held only 300 out of the 7,800 miles of railroad right-of-way gained by all nations.[19]

Looking back over his years in the Middle Kingdom, Denby realized that his efforts in behalf of American business had not achieved what he had hoped to accomplish. When he arrived in Peking in 1885, United

States exports to China and the British colony of Hong Kong, which reexported many goods to China, totaled about $10.5 million for the year. In 1898, American exports to China and Hong Kong reached almost $16.3 million. While this growth was notable and had occurred primarily since 1895, the 1898 figure represented less than 2 percent of all U.S. exports and was $5 million less than U.S. purchases from the same places. Thus far, the fabled China market was limited and, in fact, was not even paying for itself.[20]

Denby saw the rich and protected home market in the United States as one reason for the reluctance of private enterprise to cultivate new foreign trade and investment possibilities. During the American China Development Company's negotiations, he almost despaired at the unwillingness of the entrepreneurs to risk short-run profitability in order to gain a foothold in what he believed would eventually be a valuable market. The minister also blamed his government superiors in Washington for insufficiently backing his efforts. Denby thought that the State Department's adherence to a policy of noninterference placed American business at a disadvantage. He argued that unless the United States government would accept some official responsibility for the nation's commerce in East Asia, Americans could not reap the benefits available there. The State Department stubbornly held, however, to a position of limited or negligible involvement in affairs outside the Western Hemisphere. On commercial issues, Washington's official policy in China before 1898 was generally neither cooperation nor competition with other nations, but rather independent inaction.[21]

In addition to American commercial interests, Denby energetically supported missionary activities, primarily because he viewed the missionaries as pious "pioneers of trade and commerce." Believing that the spiritual benefits of Christianity were obvious and that as a government official he could not express religious opinions, he refrained from comment on the missionaries' religious endeavors. On humanitarian grounds, he argued that missionary schools and hospitals "constituted some compensation to China for the wrongs the foreign association has entailed."[22] With unrestrained cultural arrogance, Denby informed Washington that "the educated Chinaman, who speaks English, becomes a new man; he commences to think."[23] It was the link between Christianity and commerce, however, that most fascinated

Denby, and it was a theme to which he often referred. In a classic American convergence of ideals and interests, he proclaimed that the missionary "is the forerunner of commerce. . . . The drummer follows behind, and foreign commerce begins. From the missionary dwelling there radiates the light of modern civilization."[24] To Denby, civilization meant specifically "commerce, trade, a market for manufactured articles." For this reason, he lectured Secretary of State Gresham: "In the interest, therefore, of civilization, missionaries ought not only to be tolerated, but ought to receive protection."[25]

Missionaries, especially as targets of antiforeign riots, presented the United States legation with constant problems during Denby's term in China. Serious assaults, which included numerous fatalities and extensive destruction of mission properties, occurred throughout the empire. "Poor Burlingame's 'cross' shines on the hills of China, only when the population burn it!" lamented Robert Hart in 1891.[26] His reference was to Anson Burlingame's assertion in 1868 that the Chinese were ready for Christian missionaries "to plant the shining cross on every hill and in every valley."[27] Burlingame had exaggerated, of course, and the bloody Tientsin massacre of 1870 had graphically illustrated the opposition that foreign missionaries could encounter in China. Still, propelled by a growing evangelical movement in England and America and protected by the Western treaty system, Protestant missionaries in the Middle Kingdom grew in number from 81 in 1858 to a total of 1,296 by 1889. During the 1890s the number climbed rapidly upward, to 2,818 by 1900, and although the majority were British, almost half were American. In addition, there were 759 European priests serving as Roman Catholic missionaries throughout the country in 1896–1897. This growth increased the opportunities for incidents, especially since many of the new missionary stations were in the interior, where they made easier targets than merchant establishments in the treaty ports. The number of Protestant and Catholic converts was also growing and may have reached 850,000 by 1900, but the threat to Confucian orthodoxy remained relatively small. Expansion of the foreign proselytizing effort did not explain by itself the hostility that often greeted the disseminators of the Gospel; the issues extended beyond religion.[28]

"It is not because of his religion," Denby pointed out, "that the missionary is attacked by mobs, it is because of his race. It is the foreigner, and not the Christian, against whom the mobs are gathered."[29] Antimissionary riots were symptomatic of the growing Chinese frustration both with increasing foreign pressure and with the internal weakness of the Ch'ing Dynasty. Denby contended that the riots were not spontaneous but were planned and organized with the full knowledge of local officials, who resented missionary interference in local affairs and who also lost patience with the Peking government's inability to control foreign activity. After several years in China, the American minister realized that the antagonism toward Christian missionaries was part of "a widespread belief in China that international intercourse is injurious to her interests."[30] Inherently hostile toward all foreigners, many in the gentry class viewed missionaries supported by foreign governments as another manifestation of Western imperialism.[31]

Although he maintained a positive attitude toward missionaries, Denby feared their "intemperate zeal." He was concerned that their determined but unauthorized efforts to reside in the interior endangered not only the missionaries themselves but also the goodwill necessary for commercial relations. Denby warned them that extraterritoriality was inoperative away from the treaty ports and consular courts. Yet he argued their claims before the Tsungli Yamen even when he thought they were wrong, in order not to betray any hint of American weakness. For example, Denby pressed a case, which he personally considered to be "imprudent," for the American Presbyterian missionaries at Tsinan. In 1887 they tried to occupy some property using a deed that the Chinese considered invalid. Finally, after four years of effort, Denby arranged a compromise settlement with the authorities and confided to Washington his fervent hope that the Tsinan missionaries "will not get into any more trouble."[32]

When riots imperiled foreign lives and property, Denby advocated the use of force and joint action by the treaty powers. In such cases he contended that "an appeal to the 'gunboat' policy may be justified. A city in which a serious antiforeign riot occurs may be battered down."[33] Denby argued that united action was necessary to prevent the Tsungli Yamen from exploiting the rivalry among the European powers. The State Department disagreed. In 1886 Secretary Bayard instructed Denby to avoid joint action. The department held that the United States shared a common problem but not a common responsibility with the other powers. The United States would cooperate with the other nations if Americans were involved in an incident, but would not cooperate if its citizens were not personally affected.[34]

In the spring of 1891, widespread uprisings broke out in several places along the Yangtze River. The causes of these riots were complex. Various secret societies, some intent upon toppling the ruling dynasty and others seeking to defend it, spread anti-Christian propaganda to incite the masses. These instigators distributed pamphlets that were intended to manipulate the people's superstitious fears by depicting the Western missionaries as evil and dangerous. Rumors frequently circulated, as they had at Tientsin in 1870, that foreigners boiled Chinese corpses to make soap or plucked out the eyes of little children to concoct medicines. Although British and French mission buildings were the primary targets of the resulting violence, there were also some European deaths and injuries. In May a mob burned and looted the American Methodist Girls' School at Nanking, but there was no loss of life. Bayard's previous instructions notwithstanding, Denby did not hesitate to join with the European ministers in protests to the Tsungli Yamen even before Americans became involved. Following the attack on the American school, he telegraphed the navy to request that the USS *Monocacy* be sent to Nanking and expressed hope that the gunboat would "arrive in time to overawe the populace."[35]

Missionaries throughout the Yangtze region evacuated to Shanghai, and tension remained high throughout the summer of 1891. On several additional occasions, Denby joined with the other ministers in making representations to the Chinese government. Meanwhile, in numerous dispatches to the State Department, he argued that collective action and force be used to put down the riots. "I should not regard it as unfortunate," he informed Washington, "if a gunboat were to open with cannister on a mob caught in the act of destruction."[36] Secretary of State Blaine replied emphatically: "This Government does not wish to make war on China. Take no further joint action with other powers until further advised."[37] Denby dutifully obeyed this instruction, but after the riots subsided that winter, he credited the return of peace to the presence of warships and the unity of the foreign representatives.[38]

Following the Sino-Japanese War, a number of antiforeign uprisings again broke out. Most of these incidents occurred in Szechwan and Fukien provinces during the summer of 1895, and as in the riots four

The USS *Monocacy*, the gunboat that Denby requested during the antiforeign riots of 1891, had also been part of Frederick Low's mission to Korea in 1871. *Naval Historical Center.*

years earlier, there were several causes. In addition to agitation by secret societies and the old rumors about kidnapping children for diabolical purposes, a new notion circulated that all foreigners must be driven out because the British, French, and Americans had not helped China against Japan. In these disturbances not only was there extensive property damage, but several British missionaries died, and one injured American woman barely escaped death. Although United States citizens were fortunate that their losses were not heavier, Denby was outraged that "peaceable foreigners are periodically burnt out of house and home and subjected to untold suffering." Placing the blame on xenophobic local officials and an ineffective central government in Peking, he predicted that unless the Western nations did "something open, bold, and aggressive," these atrocities would continue until "the treaties and Imperial proclamations are waste paper."[39] Similar appeals from missionary boards and societies in the United States buttressed the minister's strong demands for action. As he had done in response to earlier incidents, Denby specifically advocated the use of force and joint action. He pointed out that restraint in 1891 had not prevented the problem from recurring, and he again recommended that after a riot the town should be "battered down by the ships of the injured nationalities."[40]

Secretary of State Olney disapproved the use of force—either alone or in conjunction with other nations—but he did share Denby's concern for finding ways of preventing future riots.[41] American officials in Washington agreed with the minister that local and provincial Chinese authorities could protect foreigners but refused to do so. Both Denby and the State Department considered these mandarins as guilty of murder and destruction as the mobs that actually committed the assaults. "The first head demanded by a foreign power after a riot," Denby concluded, "should be, not that of an obscure rioter, but of the highest official in the locality."[42] After the Szechwan riots, the State Department sustained Denby's view: "If the connivance of high Chinese officials in this antiforeign demonstration be reasonably shown, stern reprobation and punishment must be expected, with due reparation and safeguards for the future."[43] Despite such demands, the Chinese government was reluctant to punish officials, especially those of high rank, since it feared the undermining of imperial authority.

Because of the 1895 uprisings, foreign residents of the treaty ports repeatedly pressed their governments for thorough investigations and stern action against any Chinese, regardless of rank, who was involved. In July 1895, American missionaries in Shanghai petitioned Denby for an independent American inquiry. Since the Chinese mob made no distinction between nationalities, Denby argued that instead of each nation acting separately, a joint Western commission should be established. He suggested to Washington that the United States initiate this international investigation. If a multinational commission was impossible because of European rivalry, Denby recommended a joint American-British investigation. When some American missionaries mistakenly charged that the minister had failed to heed their concerns, Denby reminded Washington of his suggestion that the United States assume the lead in a riot probe, and he reiterated: "I still think that an international commission . . . is desirable."[44]

The British minister in Peking, Sir Nicholas O'Conor, reported privately to London that Denby's zeal in pursuing this investigation was because "he avows frankly that he owes his last appointment [i.e., reappointment] to the missionary interest . . . and is bound to play up to them as much as possible."[45] Supported by the presence of British naval vessels at Wuchang, O'Conor threatened the Tsungli Yamen with forceful action by the British admiral if the mandarins implicated in the riots were not punished. Denby and French minister Auguste Gérard made separate demands for punishments, and in the fall of 1895, Peking ordered the ex-governor general of Szechwan and six other officials degraded. The imperial authorities executed thirty-one of the actual rioters in Szechwan and Fukien and banished or imprisoned another thirty-nine. Although the British naval threat undoubtedly prompted these penalties, Gérard sought to take credit for the settlement while simultaneously charging that O'Conor had interfered with Chinese sovereignty. Denby, too, was not reluctant to claim credit for "having broken through Chinese obstinancy" and for winning a diplomatic victory in this case.[46]

Aside from demanding the punishment of officials, the State Department disagreed with Denby on the best method of preventing future riots. Washington vetoed his suggestion for an international commission and gave only qualified endorsement to cooperation with the British in the Fukien case. In reference to the Fukien riots, Acting Secretary Alvey A. Adee telegraphed the minister in August 1895 that he could "consult" and "cooperate" with the British envoy to protect the welfare of United States citizens, but "otherwise you will act independently and carefully, abstain from joining any course or policy which . . . does not concern those of the United States."[47] After Secretary of State Olney resumed charge of the department in September, his instruction to Denby was even more peremptory: "Proposition to arrange Szechuan investigation with British consul Chungking not entertained. Press independent commission."[48]

Olney clearly desired to avoid any overt association with Britain in China. On July 20 he had sent a diplomatic note to London that President Cleveland called the "twenty inch gun." This diplomatic salvo bluntly declared that the United States was "practically sovereign" in the Western Hemisphere and in effect demanded that Britain agree to arbitration in its dispute with Venezuela over the boundary of British Guiana. In political trouble because of the floundering economy, Cleveland was also on the defensive against Republican charges of foreign-policy weakness for his failure both to annex Hawaii and to oppose the recent landing of British marines in Nicaragua. Among the several reasons, then, why the administration had sent the stern note on Venezuela were the domestic political benefits of appearing to have an effective foreign policy and simultaneously twisting the tail of the bullying British lion. Reflecting similar political motives, Olney explained to Denby that the State Department opposed joining with Britain in the Szechwan investigation because of the need for "an impressive demonstration." It was important, according to the secretary of state, to convince the Chinese that the United States could act alone as "an effective factor in securing due rights for American residents in China."[49] Like Olney's Venezuelan note, his language sounded bold, but in reality the secretary was striving primarily to establish an image as much for domestic as for foreign consumption. The "crucial test," he instructed his activist minister in Peking, was whether "the attitude"—he did not say "ability"—of the United States to protect its citizens "be conspicuously manifested." If so, he continued, then "the necessity for such procedure on our part will, in all probability not recur."[50] On the issue of antiforeign riots, as on commercial questions, the State Department usually overruled Denby's preference for gunboats and joint action, and it doggedly maintained the United States' limited and independent policy position in China. More concerned about partisan politics and events elsewhere in the world, Washington was not as eager as its envoy in Peking to plunge the United States into international crosscurrents in East Asia.

Unable to agree on how to promote business or protect missionaries, Denby and the State Department also differed on America's appropriate response to war in Asia and the threatened dismemberment of China. For Denby, the war between China and Japan in 1894–1895 and the ensuing foreign scramble for economic and territorial concessions from the impotent Chinese government meant that the United States had to assume a more active defense of its interests in the Middle Kingdom. In Washington, however, the war and the resulting increase in international rivalry did not loom as large or as ominous. While Denby watched his colleagues in other legations demand and receive control of harbors, leases of railroad rights-of-way, and other concessions from the emperor's government, his cries of alarm about the

future of American economic opportunity seemed to go virtually un-
heeded by Washington.

Forty years before the Sino-Japanese War, American commodore
Matthew Perry made the first Western treaty with Japan. China's
island neighbor then faced the challenge of finding an effective way to
defend its interests and traditions against powerful, persistent intrud-
ers. Unlike the Middle Kingdom, Japan overcame the initial instinct to
resist Western ideas; following governmental reorganization in 1868, it
adopted a variety of Occidental political, economic, and military concepts to strengthen and enrich the nation. The success of these reforms became strikingly apparent when Japan so easily defeated its
much larger adversary in the 1894–1895 war. The causes and results of
the conflict revealed that, from its Western role models, Japan had
learned well the lessons of imperialism.[51]

Korea was the specific source of friction that generated the Sino-
Japanese hostilities. Lying between China and Japan, the peninsula
was like a dagger pointing at the heart of both countries. In the 1880s
and early 1890s, Peking still maintained its traditional claim of suzerainty over the Hermit Kingdom, but between 1876 and 1886, the government in Seoul made treaties with Japan, the United States, and
several European nations that presupposed an unencumbered Korean
sovereignty. Assuming Korea to be an independent nation, Japan pursued its own strategic and economic interests there and became increasingly involved in the internal affairs of the peninsula. To counter
this Japanese activism, Peking stationed a "resident" (or commissioner) in Korea in 1885 to oversee China's interests and to supervise
the Korean government. The stage was set for an eventual confrontation, and it came in June 1894, when both China and Japan dispatched
troops to the peninsula for the protection of their respective subjects
during a rebellion. The uprising ended quickly, but Tokyo was determined to terminate China's self-proclaimed control over Korea and
therefore would not withdraw its troops until Peking recognized Korean independence. The Chinese refused, tension increased, and war
appeared imminent.[52]

Aware that war would stimulate European ambitions and rivalries
and also endanger U.S. citizens and their activities, American representatives in Asia had sought for years to resolve peacefully the con-
tinual disputes between China and Japan. In this current crisis, the

Chinese government was agreeable to a simultaneous withdrawal of troops from Korea, but the U.S. ministers in Seoul and Tokyo reported to Washington that Japan was determined to keep its forces in the peninsula until its demands were met. Britain, France, and Russia were inclined to take up China's cause, since a Japanese success would threaten their interests in Korea, and also because a desperate China might be induced to grant them concessions in return for help. In July 1894, the British government asked Washington if the United States would join an effort to mediate the conflict. Also in July, Charles Denby, Jr., who was chargé d'affaires in Peking while his father was home for a kidney-stone operation, informed the State Department of a Chinese request for help from the Western nations in arranging a Japanese withdrawal. Although willing to extend its good offices in order to avert a war, the United States government desired to observe a strict neutrality. Hoping to steer clear of European political conflicts, the Cleveland administration adamantly maintained "that in no event could we intervene jointly with other powers."⁵³ Initially, then, Secretary of State Gresham made only a "strong but friendly representation" to Japan for restraint, while emphasizing that the United States acted solely as a "friendly neutral."⁵⁴

Following Japan's sinking of a Chinese troopship carrying reinforcements to Korea, both nations declared war on August 1, 1894. Inflicting heavy casualties on the Chinese, Japan quickly displayed its military and naval superiority. In August and September, Japanese forces smashed the enemy in Korea and the surrounding seas. Although press and governmental opinion in Europe and the United States tended to view the Westernized Japanese as the agents of progress in this war, Japan's overwhelming domination of the battlefront raised grave concerns. In October 1894, the British and Chinese governments both circulated inquiries about the possibility of a British, French, German, Russian, and American intervention to end the war quickly. These two proposals contained similar suggestions that China would agree to recognize Korean independence and pay an indemnity in return for a restoration of peace. China's motive understandably was to end hostilities before incurring more devastating losses in lives, territory, and prestige. London hoped that its Occidental rivals would agree to help halt the Japanese advance before the island empire appropriated Manchuria and other valuable Chinese real estate coveted by Western interests. In an article in the *Journal of Commerce* in November 1894, George Seward endorsed American participation in the European mediation effort. In replying to the Chinese and British proposals for a mediated settlement, Secretary of State Gresham made clear that the United States would take no steps inconsistent with strict neutrality and could not agree to joint action with the European powers. To explain the administration's decision, the cautious Gresham cited a basic maxim of American foreign policy: "With a few exceptions the record of our diplomatic history shows no departure from the wise policy of avoiding foreign alliances and embarrassing participation in guaranteeing the independence of distant states."[55] Affirming that President Cleveland desired a speedy peace, however, Gresham indicated that the United States would willingly act alone as a mediator.[56]

Having recuperated from his surgery, Colonel Denby returned to Peking in late October 1894, just in time to advance the American mediation effort. The minister also disliked joint mediation, but for a reason different from Washington's. Suspicious of the other countries' professed desires to preserve the Chinese empire, Denby feared that they might use intervention as an excuse for gaining selfish advantages. The United States had to act alone to end the war, in his opinion, in order to protect both Chinese and American interests. Although Gresham conceived of independent action as a way to limit U.S. involvement in the international complexities of the war and to serve the noble cause of peace, the always zealous Denby perceived an opportunity to expand American influence in East Asia and gain some personal acclaim in the process. Denby had served almost ten years as U.S. envoy, and his seniority made him dean of the diplomatic corps in Peking—a role he seemed to relish. As the peacemaking process began in November, the minister wrote an old friend in Indiana:

> My friends of the Yamen are grown up children, absolutely ignorant of international law, and they look to me as their teacher and guide. They follow all my counsels, copy my papers, and send them, always interlarding them with compliments and thanks to the U S and to me personally.[57]

Because of his vanity and his prejudices, Denby failed to notice that the mandarins' flattery was a traditional method for the management of barbarians. Chinese officials considered the American "pompous, austere, and unbending," but recognized that in their present crisis he could be useful.[58]

Despite the high hopes of Denby and the Chinese that somehow the United States could slow the Japanese steamroller, Tokyo's forces captured Port Arthur and Talien (Dairen) in November. At the same time, Japan rejected the idea of a mediated settlement and demanded instead that China sue for peace. Having no real alternative, Peking agreed to negotiate directly. With Denby and U.S. minister Edwin Dun in Tokyo acting as messengers, not mediators, the belligerents began preliminary steps toward a peace settlement. Throughout the winter of 1894–1895, the Chinese delayed and maneuvered diplomatically in hopes of gaining a better result. Much to the chagrin of Gresham, who clung to American impartiality in the proceedings, Denby offered the Chinese substantive suggestions on negotiating tactics and peace terms. With the Japanese forces continuing their forward advance into China, time ultimately ran out for Peking. In February 1895 Weihaiwei fell, and Japan's army was threatening Tientsin and Peking. In March the old viceroy and diplomat Li Hung-chang sat down in the Japanese port city of Shimonoseki with Prime Minister Ito Hirobumi of Japan, and on April 17 they signed the treaty that concluded the war. Neither Denby nor any other third party stood between the negotiators, and Ito exacted harsh terms. The Treaty of Shimonoseki provided for Korean independence; Japanese possession of Liaotung Peninsula, with the strategically and economically valuable harbors at Port Arthur and Talien; the transfer of Taiwan and the Pescadores to Japan; a $150 million indemnity for the victor; and new foreign manufacturing concessions in the treaty ports.[59]

"The Japanese war was the beginning of the end for China," Denby later recalled, because "nations of the world had learned the lesson that she could not fight, and were prepared on the slightest pretence to seize her territory."[60] The minister's initial apprehensions about European cupidity were quickly confirmed a few days after the signing of the Treaty of Shimonoseki. Moving to protect their own proprietary interests, Russia, France, and Germany pressured Japan into returning Liaotung Peninsula to China.[61] Gresham had warned Japan from the beginning of the crisis to exercise restraint, but the Cleveland administration had basically adhered to the conservative American diplomatic tradition of nonintervention and had refused to assume any responsibility for the events in Asia. Washington's approach reflected the reality that the United States could not determine the outcome of the conflict, as Denby found when he attempted to mediate. Still, the Sino-Japanese War of 1894–1895 proved to be a turning point in East Asian history. Domestic pressure mounted for reform of the Ch'ing Dynasty; Japan actively entered the imperialistic competition in the area; and the European powers descended upon the impotent Middle Kingdom in a quest for new privileges. Denby's fears for American interests appeared justified.

During 1895–1897, Westerners, including Americans, skirmished over who would secure the profits of loans, railroad contracts, and other concessions from the Peking government, which was financially over-burdened by the costs of the war and indemnity. Finally, in November 1897, a scramble among Europeans for separate economic spheres of influence began in earnest. It started when Chinese robbers killed two German missionaries in southern Shantung. German troops im-mediately occupied Kiaochow Bay, a harbor Germany had long coveted for economic and strategic reasons. Hoping for Russian assistance, the Chinese at first refused to negotiate. No third-party intervention was forthcoming, and in March 1898 Germany secured a ninety-nine-year lease to the entrance of Kiaochow Bay. Using similar pretexts, other European powers quickly followed Germany's example. In less than three weeks, Russia grabbed the tip of Liaotung Peninsula, including Port Arthur and Talien. In April France took Kwangchow Bay, and Britain leased Weihaiwei and extended its Kowloon lease to include the entire peninsula. China's existence as a nation was threatened, and Denby reported to Washington: "The foreign powers in their contest with each other are merely making China a battlefield."[62]

This "spectacle of foreign rapacity and unscrupulousness" horrified Denby. Not expecting Peking to regain control over the territory within the foreign spheres of influence, he hoped only that the status quo could be preserved and that the total dismemberment of China could be prevented. If actual partition resulted, Denby warned, not only China but the powers themselves would suffer. He believed that China could advance on its own like Japan, if only given the opportu-nity. Rather than robbing the Middle Kingdom of its territory, the powers should have been helping Peking to strengthen the central government. A stable China, Denby contended, would prosper and grow rich as both a consumer and exporter.[63]

Specifically, Denby feared that partition would destroy the China market for Americans. Deeply involved in his own efforts on behalf of such firms as the American China Development Company, the minister warned that the division of China into "hostile camps" would mean "the suicide of commerce." Although he was "very thoroughly aware that since [George] Washington's Farewell Address was uttered" the United States had refrained from "interfering in the affairs of foreign powers," Denby expressed alarm in January 1898 that this self-denial weakened American influence and made the United States a "quantite negleable." His French ability may have been *negligeable*, but Denby's concerns were *abondant*. He respected the "sanctity of the Farewell Address," but asked the State Department "whether there is some middle ground on which we may stand with advantage. Our interests in China are considerable. . . . Partition will destroy the markets."[64] Denby did not elaborate on what this "middle ground" should be, but in a later dispatch he emphasized the importance of "the autonomy of China" as part of America's "access" to the China trade. In reply, Secretary of State John Sherman made no reference to Denby's comments on the Farewell Address. The secretary complacently reported only that Germany had assured the U.S. ambassador in Berlin that foreign trade was in no danger. Although many American business spokesmen were echoing Denby's anxiety, Sherman doubted that a European partitioning of China was likely. Even if it occurred, he informed a *Philadelphia Press* interviewer, it might help rather than hurt American commerce.[65]

In July 1898, the frustrated Denby left Peking to make way for Edwin H. Conger, the new Republican choice for the post that the Indiana Democrat had held for so long. The selection of the diplomatically experienced Conger pleased American businessmen, but in the summer of 1898 the State Department gave no indication that, in order to protect commerce, it was prepared to abandon the time-honored policy of avoiding foreign entanglements. On the other hand, when Denby relinquished his diplomatic position, the United States was engaged in a war with Spain that was already transforming American foreign policy. Although it began over a complex of humanitarian, commercial, and strategic issues involving Cuba, the Spanish-American War quickly encompassed America's Pacific pathway to Asia. In May 1898, Commodore George Dewey's Asiatic Squadron demolished the Spanish fleet at Manila Bay, and in July the United States annexed the Hawaiian Islands to safeguard the route to the Philippines. These dramatic developments offered the United States for the first time the possibility of an Asian outpost—an American Hong Kong—from which to exercise a unilateral defense of its interests. Denby thrilled to the news: "When Dewey's guns boomed over Manila Bay . . . we held our heads high at Peking, and hailed the echoes of American artillery as the signals of a new career, and a power hitherto undreamt of."[66] With Denby on his way out, others would translate these events into a policy for China. President McKinley recalled the experienced Denby to government service twice, as a member of federal commissions to investigate the conduct of the Spanish-American War and the issue of Philippine annexation. At age seventy-three, the Hoosier lawyer and diplomat was still lecturing and writing on public affairs when he died in 1904.[67]

In 1898, after thirteen years of debate between Charles Denby and his superiors in Washington, the ultimate direction of American policy in China remained undetermined. The minister advocated a vigorous policy of defense and promotion of American interests through cooperation among the treaty powers. During antiforeign riots, he signed joint warnings to the Tsungli Yamen and recommended United States participation in collective naval actions. On commercial questions, Denby eagerly joined with the other ministers in lobbying for contracts. Despite the competition among firms of various nationalities, he believed that economic cooperation was the long-range key to success. Working together, he maintained, the foreign powers could strengthen China's economy for the benefit of everyone, including the Chinese themselves. To Denby, the concession scramble following the Sino-Japanese War was a disaster that threatened not only future American commerce but also the prospects for all international trade in East Asia. He regretted to see violence replace persuasion, partition replace autonomy, and strife develop among the powers as they forced concessions from a helpless nation. Lamenting that "it was every man for himself," he urgently sought strong American action to prevent these calamities.[68]

The State Department frequently responded to the minister's activities and suggestions with indifference or disapproval. American trade in China, although growing, remained a small fraction of the overall domestic and foreign commerce of the United States. The future possibilities of a vast China market were appealing; but for the present, politicians at home preferred to proceed cautiously. Chinese antiforeignism and international rivalries in China both had been acute problems since the early 1880s, but Washington continued to pursue the limited and independent policies initiated by Angell and Young. The department did not share Denby's enthusiasm for arbitrary solutions to riots and for cooperative endeavors with the European powers. Often inexperienced in diplomacy and preoccupied with domestic politics, seven different secretaries of state reminded Denby of the United States tradition of independence in foreign affairs and avoidance of international commitments.[69]

Like his predecessors at the United States legation in Peking, Denby frequently determined the initial or short-term American position on an issue without, or in spite of, specific instructions from Washington. Afterward, the State Department would often modify his actions or reject his recommendations, and these disagreements perpetuated the ambiguities in the nation's China policy. Since on many occasions the desires of the State Department and the conduct of the minister diverged, there were, in effect, two China policies. In numerous instances between 1861 and 1898, the differing perspectives of the officials in Washington and the ministers in Peking led to conflicting assessments of the appropriate course for the United States. William H. Seward and Anson Burlingame agreed on cooperation but defined the concept in very different terms. Secretary of State Seward and his successor Hamilton Fish both opposed J. Ross Browne's preference for "menacing" the Chinese. On the other hand, Fish chided Frederick Low for not being more assertive with the imperial government. William M. Evarts and George Seward disagreed on the wisdom and methods of limiting Chinese immigration. Although the State Department most often left envoys to China on their own, Washington at times pushed and at other times restrained the ministers. Whatever the case, these periodic disagreements among American policymakers added to the internal inconsistencies in official United States efforts in China.

The great irony of Denby's stay in Peking was his claim in his memoirs that he and the envoys of other nations followed "the cooperative policy, which had been adopted in the time of Bruce and Burlingame."[70] He recounted how he and his fellow ministers would meet together, determine their course of action, and then present their joint position to the Tsungli Yamen through the dean of the diplomatic corps. This simple system, he concluded, "secured unanimity and the great influence of united action. . . . It was the world against China."[71] The methods of Denby and his colleagues had little in common with the "fair diplomatic action" of Burlingame and Frederick Bruce. The cooperative policy of the 1860s was not aimed at menacing the Chinese, and, in fact, it had precisely the opposite intent. Burlingame sought to avoid coercion and the "battering down" of Chinese villages by foreign gunboats. Denby and Burlingame differed sharply over who should participate in cooperation. For Burlingame, cooperation included the Chinese, but for Denby it did not.

Denby's views came closer to Browne's "determined moral pressure" than to Burlingame's cooperative concept. Although neither Browne nor Denby was quick on the gunboat trigger, both believed that force had its place in dealing with China. They each prescribed railroads and other Western innovations as panaceas for Chinese backwardness. Most important, the two ministers did not view the treaty system as a series of international conventions mutually regulating the relations of sovereign nations; instead, the treaties were the keys to unlock China to the West. Hence both men saw cooperation as the means for the Western nations to enforce foreign treaty privileges regardless of the desires of the Chinese. Denby drew the line when partitioning appeared imminent, but his concern then was more that America would be forced out than that China would not survive. Denby took a page from George Seward's book and made altruism another name for expediency.

The original disagreement between Browne and Burlingame was still present in American policy considerations in 1898. Denby advocated force, but Washington favored forbearance. In the 1890s, as in the 1860s, however, the choice was not that clear-cut. The alternatives were not simply an active or a passive policy.[72] For the United States to do nothing would leave the fate of American interests in the hands of other governments. To do something meant an American commitment, however small, to either China or the treaty nations—a commitment that the limited activity of the United States in China could scarcely justify. European and Japanese ambitions threatened future American access to the Middle Kingdom; the Ch'ing Dynasty's political infirmity imperiled China's sovereignty; and the United States' naval demonstration at Manila Bay emboldened America's conceptions of its own power and influence in Asia. Should the United States follow the European example and seek its own sphere of influence or, at least, make some accommodation with the European spheres irrespective of Chinese rights? Should the United States chart a separate course that equated American interests with the maintenance of China's sovereign control over its own territory? The latter choice was compatible with the American ideals of self-determination, nonintervention, and mutual respect among nations that Burlingame had advanced. The other alternative of aligning with European imperialism had often served the United States well and reflected the common belief among Westerners, as Browne had exemplified, that China was incapable of developing its own resources and potential. Eight American ministers plenipotentiary in Peking, beginning with Burlingame and Browne, had grappled with these same choices between idealism and imperialism. The American dilemma in China remained unresolved in 1898, but the time for decision was near.

CHAPTER EIGHT

Epilogue:

THE DILEMMA BECOMES THE POLICY IN JOHN HAY'S OPEN DOOR NOTES

ON JULY 3, 1900, Secretary of State John Hay formally announced to the world that the United States sought to "preserve Chinese territorial and administrative entity" and to "safeguard . . . the principle of equal and impartial trade with all parts of the Chinese Empire."[1] Hay's inspiring declaration of magnanimous goals, made fittingly on the eve of Independence Day, was contained in the second of his two Open Door Notes of 1899 and 1900. Confronted by both international and domestic pressures for some American response to the threatened dismemberment of the Middle Kingdom, Hay decided to send these famous notes to the European powers and Japan in a diplomatic effort to forestall partitioning. In determining what course to take, the secretary of state wrestled with the persistent quandary that had plagued American policy since 1861: how to assert and protect American rights without assuming a burdensome and exclusive commitment either to China or to the other treaty nations. Hay's notes were an attempt to bridge the gap between these alternatives; they assumed that the preservation of China's sovereignty and the continuation of foreign commercial access to China were complementary. Hay's initiatives blended masterfully the ideals and self-interests of the United States and eventually became part of the nation's foreign-policy canon. The

Open Door Notes articulated a policy that was as American as the Fourth of July and that brought into one concise focus the competing strains in the preceding forty years of U.S. diplomacy in China.

Before becoming secretary of state in September 1898, John Hay was United States ambassador to Great Britain. While the increasingly complicated situation in China was not the reason that President William McKinley selected Ambassador Hay to head the Department of State, the appointment reflected the president's acute awareness of the importance of foreign affairs in the wake of the Spanish-American War. McKinley chose Hay on the basis of his "world travel, urbanity, intelligence, and diplomatic experience."[2] Although Hay was not an expert on East Asia, the new secretary brought to his post some knowledge of current issues in the Orient, gained through correspondence and conversations with informed observers.[3]

After his transfer to Washington, Hay of course received numerous reports and recommendations from America's representative in Peking. Continuing Charles Denby's warnings of the dangers to American interests, Edwin H. Conger responded even more emphatically to the concession scramble than had his predecessor. The new minister advised the new secretary of state that "the integrity of China can easily be preserved by an alliance of a few of the great powers." Apparently oblivious to his own disregard for China's integrity, Conger also recommended in the same dispatch that "we ought to be ready, either by negotiation or actual possession, to own and control at least one good port from which we can potently assert our rights and effectively wield our influence."[4] While opposing "permanent ownership of territory," he argued that "a strong foothold here by the United States . . . might compel them [the European powers] to keep permanently open doors for our commerce."[5]

Conger also sent Hay detailed accounts of the activities and opinions of Lord Charles Beresford, who toured China during the winter of 1898–1899 as a representative of the Associated Chambers of Commerce of Great Britain. A former admiral and member of Parliament, Beresford knew Hay from London, and the secretary of state hosted a luncheon for him when he visited Washington in February 1899. Beresford pointed the finger of guilt at Russia as the primary threat to the status quo in China and recommended that the United States join with

Britain, Germany, and Japan to protect their interests "by assuring to China a stable Government, free from constant harassment of movement from without for territorial acquisition."[6] Without the abolition of spheres of influence, Beresford predicted, trade would be interrupted and relations among the powers would become strained. If Chinese territorial integrity could be maintained and trade opened to everyone, he contended, the whole world would benefit.[7]

In addition to Beresford and Conger, many American businessmen systematically lobbied the State Department for protection of the China trade. In June 1898, representatives of several firms with financial interests in China created the American Asiatic Association. This pressure group had several branch offices, a permanent staff, and its own journal, and it was in full operation by the time Hay assumed his new post. Admitting frankly their concerns about their own interests in the China market, these business spokesmen presented a strong case to the secretary of state. The business lobbyists made effective use of a large amount of data to support their arguments. Although the existing United States trade with China was small, they contended that the potential market was "simply incalculable." The annual report of the harbor master at Hong Kong for 1898, released only a month before Hay sent his first Open Door Note, typified the statistics being cited. The *New York Times* announced on page one that this report

> shows an increase in American shipping in 1898 over 1897 which has all taken place since August, or within a period of four months. The increase for 1899 will be fully double that of 1898 because of the large number of ships plying between Manila and Hongkong. . . .[8]

From the perspective of 1899, the China market appeared to be a very real interest of the United States.[9]

A new aggressive spirit in the United States completed the setting within which the Open Door Notes were written. The Spanish-American War, and particularly Commodore George Dewey's victory at Manila Bay, prompted an obvious shift in the thinking and forms of expression of many Americans. Ratified by a very slim margin in February 1899, the treaty that ended the war with Spain transferred possession of the entire Philippine archipelago to the United States.

Charles Denby expressed a widely shared belief when he declared: "Since 1898 everything has changed in the Far East. . . . The United States has become an Asiatic power."[10] In explaining how this development affected China, the former minister boldly asserted that the establishment of an American "foothold in the East," which he noted was only six hundred miles from China's coast, decreased the possibility that other nations would partition the Middle Kingdom. This sense of power and self-assertiveness found its way onto the editorial page of the usually restrained *New York Times,* which termed Dewey's victory the "key" to the open door in China.[11]

Events in the spring of 1899 injected additional and greater urgency into the existing diplomatic, commercial, and chauvinistic pressures for American action in China. After several incidents of antiforeign violence, Germany sent troops into the interior of Shantung in March. At about the same time, and with British support, Italy demanded possession of Sanmen Bay. In April 1899, London and St. Petersburg mutually agreed to separate spheres for railroad development. Her Majesty's foreign office promised not to impede Russia "north of the great wall," and in return the czar's government pledged not to compete with Britain in the Yangtze Valley. This deal certainly "muddled" London's traditional role as a defender of free trade. The British government hoped that free trade could be preserved in China, but London had avoided confronting the continental powers over the spheres of influence and, in fact, had claimed its own "compensatory concession" at Weihaiwei and made the railroad deal with Russia in case partitioning occurred. In spite of Peking's successful rebuffing of the German and Italian moves, the actions of Britain, Russia, Germany, and Italy dimmed American hopes for the maintenance of open commerce. In the spring of 1899, the breakup and disappearance of China itself appeared imminent, unless someone could devise a means to reverse the escalating international rivalry in East Asia.[12]

Two additional events set the stage for an American diplomatic initiative. In August, Philippine Commission chairman Jacob Gould Schurman returned from Asia and reported that "the future of China was the one overshadowing question." A trusted administration confidant, Schurman specifically linked China's sovereignty and free trade in his policy recommendation: "China . . . should maintain its independent position, but its doors should be kept open."[13] The same month, the Russian czar issued a ukase declaring Talien a free port. This Russian action held out a slim hope that an international accord might still be possible, but only if some country moved quickly to take the initiative.[14]

On August 24, 1899, Hay asked William W. Rockhill, his Far Eastern advisor, to prepare an instruction to the United States ambassadors in Great Britain, Germany, Russia, and France. Rockhill, who had served under Young and Denby in China, drafted what became known to the world as Hay's first Open Door Note. Many historians have given Rockhill and his close friend Alfred E. Hippisley, an English officer in the Chinese customs service since 1867, primary credit for the substance of the note. These standard accounts emphasize the following: During the summer of 1899, Rockhill and Hippisley carried on an extensive correspondence on the China question, and in his August 21 letter, Hippisley enclosed a detailed memorandum of policy suggestions. Rockhill sent copies of some of these letters to Hay, both directly and through Assistant Secretary Alvey A. Adee. In reply to Hay's August 24 request, Rockhill prepared a memorandum that borrowed heavily from the one that Hippisley had sent on August 21. McKinley approved Rockhill's memorandum, and Rockhill then drafted the actual instructions to the U.S. ambassadors in London, Berlin, and St. Petersburg. After Adee made a few minor corrections, John Hay signed the instructions and dispatched them on September 6, 1899. In November the same communication also went to the American envoys in France, Japan, and Italy.[15]

The major problem with this scenario is the almost negligible role assigned to John Hay. Diplomatically experienced and at the height of his career, the secretary did not suddenly become a nonentity in his own department. In 1899 the State Department was still a simple organization, with no Division of Far Eastern Affairs, which was not created until 1908. Having a minimal foreign-policy bureaucracy, the secretary himself made almost all departmental decisions. Although not an East Asian expert like Hippisley and Rockhill, Hay was well versed in the specifics of the situation in China. In fact, given all the pressures on him, he could scarcely have avoided confronting the China question. Receiving information on policy alternatives from many sources other than Rockhill, Hay undoubtedly realized that eventually he would have to respond officially to the creation of European spheres of influence in China.[16]

Hay gave the China problem a great deal of thought. As early as March 1899, before Rockhill or Hippisley was even available for consultation, he was wrestling with the difficult choices that the issue involved. When Germany sent troops into Shantung and Italy demanded its own harbor in China, Hay informed Paul Dana of the *New York Sun* that the administration was "opposed to the dismemberment of that Empire" and that the American people would not countenance U.S. participation "in the great game of spoliation now going on." He quickly added, though, that "we are keenly alive to the importance of safeguarding our great commercial interests in that Empire." Here, six months before Rockhill and Hippisley composed their memoranda on China, the secretary of state himself concisely stated the substance of the Open Door Notes: an affirmation of support for China's territorial integrity and a defense of American commercial rights in the Middle Kingdom. Hay's coupling of China's survival with the protection of American interests mirrored the recommendations that he had received from Conger, Beresford, and Schurman. The problem was how to accomplish these goals. Hay knew what was at stake but also realized that his alternatives were severely limited. Although he did "not consider our hands tied for future eventualities," Hay explained to Dana that "for the present our best policy is one of vigilant protection of our commercial interests, without formal alliances with other Powers interested."[17]

The China policy that Hay personally favored was an alliance with Britain. While ambassador to England, he had publicly urged an Anglo-American "partnership in the beneficent work of the world," but at that time the McKinley administration had reaffirmed the century-old American tradition of "avoiding interference or connection with European complications."[18] Although Hay was now in charge of the nation's foreign relations, he knew that those journalists and politicians who had "a mad-dog hatred of England" would scream "subservience to Great Britain" if he officially proposed an alliance with Britain. Other possible alliances did not square with Hay's own biases. He considered Russia the chief aggressor in China, France the "harlot" of Russia, and Germany too self-seeking. Although briefly contemplating a joint effort with England, Germany, and Japan, he finally gave up all thoughts of an alliance. He later complained to former Secretary of State John W. Foster:

> All I have ever done with England is to have wrung great concessions out of her with no compensation. And yet, these idiots say I'm not an American because I don't say, "To hell with the Queen," at every breath. . . . That we should be compelled to refuse the assistance of the greatest power in the world, *in carrying out our own policy,* because all Irishmen are Democrats and some Germans are fools—is enough to drive a man mad. Yet we shall do what we can.[19]

In August 1899, when he asked Rockhill to draft a statement on China, John Hay found himself in a difficult position. Although Rockhill warned him that Britain was "as great an offender in China as Russia itself," Hay's own pro-British biases caused him to seek a policy close to that of England. Anglo-American relations were improving, and Hay desired to maintain movement toward a rapprochement, even if an alliance was impossible. He could expect political support for such a course from the American Asiatic Association, which viewed Britain as a commercial ally and had endorsed Beresford's proposals for closer Anglo-American cooperation. On the other hand, William Jennings Bryan's free silverites disliked England because London supported the gold standard. Hay was well aware that others with a long-standing distrust of Britain, such as Irish-Americans, would most likely vote against any administration that appeared to be pro-British. With the elections of 1900 approaching, it seemed preferable that the United States act alone to defend its interests, but not necessarily by claiming a territorial concession as Conger had suggested. Even after the Spanish-American War, the tradition of limiting America's foreign commitments was still strong. What Hay needed was a stopgap to satisfy his complex requirements. The measure had to be clearly American in origin but compatible with British policy; it had to be assertive but free of unnecessary risks and obligations. He found it in the Rockhill-Hippisley memorandum, but the secretary of state himself made the decision to act and set the parameters of that action.[20]

Hay proceeded quickly to implement the Rockhill-Hippisley draft, because he saw it as a limited and expedient, if not too promising, attempt to satisfy the need for some kind of American move. The Open

Door Note of September 1899 acknowledged the existence of the spheres of influence and made no attempt to terminate them. The State Department instructed the American envoys to request from the other powers formal, written assurances that the commercial rights of all nations would be respected within the spheres of influence and leased territories. In effect, the United States' proposition paralleled London's acquiescence to the spheres but sought a reaffirmation of the unimpeded access to China's markets that the Western treaty system had always guaranteed. In addition, there was an implicit connection between the Open Door policy and China's integrity. The carefully worded note stated that the United States would "in no way commit itself to a recognition of exclusive rights of any power within or control over any portion of the Chinese Empire." Clearly the future welfare of China itself was an integral part of Hay's effort in 1899, but it was the danger to American, not Chinese, interests that selfishly motivated the secretary of state's appeal to the powers. His instruction to America's diplomats told them to convey Washington's explicit concern that "complications arising between the treaty powers" might "imperil the rights insured to the United States under our treaties with China." The stated purpose of the Open Door Note was to protect U.S. interests within the spheres, preserve an "open market for the commerce of the world," reduce international friction, and facilitate efforts for "strengthening the Imperial Government and maintaining the integrity of China." These were ambitious objectives to be accomplished merely by an exchange of diplomatic notes.[21]

As Washington expected, the other nations responded to Hay's initiative with varying degrees of enthusiasm and concurrence. The British prime minister informed American ambassador Joseph H. Choate on November 30 that his government would make the desired pledge of open commerce in regard to Weihaiwei, future leases, and spheres of interest, if other powers made similar pledges. The omission of Hong Kong and Kowloon from this list was clear to all. Germany, France, Italy, and Japan agreed to the equality of trade and navigation for all nations in China, provided that all governments assented. In December, Count Michael Muraviev, the Russian foreign minister, asserted that the czar's designation of Talien as a free port was proof of Russia's "firm intention to follow the policy of the open door." As Britain had done with Hong Kong, Russia clearly exempted Port Arthur from its pledge. Muraviev promised only that his government would claim no special privileges for its own subjects in any ports "now opened or hereafter to be opened to foreign commerce by the Chinese Government, and which lie beyond the territory leased to Russia."[22] Choosing to recognize the assurances rather than the omissions in the responses, Hay publicly announced the treaty nations' "final and definitive" assent to the Open Door on March 20, 1900.[23]

The Open Door Note of September 1899 contained no specific promises to China itself. Hay did not even inform the Chinese government of the note's contents until November, when newspaper accounts prompted Wu Ting-fang, the Chinese minister in Washington, to question the secretary of state about what was happening. Hay reassured Wu that the United States was not contemplating participation in a European dismemberment of China, as the press had rumored. Hay could not have eased Chinese concerns entirely, though, because he added that, if the United States "should desire any [future] conveniences or accommodations on the coast of China," it would raise the subject directly with the Chinese government. Almost as an afterthought, the secretary of state also expressed hope that Peking "would cooperate with us in gaining the assurances we desired from the European powers" of an open door for trade.[24] Hay contemplated no special commitment to China, and in fact, George Seward sharply criticized Hay for not taking the opportunity to exert U.S. influence against "all spheres of influence movements, and all they imply."[25] Hay's diplomatic correspondence with Britain and Russia specifically mentioned that the integrity of the Middle Kingdom was threatened, but he sought no explicit guarantees from the powers to respect China's sovereignty other than in tariff collection, which was actually performed by Westerners who staffed the imperial customs service.[26]

Although Hay's cautiously worded request to the other powers entailed little risk for the United States, the Open Door Note did seem to imply that the State Department was formally committing itself, contrary to tradition, to joint international action. The instructions to the ambassadors in London and Berlin indicated a desire for British and German help in gaining agreement by other nations to the American appeal. No such request appeared in the correspondence addressed to St. Petersburg, suggesting that the United States was possibly attempting to mobilize the influence of other countries to preempt expected Russian resistance. After all the nations had replied, Hay speculated that Russia had agreed to the Open Door only because it assumed that the other governments would decline and thus the whole declaration would come to nothing. He later termed Russian promises as "false as dicers' oaths." "If now they [the Russians] choose to take a stand in opposition to the entire civilized world," he confided in April 1900 to Ambassador Henry White in Berlin, "we shall then make up our minds what to do about it. At present I am not bothering much."[27] Although he seemed to imply a possible alliance against Russia, Hay did not seriously harbor such thoughts, and he resigned himself to America's inability to control the Chinese situation. The Open Door Note of 1899 was a new departure for the State Department in pursuit of the old design for free trade in China. This move fell far short, though, of the kind of official cooperation that Denby had urged throughout his career in Peking or that Hay himself actually preferred.[28]

Hay received considerable public acclaim for his diplomatic accomplishment. A Republican spokesman declared that the secretary of state's Open Door Note, which followed on the heels of what Hay himself termed a "splendid little war" with Spain, "supplements and complements the work of our army and navy. A year ago no nation would have listened to a proposition of this kind, but the whole world listens to the United States now."[29] In spite of such accolades, Hay knew that the pledges he had received from the other nations were worth very little. He was more hopeful that the Open Door initiative would improve relations with Britain and help the Republican party in the upcoming elections. Democratic campaigners were characterizing Hay's note as a demonstration of Anglo-American solidarity and were accusing the Republicans of an "ill-concealed" alliance with Great Britain. Despite these partisan blasts, Hay's mail indicated that many voters would "give the administration credit" at the polls in November for its "defense of American trade in the Far East."[30]

In the summer of 1900, with China already a prominent issue in American politics and foreign policy, the dramatic and ominous Boxer Uprising occurred in Peking. The newest episode in a half-century of antiforeignism, this massive outbreak of violence escalated rapidly into a major international complication of the type that Hay's Open

Door Note had sought to prevent. Instigated by an intensely xenophobic secret society known to Westerners as the Boxers, this upheaval represented a nascent Chinese nationalism and not simply superstitious fear. The Boxer leaders believed that they and their followers were "Celestial soldiers" with divine orders to annihilate all foreigners, but many conservative Chinese officials joined or condoned the Boxer Uprising for what were clearly patriotic motives. T'ing-yung, a mandarin who actually led a Boxer band in a murderous assault on Christian missionaries, explained afterward to Western soldiers: "You people have insulted us too much, so who would not take revenge when he gets the chance."[31] Following the humiliation by Japan in 1894–1895, China had experienced mounting internal conflict between officials such as T'ing-yung who advocated militant resistance to all external pressures and other mandarins who favored internal reforms as the best means of protecting China's interests. In September 1898, the old empress dowager Tz'u-hsi had intervened directly to squelch a major reform movement, and since that time many Ch'ing officials had openly espoused antiforeignism as the best method of defending China's traditional political order. It was this obvious connivance of Chinese leaders with the xenophobic forces that made the Boxer Uprising so diplomatically explosive.[32]

By June 1900, Boxers were streaming into Peking on a rampage of destruction and killing. In and around the capital, bands of Boxers burned churches and other foreign property and then turned their rage toward the walled compounds of the foreign legations. There were several attacks on the small detachment of legation guards, and on June 20 Boxers murdered Minister Clemens von Ketteler of Germany. Rather than suppressing this mob violence, the imperial court encouraged it. Although not entirely convinced that the Boxers would triumph, Tz'u-hsi wanted to believe that they had magical powers that would enable them to rid China of the oppressive barbarians. On June 21 she actually declared war on the foreign powers and incorporated the "righteous" Boxers into the imperial army. The "war" remained confined to the Peking area, because more temperate Chinese leaders in central and south China declared their neutrality. For fifty-five days, the imperial forces in Peking and 200,000 Boxers besieged the foreign legations. A joint military force of Japanese and Western troops that numbered 18,000 men, including 2,100 Americans, as-

This bronze lion guarded the entrance to the private living quarters of Empress Dowager Tz'u-hsi in the Imperial Palace.

sembled at Taku and fought its way inland. The international expedition relieved the besieged legations on August 14; the disguised empress dowager fled from the city the next morning.[33]

The Boxer Uprising presented Secretary of State Hay with a policy predicament. News of von Ketteler's murder and disruption of direct communication with the legations in Peking created genuine fear that Conger and the other foreign envoys were also dead at the hands of fanatics acting on behalf of the Chinese government. Newspaper accounts described "heads carried on spears." If this macabre scenario proved to be true, the international relief force gathering at Taku could become the vanguard for a full-scale war with China. Given the recent history of concession taking in the Middle Kingdom and the presumed inability of China to mount a successful military defense, such a war would almost certainly end with the dismemberment of the tottering empire. As Hay's Open Door Note of September had revealed, the State Department believed that a breakup of China would be disastrous. If partition occurred, domestic politics would prevent the United States from claiming its own enclave. The Philippine annexation and continued military involvement there had already led Democratic party leaders to campaign against further attempts to acquire territory in Asia. At the same time, public opinion would expect some forceful reaction by Washington if the Boxer atrocities included American victims. With the Republican and Democratic national conventions meeting in June and July, the presidential campaign season of 1900 was underway, and the McKinley administration could not overlook political considerations. Where in this maze was a policy move that would further both the president's political position and the nation's foreign interests?[34]

On July 3, 1900, Hay responded to these complexities with a bold, even stirring, circular telegram that became known as the second Open Door Note. Addressing the American representatives in the six nations that had received his first note plus the envoy in Austria-Hungary, Hay instructed the diplomats to communicate the telegram's contents to their host governments. Dropping the cautious phrasing of his 1899 initiative, the secretary of state explicitly linked the preservation of "Chinese territorial and administrative entity" with the need to "safeguard for the world the principle of equal and impartial trade for all parts of the Chinese Empire."[35] This appeal to principle and philanthropy—to respect for free trade and China's sovereignty—could be expected to satisfy the American people in an election year. In rebuttal to the Democrats' criticisms of McKinley's Philippine policies, Republicans trumpeted Hay's telegram as proof of the administration's anti-imperialism. A few days after distributing the second Open Door Note, Hay candidly admitted to his close friend Henry Adams that "the ideal policy is . . . to do nothing, and yet be around when the watermelon is cut." He hastened to emphasize that the United States wanted no watermelon but only desired to be seen in brightly "colored circles on occasions of festivity." "We strive to please the public," he explained to Adams and then added peevishly: "I take refuge in a craven opportunism. . . . Always doing the thing I know is wrong must be in time ruinous to the Immortal Soul—but that I can charge to the American people whose fault it is."[36]

Hay's pronouncement of July 3 reiterated traditional American ideals and, if his goals could be realized, would simultaneously secure

U.S. interests. The critical question was the feasibility of his stated desires. Because the Boer War in southern Africa had preempted London's attention, and because American politics proscribed a formal U.S. alliance with Britain, Hay could not propose joint Anglo-American action, but he could assume that a unilateral U.S. move to forestall partitioning would have British support. Reading Choate's reports from London, Hay knew that the British desired to prevent partitioning in order to keep open the commercial door. Although Hay often equated American and British interests, Choate also reminded the secretary of state that London had its own "earmark" on spheres in Weihaiwei and elsewhere, in case China was carved up. Washington would have to act alone and could not rely on jackal diplomacy.[37]

The United States had a large number of troops—some 60,000—in the Philippines. Although the administration could not transfer them to China without risk of losing control of the islands, the American forces in the western Pacific and those in the joint rescue expedition to Peking made the United States a visible factor in the military power balance in China. Hay and his advisor Rockhill were keenly aware of the delicate balance of power that existed among the various European nations and Japan. Believing that difficulties in the current campaign against the Boers negated British influence, Hay exclaimed on June 15: "If Russia and Germany arrange things, the balance is lost for ages."[38] The East Asian equilibrium was so close, though, that even a vague demarche by the United States might prompt caution in foreign chancelleries. Consequently, a bold, unilateral declaration of intent by the United States might be just the thing to keep attention focused on the Boxer menace and to prevent foreign intervention from broadening to all of China. Hay's circular telegram argued for "peace with the Chinese nation" and insisted that the "virtual anarchy" in Peking meant that the "local provincial authorities," who had disassociated themselves from the imperial war decree, "represented the Chinese people, with whom we seek to remain in peace and friendship."[39] A United States initiative might preserve cooperation among the powers and curb competition for selfish advantages. The Open Door Note of July 3 did not request formal replies but emphasized the need for nations "to act concurrently," and several days later, Hay wrote to St. Clair McKelway of the Brooklyn Eagle: "We have been particularly anxious to avoid, and even to do what we could to prevent a splitting up of the powers into groups and combinations, and so far successfully."[40] Hay's analysis was not new; for years American diplomats had sought Western restraint and cooperation in China as the best means of securing U.S. interests. The second Open Door Note managed to combine this proven technique of protecting the nation's interests with the well-established tradition of American magnanimity and adherence to liberal political principles.[41]

Contemporary assessments of Hay's handiwork varied widely. His friend Brooks Adams believed that the secretary of state had single-handedly blocked Russian and German ambitions in China. Proclaiming that the United States held "command in the East," Adams praised Hay: "Your policy will prove to have carried us round one of the great corners of our history. The further we go forward, the larger your conception will look."[42] An enthusiastic Kentuckian wrote to Hay that the "notice to European powers . . . is a greater document than the Declaration of Independence, and as a democrat I'll endorse it at the polls."[43] Charles Denby, on the other hand, criticized Hay's actions as too pro-British, too anti-Russian, and not sufficiently keyed to America's own self-interests. The former minister complained that the State Department remained "discreetly silent" about the British presence in Hong Kong and Weihaiwei while it manifested inordinate concern about Russian encroachments in Manchuria. Recalling Russia's friendship for the North during the Civil War, Denby claimed that St. Petersburg still "notoriously values our friendship." Hence, he recommended that the United States would best serve its own interests by openly proclaiming "that we are as friendly to Russia as we are to England."[44] Josiah Quincy, a former assistant secretary of state, penned a similar critique of Hay's policy, which he charged was "too political in character." Terming Russian activity in Asia "natural and legitimate," Quincy argued that "friendly relations with Russia" were essential to American diplomacy.[45] These reactions, both positive and negative, to the Open Door Notes highlighted the pro-British biases of Hay's diplomacy and dramatized the extent to which Hay himself determined policy.

In analyzing the Open Door concept, historians have characterized it as everything from an "antiquated" policy that had no future to "a brilliant economic stroke which led to the gradual extension of American economic and political power throughout the world."[46] Most historians who ascribe to some form of the first view either assert or imply that, under the influence of Rockhill and Hippisley, Hay entered into the Open Door initiative understanding neither the situation in China nor the implications of the Open Door Notes for overall American foreign policy. Such assessments place a heavy burden of responsibility on the notes for creating a myth of American influence in a region where the power and interests of the United States were in fact limited.[47] On the other hand, many historians who believe that Hay responded with reason and purpose to the pressures for an American policy in China consider the Open Door Notes a first step toward "informal empire" or "the overseas expansion of the American economic system." This interpretation detects a direct connection between America's rapidly expanding economic power in 1899–1900 and Hay's appeal for the protection of future U.S. commercial access to East Asia. Avoiding traditional colonization in the form of leaseholds or spheres of influence, the Open Door Notes were, according to this view, a clever and "interesting hybrid of anti-colonialism and economic imperialism."[48]

Hay's own view of his work was rather unassuming. His diplomacy was a practical attempt to make the best of a bad situation, but he certainly did not consider it brilliant. Because American politics and traditions prevented the use of formal alliances, Hay asked plaintively: "Is it of any avail to me to see . . . the only safe course to take, when I know it will not and cannot be taken?"[49] With a feeling bordering on futility, Hay knew that factors extraneous to either the United States or even East Asia would largely determine whatever degree of success his policy enjoyed. When Britain and Germany concluded an agreement in October 1900 to respect the Open Door and China's integrity, Hay was immodestly heartened that "these two great Powers, who are not dependent upon Senates, [had] come together & form[ed] a compact to confirm and fortify my work."[50] Although pleased by the Anglo-German accord, the secretary of state suspected "ulterior intentions" and interpreted the "whole scheme" as a German effort "to guard herself against being discriminated against in the trade of the Yangtze Valley which England has preempted as her sphere of influence."[51] Hay could see for himself that the checks and balances stimulated by European rivalries were as much responsible for preventing the partitioning of China in 1900 as were the Open Door Notes.

Hay made his decisions in 1899 and 1900 based upon a pragmatic assessment of American choices. Despite its apparent cleverness, his approach was tentative, ad hoc, and ambiguous. Although the American Asiatic Association was lobbying to convince government officials of the potential of the China market, in March 1899 Congress refused an administration request to fund an investigation of commercial prospects in East Asia. A few days later, the secretary of state admitted that, even with the race for economic concessions underway, it was "not very easy to formulate with any exactness the view of the [U.S.] Government in regard to the present condition of things in China."[52] In addition to the uncertainty in official circles, most of the business community was not displaying any particular eagerness to rush into the China market. Despite much talk of underconsumption at home and the need for foreign markets, the home market continued to be the major concern of American business. Why should New York entrepreneurs take the slightest risk on a venture in Shanghai when they could be practically guaranteed a handsome return on a deal in Pittsburgh? Most American businessmen were not willing to bear the burden of "informal empire."[53]

John Hay sent the Open Door Notes because he felt that doing something, even if it was inadequate, was better than doing nothing. As secretary of state, he could not avoid the responsibilities of his office. The clamor for an American response to events in China was increasing at the same time that the elections of 1900 were approaching. Hay was a politician as well as a diplomat, but his Open Door initiatives were not simply gestures made for the sake of political expediency, nor were they issued in an absence of mind. Hay carefully considered his options, and realizing that the United States had only limited influence in Asia, he responded to the pressures for a policy with a simultaneous display of bravado and caution.

The Open Door Notes elevated the persistent American dilemma in China to an American policy doctrine. Hay tried to establish a position between involvement and noninvolvement. He abandoned the State Department's traditional caution about international cooperation but did not adopt Denby's tactic of joint action or any arrangement that might appear to be an alliance. Avoiding a binding commitment to either the treaty nations or to China, he initially did not even bother to consult or inform the Chinese about the Open Door correspondence.

At the same time, he refused to concede that American economic and strategic interests in East Asia were limited or any less pressing than those of Russia, England, and Japan. Hay identified the United States with two principles—free trade in China and the integrity of the Middle Kingdom. America had neither the power nor the will to sustain either of these goals, but Hay's rhetoric raised the expectation of an American commitment in China while veiling the reality of noncommitment. As a result, the United States began the twentieth century possessing a China policy with laudable objectives that merged U.S. interests and ideals. What was good for China was good for the United States, and vice versa. This doctrine was so exceedingly attractive that it obscured the lesson of the preceding forty years that it might not be feasible.

Because of the conflict between imperialism and idealism, the United States did not settle upon a definitive policy in China between 1861 and 1898. The eight American ministers in Peking during those years vacillated between the competing standards of upholding Western solidarity under the unequal treaties and respecting Chinese sovereignty, without binding the United States to either alternative. At times American representatives hesitated to align their government with imperialistic European policies, but on the other hand, to side with China as a matter of principle risked advantages that the United States gained from unity with the Western powers. Anson Burlingame's cooperative policy included the Chinese authorities as equal participants and attempted to ease the impact of the treaties that the West had imposed upon China. Conversely, J. Ross Browne excluded the Peking government from the cooperative policy and favored joint foreign pressure to expand Western treaty privileges. Frederick F. Low and Benjamin P. Avery experimented with several compromise positions between those of Burlingame and Browne but failed to arrive at a satisfactory policy. Until the threat of impeachment made him more cautious, George F. Seward advocated both enforcement and evasion of the treaties, in accordance with which course was most useful for particular American interests. The efforts of James B. Angell and John R. Young to establish an independent American position in China limited the United States commitment to the Western treaty system even more than had Seward's expediency. Despite these attempts at a uniquely American approach, the United States did not divorce itself from the treaties. Charles Denby worked hard to keep his nation an active participant within the foreign system, which he described as the West united against China. The State Department repeatedly disagreed with Denby's activist approach, and in fact, from 1861 to 1898 the differing perspectives of American officials in Washington and the envoys in Peking often exacerbated the ambiguity in the nation's China policies. Although U.S. diplomats frequently joined with other envoys to confront the Peking government, Washington often declared its adherence to the doctrine of no foreign entanglements and its respect for China's sovereign rights. On the other hand, congressional exclusion of Chinese immigrants conflicted with the beneficence that many Americans liked to ascribe to their nation's conduct. Both in Peking and in Washington, American expressions of altruism often appeared to be more self-serving than self-evident.

As a result of American ambivalence toward both China and the treaty nations, continuity was often lacking in U.S. policy.[54] The United States did not have a consistent answer to its persistent quandary between self-interest and selfless idealism. In China this dichotomy often emerged as a choice between force and forbearance. Almost every American envoy in Peking had a different opinion on the use of naval and military power. Other nations demonstrated that gunboats and marines, or even outright war, as in the case of France and Japan, could be used successfully against a weak China. Burlingame opposed force except in self-defense; Browne considered Western coercion in China unavoidable; and Low first criticized French intimidation at Tientsin and then used gunboats himself in Korea. George Seward argued that the mere threat of coercion was sufficient, and Young was torn between an instinctive aversion to military pressure and the knowledge that it worked. Denby recommended leveling villages during riots but disapproved of war with the Chinese government. The United States seldom employed armed force in China, but American officials did not disavow foreign privileges gained forcefully by other nations. Hence, despite America's relatively peaceful behavior, the ever-expanding and interlocking system of foreign advantages in China involved the United States in Western imperialism. Over the course of the nineteenth century, Britain, France, Russia, Germany, and Japan secured favorable treaty arrangements, possession of key bases such as Hong Kong and Port Arthur, economic concessions, and spheres of influence. Although the United States never attempted to dominate or control Chinese territory, participation in the treaty system and belief in Western superiority meant that Americans could not escape obvious association with imperialism in China.

By the time John Hay became secretary of state in 1898, the escalating European scramble for economic and strategic advantages in China threatened to destroy the old empire's political and territorial integrity and possibly to obliterate American economic opportunity in the process. To protect present and future U.S. interests, Hay seemed to face a choice of either aggressively joining or actively opposing this imperialistic assault on China, but he selected another option. Responding with the Open Door Notes, Hay adopted a position that incorporated elements of several previous American policies. He expressed concern about China's survival, but tended to treat China more as a passive object than as a nation. Hay's noble rhetoric was reminiscent of Burlingame's cooperative approach but lacked Burlingame's sincerity. Like Browne, Hay sought to protect American interests with little regard for China, but Hay did not mimic Browne's counsels of coercion. Hay carefully avoided any commitment to preserving Chinese sovereignty, but he would not follow those nations that were taking concessions from China. His initiative was, in fact, an attempt at American leadership in China. In the 1860s, Burlingame exercised leadership among the Western diplomats in Peking; Avery later tried to lead; and George Seward clearly followed British minister Thomas Wade like a jackal trails a lion. Similarly, various secretaries of state provided differing precedents for the proper U.S. relationship with the other treaty powers in China. William Seward, for example, thought of cooperation as going along with Britain, but William Evarts and Richard Olney sought to disassociate the United States from England. Despite his earnest desire for closer Anglo-American relations, Hay avoided any formal arrangements with London or any other dramatic departure from accepted American diplomatic practices. His policy was remarkably restrained for an era of vigorous expansionism by many nations, including the United States itself during the war with Spain. Although more assertive of American commercial rights than previous statements by Washington, the Open Door Notes were an attempt to preserve more than to expand the modest American stake in China.[55] Hay did not choose to join with European imperialism, but neither could he entirely separate the United States from it.

Not a narrow economic determinism but rather a broader and even more compelling cultural attitude shaped American imperialism in China. In an emotional, spread-eagle speech in January 1900, Albert J. Beveridge reminded his United States Senate colleagues that "just beyond the Philippines are China's illimitable markets," but the senator's grand vision extended far beyond an expanding American commercial empire. "We will not abandon our opportunity in the Orient. We will not renounce our part in the mission of our race, trustee, under God, of the civilization of the world," he trumpeted.[56] Few people had the senator's talent for oratorical excess, but his sense of mission had many adherents. In the closing years of the nineteenth century, few Americans admitted supporting crass economic imperialism, because the nation's motives abroad were a much more complex mixture of economic, racial, philosophical, religious, and historical determinants. Many Americans believed that their nation was the epitome of moral and material success, that it was the most generous and just of all nations, that its superior qualities enabled and obligated it to help the backward peoples of the world, and that social and economic progress benefited everyone. These assumptions were by no means unique to the United States. This cultural chauvinism linked American and European imperialism, but for Americans it was part of a dilemma. Although in many ways intrinsically American, imperialism conflicted with a different and equally basic American idealism.[57]

From Burlingame through Denby, the United States ministers in Peking had a "sweet and sour" China policy. Their widely varying recipes combined in differing proportions the philanthropic ideal of self-determination for all peoples and the pursuit of U.S. interests. In assessing these two considerations, American envoys desired the protection of their nation's limited interests without an overreaching commitment to either the Chinese or Western governments. Declining to choose between the seemingly incompatible alternatives of China's integrity and foreign privileges, Hay formally merged them. Although his effort to create a consensus policy might appear at worst hypocritical or at best indecisive, it was as American as the Declaration of Independence. The secretary of state found no conflict between

American ideals and interests. The idealism and imperialism inherent in Hay's Open Door Notes were part of the nation's historic paradox between its altruistic motives and its own aggrandizement.

America's ambient policy drift between being referee and participant in China finally led the United States into implied commitments that it had studiously avoided throughout the nineteenth century. As a result, the United States bequeathed itself a debilitating legacy for the twentieth century. By identifying American interests and welfare with abstract ideals, the United States embarked upon a course in East Asia that would eventually become part of a broader effort of global proportions. Washington was declaring that universal respect for the sovereignty and inviolability of nations was not only an American desire but a stated goal of United States policy. If this grand objective could be achieved, American values of social justice and political self-determination and their self-proclaimed benefits would be possible for others. Simultaneously, the United States' own economic and security interests would benefit from the international peace, stability, and progress that would flow from this idyllic condition. As the twentieth century dawned, the United States was proclaiming its allegiance to peaceful, moral, legal principles of international conduct. In two world wars, in Korea and Vietnam, and in countless other conflicts of smaller proportions, the United States sought to export its ideals throughout the world. As in the Open Door Notes in China, the United States equated those ideals with its own self-interest—becoming simultaneously self-righteous and self-serving. Through the eyes of many in the world and in the United States, this conduct was imperialism. In official American policy, it was idealism. In truth, it was both imperialism and idealism.

APPENDIX

United States Ministers to China, Secretaries of State,
and Presidents, 1861–1901

Minister to China	Secretary of State	President
Anson Burlingame, 1861–67	William H. Seward, 1861–69	Abraham Lincoln, 1861–65
J. Ross Browne, 1868–69		Andrew Johnson, 1865–69
Frederick F. Low, 1869–74	Hamilton Fish, 1869–77	Ulysses S. Grant, 1869–77
Benjamin P. Avery, 1874–75		
George F. Seward, 1876–80	William M. Evarts, 1877–81	Rutherford B. Hayes, 1877–81
James B. Angell, 1880–81	James G. Blaine, 1881	James A. Garfield, 1881
John R. Young, 1882–85	Frederick T. Frelinghuysen, 1881–85	Chester A. Arthur, 1881–85
Charles Denby, 1885–98	Thomas F. Bayard, 1885–89	Grover Cleveland, 1885–89
	James G. Blaine, 1889–92	Benjamin Harrison, 1889–93
	John W. Foster, 1892–93	
	Walter Q. Gresham, 1893	Grover Cleveland, 1893–97
	William B. Olney, 1895–97	
Edwin H. Conger, 1898–1905	John Sherman, 1897–98	William McKinley, 1897–1901
	William R. Day, 1898	
	John Hay, 1898–1905	

NOTES

1. IMPERIALISM AND IDEALISM

1. William Woodruff, *America's Impact on the World*, pp. 5–6, 44–46; Michael Kammen, *People of Paradox*, pp. 211–24; Felix Gilbert, *The Beginnings of American Foreign Policy*, pp. 135–36; Morrell Heald and Lawrence S. Kaplan, *Culture and Diplomacy*, pp. 4–5.

2. Richard W. Van Alstyne, *Genesis of American Nationalism*, pp. 58–114; Frederick Merk, *Manifest Destiny and Mission in American History*, pp. 261–66; Heald and Kaplan, *Culture and Diplomacy*, pp. 8–9.

3. Woodruff, *America's Impact*, pp. 180–81; Kammen, *People of Paradox*, pp. 292–98; Rush Welter, *The Mind of America, 1820–1860*, pp. 45–74.

4. Charles Denby, *China and Her People*, Vol. 2, pp. 38–39.

5. Akira Iriye, *Across the Pacific*, pp. 3–7, 17; Jerome Ch'en, *China and the West*, pp. 39–48; John King Fairbank, *The United States and China*, pp. 307–20; Milton Plesur, *America's Outward Thrust*, pp. 214–20; William H. Goetzmann, *When the Eagle Screamed*, pp. 92–94.

6. Robin W. Winks, "Imperialism," pp. 253–70; Akira Iriye, "Imperialism in East Asia," pp. 130–31; Marilyn Young, "The Quest for Empire," pp. 131–42; William Appleman Williams, *The Tragedy of American Diplomacy*, pp. 60–61, 82; John King Fairbank, *China Perceived*, p. 99; Fairbank, *United States and China*, pp. 169–70, 451–52; Heald and Kaplan, *Culture and Diplomacy*, p. 121; Woodruff, *America's Impact*, p. 48.

7. J. Ross Browne, "Under the Dragon's Footstool," *Overland Monthly* 6, no. 3 (March 1871): 238; Denby, *China and Her People*, Vol. 1, pp. 19–23.

8. Walter A. Burlingame to Isaac Livermore, 12 December 1866, Burlingame Family Papers, Syracuse University Library; Alexander Michie, *The Englishman in China*, Vol. 2, p. 143; L. C. Arlington and William Lewisohn, *In Search of Old Peking*, pp. 1–3, Denby, *China and Her People*, Vol. 1, p. 26.

9. Michie, *Englishman in China*, Vol. 2, pp. 143–44; Chester Holcombe, *The Real Chinaman*, pp. 323–24.

10. John King Fairbank, "A Preliminary Framework," pp. 1–2.

11. Ibid., pp. 2–4, 19; Ch'en, *China and the West*, pp. 25–27; Earl Swisher, *China's Management of the American Barbarians*, pp. 41–42; Mark Mancall, "The Persistence of Tradition in Chinese Foreign Policy," pp. 16–22.

12. Frederick Wells Williams, *Anson Burlingame and the First Chinese Mission to Foreign Powers*, p. 30; Jane Burlingame to Edward Burlingame, 10 February 1864, Burlingame Family Papers, Library of Congress; Michie, *Englishman in China*, Vol. 2, pp. 139–40, 145; Denby, *China and Her People*, Vol. 1, pp. 29–30.

13. Sarah Pike Conger, *Letters from China*, p. 67; Juliet Bredon, *Peking*, pp. 36–49; Arlington and Lewisohn, *Old Peking*, pp. 5–16; Denby, *China and Her People*, Vol. 1, pp. 30–40, Vol. 2, p. 195.

14. Te-kong Tong, *United States Diplomacy in China, 1844–60*, pp. 3–4, 285; John King Fairbank, *Trade and Diplomacy on the China Coast*, pp. 3–22.

15. Tong, *United States Diplomacy*, pp. 115–218.

16. Ibid., pp. 223–34, 280–82; Swisher, *China's Management*, pp. 505–506; Henri Cordier, *Histoire des Relations de la Chine avec des Puissances Occidentales, 1860–1900*, Vol. 1, pp. 1–11, 18–20, 40, 90–99.

17. China, Imperial Maritime Customs, *Treaties, Conventions, etc., between China and Foreign States*, Vol. 1, pp. 29–46, 159–64, 212–29, 238–42, 509–23, 602–23, 673–78.

18. Fairbank, *China Perceived*, pp. 85–101; Warren I. Cohen, *America's Response to China*, p. 29; Fairbank, *United States and China*, pp. 312–15; Swisher, *China's Management*, pp. 172–78; Heald and Kaplan, *Culture and Diplomacy*, pp. 101–102.

19. For some of these widely accepted interpretations, see Tyler Dennett, *Americans in Eastern Asia*, pp. v–vii, 677–80; Cohen, *America's Response*, pp. 8–65; Fairbank, *United States and China*, pp. 308–23. Paul H. Clyde has also examined this period of Sino-American relations in a series of articles that did not attempt an overall policy evaluation but that were intended to stimulate research. See Paul H. Clyde, "The China Policy of J. Ross Browne, American Minister to Peking, 1868–1869," pp. 312–33; "Frederick F. Low and the Tientsin Massacre," pp. 100–108; "Attitudes and Policies of George F. Seward, American Minister at Peking, 1876–1880," pp. 387–404.

20. The need for research on this question and others has been pointed out in Kwang-ching Liu, "America and China: The Late Nineteenth Century," pp. 34–96.

21. Ch'en, *China and the West*, pp. 75–82; Swisher, *China's Management*, pp. 47–49; E. V. G. Kiernan, *British Diplomacy in China, 1880 to 1885*, pp. 274–77.

22. Dennett, *Americans in Eastern Asia*, pp. 669–74; Tong, *United States Diplomacy*, p. 284; James A. Field, Jr., "American Imperialism: The Worst Chapter in Almost Any Book," pp. 660–63; Robert L. Beisner, *From the Old Diplomacy to the New, 1865–1900*, pp. 34–39, 80–81.

23. Williams, *Tragedy of American Diplomacy*, pp. 39–43; Thomas J. McCormick, *China Market*, p. 107; Walter LaFeber, *The New Empire*, pp. 410–11.

24. Richard Hofstadter, "Manifest Destiny and the Philippines," pp. 173–200; Julius Pratt, *The Expansionists of 1898*, pp. 1–33, 360; Marilyn Blatt Young, *The Rhetoric of Empire*, pp. 1–13.

2. "FAIR DIPLOMATIC ACTION"

1. Anson Burlingame obituary, unidentified Detroit newspaper, no date, Burlingame Family Papers, Library of Congress.

2. Robert F. Lucid, ed., *The Journal of Richard Henry Dana, Jr.*, Vol. 2, p. 567; Frederick Wells Williams, *Anson Burlingame and the First Chinese Mission to Foreign Powers*, pp. 3–8; Burlingame obituary, Burlingame Family Papers, Library of Congress.

3. William Stevens Robinson, *"Warrington" Pen Portraits*, pp. 427–28;

Henry Wilson, *History of the Rise and Fall of the Slave Power in America,* Vol. 2, pp. 308–309; Lucid, *Dana,* Vol. 2, pp. 636–37; *Kossuth in New England,* pp. 10, 63–64, 283; *Boston Daily Advertiser,* 16 November 1854.

4. James E. Campbell, "Sumner-Brooks-Burlingame or the Last of the Great Challenges," pp. 435–73; Williams, *Burlingame,* pp. 8–13; *Congressional Globe,* 34th Cong., 1st sess., appendix, pp. 653–56; Correspondence, May–August 1856, Burlingame Family Papers, Library of Congress.

5. Williams, *Burlingame,* pp. 13–14; William Winter to Burlingame, 28 July 1856, Burlingame Family Papers, Library of Congress; *Boston Daily Advertiser,* 6 November 1860.

6. W. A. P. Martin, *A Cycle of Cathay or China,* p. 222; Burlingame to William Seward, 16 September 1862, U.S., Department of State, Despatches from United States Ministers to China, 1843–1906 (hereafter cited as China Despatches).

7. Burlingame to W. Seward, 23 December 1863 (private), China Despatches.

8. Jane Burlingame to Livermore, 12 January 1863, 13 March 1863, Burlingame Family Papers, Library of Congress; Jane Burlingame to Edward Burlingame, 10 February 1864, ibid.; Raphael Pumpelly, *My Reminiscences,* Vol. 1, p. 432; Williams, *Burlingame,* pp. 20, 26–30. For more on Burlingame's diplomatic ability, see Samuel Soonki Kim, "Anson Burlingame: A Study in Personal Diplomacy" (Ph.D. dissertation), and Telly Howard Koo, "The Life of Anson Burlingame" (Ph.D. dissertation).

9. Martin, *Cycle of Cathay,* pp. 378–79; Jane Burlingame to Livermore, 12 January 1863, 10–11 April 1863, 23 January 1864, Burlingame Family Papers, Library of Congress; William H. Seward, *Travels around the World,* p. 138. For an excellent study of Frederick Bruce's diplomacy, see Britten Dean, *China and Great Britain.*

10. *Congressional Globe,* 35th Cong., 1st sess., appendix, p. 291.

11. Burlingame to W. Seward, 10 April 1867, China Despatches.

12. Burlingame to W. Seward, 9 November 1864, ibid.; Pumpelly, *Reminiscences,* Vol. 1, p. 390.

13. T'ung-chih was the reign name of the emperor who assumed the throne in 1862. The standard historical work in a Western language on the restoration is Mary Wright, *The Last Stand of Chinese Conservatism.*

14. Ibid., pp. 224–28; Burlingame to W. Seward, 25 October 1862, 12 December 1862, China Despatches; Jerome Ch'en, *China and the West,* pp. 60–62; Arthur W. Hummel, ed., *Eminent Chinese of the Ch'ing Period (1644–1912),* p. 381; Tony Yung-yuan Teng, "Prince Kung and the Survival of the Ch'ing Rule, 1858–1898" (Ph.D. dissertation), pp. 107–20; Samuel S. Kim, "America's First Minister to China: Anson Burlingame and the Tsungli Yamen," pp. 87–91. It should be noted that Burlingame was America's first resident minister in Peking, and not America's first minister to China. Three of Burlingame's predecessors in China—Caleb Cushing, William B. Reed, and John E. Ward—held the rank of envoy extraordinary and minister plenipotentiary.

15. Williams, *Burlingame,* pp. 134–39.

16. W. Seward to Burlingame, 6 March 1862, U.S., Department of State, Diplomatic Instructions of the Department of State, 1801–1906, China (hereafter cited as China Instructions).

17. Ibid.

18. Burlingame to W. Seward, 17 June 1862, China Despatches.

19. Ibid.; Tyler Dennett, "Seward's Far Eastern Policy," pp. 45–62; Tyler Dennett, *Americans in Eastern Asia*, p. 410; Warren I. Cohen, *America's Response to China*, pp. 31–32; Foster Rhea Dulles, *China and America*, p. 63; Jane Burlingame to Livermore, 11 November 1862, Burlingame Family Papers, Library of Congress.

20. Burlingame to W. Seward, 20 June 1863, China Despatches.

21. Ibid.

22. Frederick Bruce to Lord Russell, 15 June 1863 (confidential), enclosed in ibid. Wright, *Last Stand*, pp. 21–42, argues that Bruce and his fellow Englishmen Rutherford Alcock and Robert Hart authored the cooperative policy. S. S. Kim, "Burlingame and the Inauguration of the Cooperative Policy," p. 353, terms Bruce's support of Burlingame's efforts as "indispensable" but attributes to Burlingame the principal "midwife's role" in the establishment of the policy.

23. Burlingame to W. Seward, 21 June 1863 (private), China Despatches.

24. Ibid.

25. W. Seward to Burlingame, 9 September 1863, China Instructions.

26. Burlingame to W. Seward, 2 July 1863, China Despatches; Jane Burlingame to Elizabeth Leland, 9 April 1864, Burlingame Family Papers, Library of Congress. The effect of *ch'ing-i* (literati opinion) on government policy is as difficult to assess in China as is public opinion elsewhere. See Lloyd E. Eastman, *Throne and Mandarins.*

27. Burlingame to W. Seward, 6 November 1863, China Despatches.

28. Burlingame to W. Seward, 27 October 1862, ibid.; Franz Michael, *The Taiping Rebellion*, pp. 170–73; Richard J. Smith, *Mercenaries and Mandarins*, pp. 107–11.

29. George Seward to W. Seward, 25 March 1864, William Henry Seward Papers, University of Rochester Library.

30. Burlingame to W. Seward, 23 June 1863, 4 June 1864, China Despatches; Jane Burlingame to Livermore, 10 April 1863, 28 April 1863, Burlingame Family Papers, Library of Congress; Smith, *Mercenaries*, pp. 111–14, 120–22.

31. Samuel Wells Williams to W. Seward, 26 June 1865, 6 April 1866, China Despatches; Williams to Hunter, 5 September 1865, ibid.; G. Seward to Burlingame, 5 June 1865, Burlingame Family Papers, Library of Congress; Williams to Burlingame, 26 June 1865, Samuel Wells Williams Family Papers, Yale University Library; Ch'en, *China and the West*, p. 324.

32. W. Seward to Charles Francis Adams, 18 August 1862, U.S., Department of State, Diplomatic Instructions of the Department of State, 1801–1906, Great Britain; W. Seward to Burlingame, 18 August 1862, China Instructions.

33. Williams to W. Seward, 26 June 1865, China Despatches; Williams to Hunter, 5 September 1865, ibid.; W. Seward to Williams, 6 November 1865, China Instructions; W. Seward to Burlingame, 17 April 1866, ibid.; Williams to G. Seward, 6 September 1865, Williams Family Papers; Frederick Wells Williams, *The Life and Letters of Samuel Wells Williams, LLD*, p. 360; Martin R. Ring, "The Burgevine Case and Extrality in China, 1863–1866," pp. 136–48. For more on the Burlingame-Williams relationship, see Martin R. Ring, "Anson Burlingame, S. Wells Williams and China, 1861–1870: A Great Era in Chinese-American Relations" (Ph.D. dissertation).

34. Burlingame to W. Seward, 10 December 1862, 11 June 1863, 20 June 1863, China Despatches.

35. Burlingame to W. Seward, 20 June 1863, 7 November 1863, ibid.; Martin, *Cycle of Cathay*, pp. 231–32, 379.

36. Burlingame to W. Seward, 7 November 1863, 23 November 1863, China Despatches; John L. Rawlinson, "The Lay-Osborn Flotilla: Its Development and Significance," pp. 58–93; Jack J. Gerson, *Horatio Nelson Lay and Sino-British Relations, 1854–1864*, pp. 188–96; Stanley F. Wright, *Hart and the Chinese Customs*, pp. 225–59.

37. Burlingame to W. Seward, 7 November 1863 (private), China Despatches.

38. Burlingame to W. Seward, 7 November 1863 (private), 14 November 1863 (private), ibid.; W. Seward to Burlingame, 8 February 1864, China Instructions.

39. Burlingame to W. Seward, 10 September 1864, 7 May 1865, 27 November 1865, 19 September 1866, China Despatches; W. Seward to Burlingame, 29 January 1866, China Instructions; Burlingame to W. Seward, 26 July 1865 (telegram), William Henry Seward Papers; "Charles Francis Adams Diary," 14 July 1865, Adams Family Papers, Massachusetts Historical Society; Gerson, *Lay*, pp. 196–201.

40. Burlingame to W. Seward, 12 December 1866, 15 December 1866, China Despatches. Bell later recommended that American troops occupy Seoul and demand satisfaction for the *General Sherman*. See Charles O. Paullin, *Diplomatic Negotiations of American Naval Officers, 1778–1883*, p. 284.

41. Burlingame to W. Seward, 31 January 1867 (private), 31 January 1867, 12 December 1866, China Despatches.

42. Jules Berthemy to Marquis de Moustier, 3 March 1867, quoted in Dennett, "Far Eastern Policy," pp. 54–56. The translation is my own; Dennett's quotation is in French.

43. Dennett, "Far Eastern Policy," pp. 54–59.

44. Ibid.; W. Seward to Burlingame, 6 May 1867, China Instructions; Frederick Low to Hamilton Fish, 1 February 1873, China Despatches; Alvey A. Adee to G. Seward, 23 February 1898, George Frederick Seward Papers, New York Historical Society.

45. Burlingame to Williams, 27 March 1869, Williams Family Papers; Williams, *Burlingame*, pp. v–vi.

46. Burlingame to W. Seward, 1 December 1865, China Despatches.

47. Burlingame to W. Seward, 23 December 1863 (private), 1 November 1861, 14 December 1861, 17 June 1862, ibid.; Michael, *Taiping Rebellion*, pp. 170–71.

48. Burlingame to W. Seward, 28 February 1866, China Despatches.

49. Burlingame to W. Seward, 28 February 1866, 1 December 1865, ibid.; W. Seward to Burlingame, 9 April 1866, China Instructions; H. H. Bell to Goldsborough, 1 March 1866, U.S., Department of the Navy, Area File of the Naval Records Collection, 1775–1910; E. Mowbray Tate, "U.S. Gunboats on the Yangtze: History and Political Aspects, 1842–1922," p. 123.

50. Bell to Gideon Welles, 18 July 1866, U.S., Department of the Navy, Letters Received by the Secretary of the Navy from Commanding Officers of Squadrons, 1841–1886.

51. Burlingame to Williams, 27 March 1869, Williams Family Papers; Williams to E. T. Sandford, 25 April 1867, ibid.; Burlingame to W. Seward, 7 March 1865, 23 April 1867, China Despatches; W. Seward to Burlingame, 23 August 1867, China Instructions; Bell to Burlingame, 4 June 1867 (private), Burlingame Family Papers, Library of Congress.

52. Williams to W. Seward, 28 November 1867, China Despatches; Burlingame to W. Seward, 14 December 1867, ibid.; Jane Burlingame to Edward Burlingame, 23 November 1867, Burlingame Family Papers, Syracuse University Library; *North China Herald*, 24 December 1867; Kim, "America's First Minister to China," p. 101.

53. Dennett, *Americans in Eastern Asia*, p. 182; Dulles, *China and America*, p. 65.

54. Williams, *Burlingame*, pp. 71–72, concludes that, since Burlingame was faced on one side with the "aggressiveness" of the Europeans and on the other side with the "repugnance" of the Chinese, there was little choice but "to await the slow progress" of cooperation.

55. Burlingame to W. Seward, 29 March 1867, China Despatches.

56. Burlingame to G. Seward, 15 June 1864, enclosed in Burlingame to W. Seward, 18 June 1864, ibid.

3. "DETERMINED MORAL PRESSURE"

1. Burlingame to W. Seward, 17 June 1862, 14 December 1867, U.S., Department of State, Despatches from United States Ministers to China, 1843–1906 (hereafter cited as China Despatches); Burlingame to W. Seward, 21 November 1867, enclosed in Williams to W. Seward, 28 November 1867, ibid.

2. *North China Herald*, 24 December 1867.

3. Ibid.

4. *Official Papers of the Chinese Legation*, p. 7; Mary Gertrude Mason, *Western Concepts of China and the Chinese*, p. 132.

5. Quoted in Immanuel C. Y. Hsü, *China's Entrance into the Family of Nations*, p. 168.

6. Knight Biggerstaff, "The Official Chinese Attitude toward the Burlingame Mission," pp. 683–89; Knight Biggerstaff, "The Secret Correspondence of 1867–1868: Views of Leading Chinese Statesmen regarding the Further Opening of China to Western Influence," pp. 122–36; Earl Swisher, *Chinese Representation in the United States, 1861–1912*, pp. 13–16; Merle Curti and John Stalker, "'The Flowery Flag Devils'—The American Image in China, 1840–1900," p. 670.

7. Frederick Wells Williams, *Anson Burlingame and the First Chinese Mission to Foreign Powers*, pp. 103–104, declares flatly that Burlingame did not receive written instructions from the Tsungli Yamen. Knight Biggerstaff, "Anson Burlingame's Instructions from the Chinese Foreign Office," pp. 277–78, notes that the instructions were filed in the imperial archives but acknowledges that there is "some doubt that he [Burlingame] knew of their existence."

8. Tony Yung-yuan Teng, "Prince Kung and the Survival of the Ch'ing Rule, 1858–1898" (Ph.D. dissertation), p. 131.

9. The United States Department of State published both letters in 1868. See U.S., Department of State, *Foreign Relations of the United States*, 1868, Vol. 1, pp. 499–500, 602–603 (hereafter cited as FRUS, followed by the appropriate year).

10. Biggerstaff, "Anson Burlingame's Instructions," p. 278.

11. Burlingame to W. Seward, 14 December 1867, China Despatches. The Chinese documents state that the mandarins were to learn from this experience, but that injunction did not diminish their official standing.

12. FRUS, 1868, Vol. 1, p. 499.

13. Ibid., p. 602.

14. Biggerstaff, "Anson Burlingame's Instructions," p. 279; FRUS, 1868, Vol. 1, p. 601.

15. *Official Papers of the Chinese Legation*, p. 27.

16. Ibid.

17. Ibid., pp. 27–28.

18. Ibid.

19. William B. Reed to Williams, 4 August 1868, Samuel Wells Williams Family Papers, Yale University Library; Williams to Robert S. Wiliams, 29 September 1868, 28 October 1868, ibid.; Williams, *Burlingame*, pp. 139–44; W. A. P. Martin, *A Cycle of Cathay or China*, pp. 376–77; Foster Rhea Dulles, *China and America*, pp. 69–73.

20. Charles I. Bevans, ed., *Treaties and Other International Agreements of the United States of America, 1776–1949*, Vol. 6, pp. 680–84; Frederick W. Seward, *Reminiscences of a War-time Statesman and Diplomat, 1830–1915*, pp. 378–79.

21. Burlingame to Williams, 27 March 1869, Williams Family Papers.

22. *Official Papers of the Chinese Legation*, pp. 37–39.

23. Ibid., p. 39; William H. Seward, *Travels around the World*, p. 257.

24. Earl of Clarendon to Burlingame, 28 December 1868, Great Britain, Parliament, *Correspondence respecting the Relations between Great Britain and China*, pp. 1–2; Burlingame to Clarendon, 1 January 1869, ibid., p. 4.

25. Count Bismarck to Burlingame, 16 January 1870, *Official Papers of the Chinese Legation*, p. 55; Burlingame to George Bancroft, 17 January 1870, George Bancroft Papers, Massachusetts Historical Society.

26. Biggerstaff, "Official Chinese Attitude," pp. 696–97; Williams, *Burlingame*, pp. 172–76, 194–97, 242–49.

27. Williams, *Burlingame*, pp. 152–53; Biggerstaff, "Official Chinese Attitude," pp. 697–98; Tyler Dennett, *Americans in Eastern Asia*, pp. 383–89; Stanley F. Wright, *Hart and the Chinese Customs*, pp. 373–75. One of the most intemperate attacks on Burlingame's mission was Johannes von Gumpach, *The Burlingame Mission*.

28. Burlingame to Williams, 23 January 1870, Williams Family Papers.

29. Ibid. Italics are in the original.

30. Quoted in Lina Fergusson Browne, ed., *J. Ross Browne*, p. 330.

31. Ibid.; Frederick Wells Williams, *The Life and Letters of Samuel Wells Williams, LLD*, p. 377; Michael Goodman, *A Western Panorama, 1849–1875*, pp. 255–57; Burlingame to W. Seward, 14 December 1867, China Despatches; Burlingame to Williams, [April 1868,] Williams Family Papers; Cornelia W. Martin to Williams, 5 September 1868, ibid.

32. "Our New Minister to China," *San Francisco Newsletter and California Advertiser*, 1 August 1868; Browne, *J. Ross Browne*, pp. xiii–xix; Goodman, *A Western Panorama*, pp. 12–28; Richard H. Dillon, *J. Ross Browne*, pp. 3–18; Francis J. Rock, "J. Ross Browne: A Biography" (Ph.D. dissertation), pp. 1–7, 52–70; Lois Rather, *J. Ross Browne, Adventurer*, pp. 9–16.

33. Quoted in Dillon, *J. Ross Browne*, p. 206.

34. Quoted in Goodman, *A Western Panorama*, p. 256; ibid., pp. 28–54, 119, 161–78, 221–51; Dillon, *J. Ross Browne*, p. x; Rock, "J. Ross Browne," pp. 23–45.

35. J. Ross Browne to W. Seward, 28 October 1868, China Despatches; Browne, *J. Ross Browne*, p. 330; J. Ross Browne, "Under the Dragon's Footstool," *Overland Monthly* 6, no. 3 (March 1871): 233–43.

36. W. Seward to Browne, 8 September 1868, U.S., Department of State, Diplomatic Instructions of the Department of State, 1801–1906, China (hereafter cited as China Instructions).

37. Browne to W. Seward, 25 November 1868, China Despatches; Nathan A. Pelcovits, *Old China Hands and the Foreign Office*, pp. 66–67.

38. Browne to W. Seward, 25 November 1868, China Despatches; Mary Wright, *The Last Stand of Chinese Conservatism*, pp. 36–37.

39. Browne to W. Seward, 2 January 1869, China Despatches; J. Ross Browne, "Under the Dragon's Footstool," *Overland Monthly* 6, no. 3 (March 1871): 233–43.

40. Browne to W. Seward, 14 January 1869, China Despatches.

41. Fish to Burlingame, 17 September 1869, U.S., Department of State, Notes to Foreign Legations in the United States from the Department of State, 1834–1906, China; Burlingame to Fish, 3 September 1869, U.S., Department of State, Notes From the Chinese Legation in the United States to the Department of State, 1868–1906; Browne to Fish, 4 June 1869, China Despatches; Burlingame to Bancroft, 31 August 1869, Bancroft Papers.

42. Browne to Fish, 15 June 1869, China Despatches.

43. Browne to Fish, 23 June 1869, 30 June 1869, ibid.

44. Browne to Fish, 5 December 1868, ibid.; Curti and Stalker, "'Flowery Flag Devils,'" p. 669; Ssu-yü Teng and John K. Fairbank, *China's Response to the West*, pp. 61–67.

45. Browne to Fish, 5 December 1868, China Despatches.

46. Ibid.

47. W. C. Ralston to Burlingame, 20 February 1867, Burlingame Family Papers, Library of Congress (Burlingame wrote a memorandum of his answer in the margin of the letter); August Heard to Burlingame, 13 July 1865, ibid.; E. L. Beard to Burlingame, 31 March 1867, ibid.; Burlingame to W. Seward, 10 March 1865, 29 March 1867, China Despatches.

48. Burlingame to W. Seward, 22 May 1867, China Despatches; W. Seward to Burlingame, 21 January 1867, 11 February 1867, 5 April 1867, China Instructions.

49. Browne to W. Seward, 1 March 1869, China Despatches; Browne to Fish, 19 June 1869, ibid.

50. Browne to W. Seward, 28 January 1869, ibid.

51. Browne to W. Seward, 1 March 1869, ibid.

52. Browne to W. Seward, 26 November 1868, ibid.

53. Browne to Charles LeGendre, 5 June 1869, enclosed in Browne to Fish, 5 June 1869, ibid.; Browne to W. Seward, 26 January 1869, 18 February 1869, 1 March 1869, ibid.; Richard O'Conner, *Pacific Destiny*, p. 162.

54. Browne to LeGendre, 5 June 1869, enclosed in Browne to Fish, 5 June 1869, China Despatches.

55. Browne to Fish, 16 June 1869, ibid.

56. Browne to Fish, 15 June 1869, ibid.

57. Browne to W. Seward, 27 February 1869, ibid.; Browne to Fish, 16 June 1869, ibid.

58. Charles D. Poston to Browne, 25 April 1869, quoted in Browne, *J. Ross Browne*, p. 343. See also Charles D. Poston, "Reminiscences," pp. 8–9, unpublished manuscript, Arizona Historical Society Library.

59. Browne to Fish, 16 June 1869, China Despatches.

60. Ibid.; Williams, *Burlingame*, pp. 203–204, attributes Browne's change to his disappointment over not finding in China the opportunity for personal profit and reputation. This motive may have been a factor, but until Howard's nomination, Browne had avoided an open attack on current policy, and he later offered to return to China after learning that Howard would not be going to Peking. Rock, "J. Ross Browne," pp. 45–46; Burlingame to Williams, 13 August 1869 (confidential), Williams Family Papers.

61. Browne to Robert Hart, 28 June 1869, and Hart to Browne, 30 June 1869, with Browne's footnotes, enclosed in Browne to Fish, 20 August 1869, China Despatches; John King Fairbank, *Trade and Diplomacy on the China Coast*, p. 462; John King Fairbank, Katherine Frost Bruner, and Elizabeth MacLeod Matheson, eds., *The I. G. in Peking*, Vol. 1, p. 121.

62. Hart to Browne, 30 June 1869, with Browne's footnotes, enclosed in Browne to Fish, 20 August 1869, China Despatches; Wright, *Hart*, pp. 367–69.

63. Hart to Browne, 30 June 1869, with Browne's footnotes, enclosed in Browne to Fish, 20 August 1869, China Despatches.

64. Ibid.; Wright, *Hart*, pp. 369–70; Fairbank, Bruner, and Matheson, *I. G. in Peking*, Vol. 1, p. 51. The defiant tone of Browne's statements reappears consistently in his writings after his return to the United States. See Browne, "Under the Dragon's Footstool," *Overland Monthly* 6, no. 2 (February 1871): 155–64, and 6, no. 3 (March 1871): 233–43; J. Ross Browne, "Experiences in China," *San Francisco Daily Examiner*, 20, 22, 27, 29 December 1870, and 3, 5, 11 January 1871.

65. Browne to Fish, 15 June 1869, China Despatches.

66. Browne to Williams, 19 July 1869, Williams Family Papers; Browne to Fish, 3 July 1869, China Despatches; Browne to Williams, 20 July 1869, ibid.

67. Browne to Fish, 21 August 1869, China Despatches.

68. Ibid.

69. Burlingame to Williams, 13 August 1869 (confidential), Williams Family Papers.

70. Browne to Fish, 20 August 1869 (telegram), 30 August 1869 (unofficial), 14 February 1870, China Despatches; Poston to Browne, 25 April 1869, in Browne, *J. Ross Browne*, p. 344; Paul H. Clyde, "The China Policy of J. Ross Browne, American Minister to Peking, 1868–1869," p. 321; Dillon, *J. Ross Browne*, pp. 205–206; Rather, *J. Ross Browne*, pp. 81–93; Allan Nevins, *Hamilton Fish*, p. 249.

71. Williams to Robert S. Williams, 24 March 1870, Williams Family Papers; Clyde, "China Policy," p. 322; Samuel S. Kim, "America's First Minister to China: Anson Burlingame and the Tsungli Yamen," p. 91.

4. DISILLUSIONMENT AND FRUSTRATION

1. John K. Fairbank, Edwin O. Reischauer, and Albert M. Craig, *East Asia*, pp. 574–75; Mary Wright, *The Last Stand of Chinese Conservatism*, p. 297; Paul Cohen, *China and Christianity*, p. 233. Nathan A. Pelcovits, *Old China Hands and the Foreign Office*, p. 87, argues, on the other hand, that the Tientsin affair did not change British policy.

2. Wright, *Last Stand*, pp. 251–95. Pelcovits, *Old China Hands*, pp. 32–97, contends that nonratification did not mean that the British Foreign Office had abandoned moderation in its China policies, and Stanley F. Wright, *Hart and the Chinese Customs*, pp. 379–84, declares that the convention was "born of the Burlingame spirit of tolerance and reciprocity."

3. Fish to Bancroft, 31 August 1869, enclosed in Fish to Low, 3 December 1869, U.S., Department of State, Diplomatic Instructions of the Department of State, 1801–1906, China (hereafter cited as China Instructions); Seward to Browne, 8 September 1868, ibid.

4. G. Seward to Fish, 22 April 1870, U.S., Department of State, Despatches from United States Consuls in Shanghai, 1847–1906.

5. Pelcovits, *Old China Hands*, p. 57; Wright, *Last Stand*, p. 252; John King Fairbank, *Trade and Diplomacy on the China Coast*, p. 375; Alexander Michie, *The Englishman in China*, Vol. 1, pp. 129–35, 163, Vol. 2, pp. 194–222.

6. Fish to Low, 3 December 1869, China Instructions.

7. Fish to Bancroft, 31 August 1869, enclosed in ibid. This long treatise was a detailed description of the State Department's China policy and was sent originally to Bancroft, U.S. minister to Germany, in order that it could be given to Burlingame.

8. Ibid.

9. Ibid.

10. Fish to Burlingame, 24 December 1869, U.S., Department of State, Notes to Foreign Legations in the United States from the Department of State, 1834–1906, China.

11. Ibid.; Walter LaFeber, *The New Empire*, pp. 32–39.

12. H. Brett Melendy and Benjamin F. Gilbert, *The Governors of California*, pp. 129–30; Eli T. Sheppard, "Frederick Ferdinand Low, Ninth Governor of California," pp. 116–25, 133–40; Bancroft Davis to Low, 29 September 1869, China Instructions.

13. Melendy and Gilbert, *Governors of California*, pp. 130–31; Sheppard, "Low," pp. 140–42; Leo P. Kibby, "Union Loyalty of California's Civil War Governors," p. 318; Hubert Howe Bancroft, *History of California*, Vol. 7, pp. 303–304.

14. Melendy and Gilbert, *Governors of California*, pp. 133–38; Kibby, "Union Loyalty," p. 319; Joseph Ellison, *California and the Nation, 1850–1869*,

pp. 204–207; Theodore H. Hittell, *History of California*, Vol. 4, pp. 366–75, 405.

15. Quoted in Melendy and Gilbert, *Governors of California*, p. 133.

16. Ibid., p. 137; Sheppard, "Low," p. 126; Hittell, *History of California*, Vol. 4, p. 404.

17. Sheppard, "Low," pp. 113–14; Low to Fish, 8 October 1869, 20 April 1870, U.S., Department of State, Despatches from United States Ministers to China, 1843–1906, China (hereafter cited as China Despatches); Burlingame to Bancroft, 15 November 1869, George Bancroft Papers, Massachusetts Historical Society.

18. Low to Fish, 10 May 1870, China Despatches.

19. John King Fairbank, Katherine Frost Bruner, and Elizabeth MacLeod Matheson, eds., *The I. G. in Peking*, Vol. 1, p. 93.

20. Low to Fish, 27 July 1870, China Despatches.

21. Low to Fish, 27 June 1870, ibid. Over two years later, Low sent the State Department a copy of the "Annals of the Society of the Holy Childhood," which he identified as the organization that sponsored "Romish" orphanages in China. The document solicited money for the purchase of children in order that they could be baptized. It stated, for example, that "with every half crown that is sent to China one infant can be bought." Low commented: "That children are purchased for these orphanages there can, I think, be no longer any question." Low to Fish, 20 November 1872, ibid. See also Cohen, *China and Christianity*, pp. 229–73; Wright, *Last Stand*, pp. 295–97.

22. Low to Fish, 24 November 1870 (private and confidential), China Despatches.

23. Low to Fish, 27 July 1870 (private and confidential), ibid.

24. Low to Fish, 22 August 1870, ibid.

25. Low to Fish, 24 August 1870, ibid.

26. Low to Davis, 10 January 1871 (private), ibid.; Low to Fish, 17 September 1870, 26 September 1870, ibid.

27. Fish to Low, 29 November 1870, China Instructions. Fish also sought to insure Western solidarity following the Tientsin massacre when he initiated correspondence in Europe aimed at a suspension of hostilities in China between France and Prussia. The two European countries made such a move even before receiving Fish's suggestion. See U.S., Department of State, *Foreign Relations of the United States*, 1870, pp. 396–98 (hereafter cited as FRUS, followed by the appropriate year); Allan Nevins, *Hamilton Fish*, pp. 915–16.

28. Fish to Low, 22 September 1870 (personal), China Instructions; Davis to Low, 19 October 1871, ibid.

29. Henri Cordier, *Histoire des Relations de la Chine avec des Puissances Occidentales, 1860–1900*, Vol. 1, pp. 386–90.

30. Low to Fish, 28 September 1870, 25 October 1870, China Despatches; Cordier, *Histoire*, Vol. 1, pp. 383–86; Jerome Ch'en, *China and the West*, p. 142.

31. Low to Fish, 27 July 1870 (private and confidential), China Despatches.

32. Low to Fish, 20 February 1871 (confidential), ibid.

33. Ibid.

34. Ibid.

35. Low to Fish, 10 January 1871, ibid.

36. Ibid. Low was more than just the "careful observer" described by Paul H. Clyde, "Frederick F. Low and the Tientsin Massacre," pp. 100–108.

37. Low to Fish, 18 August 1870, 5 December 1870, 19 December 1871, China Despatches.

38. Low to Fish, 10 January 1871, ibid.

39. Low to Davis, 10 January 1871 (private), ibid.

40. Ibid.

41. Tyler Dennett, "Seward's Far Eastern Policy," pp. 45–62.

42. Fish to Low, 20 April 1870, China Instructions; Fish to Secretary of the Navy George M. Robeson, 4 April 1870, FRUS, 1870, pp. 331–33.

43. Low to Fish, 13 May 1870, China Despatches.

44. Ibid.; Low to Fish, 16 July 1870, 22 November 1870, 3 April 1871, ibid.

45. Low to Fish, 15 June 1871, ibid.

46. Ibid.; Low to Fish, 31 May 1871, 2 June 1871, ibid.; Fairbank, Bruner, and Matheson, *I. G. in Peking*, Vol. 1, p. 61.

47. Low to Fish, 20 June 1871, China Despatches.

48. Ibid.

49. Ibid.

50. For critical evaluations of the mission, see Tyler Dennett, *Americans in Eastern Asia*, p. 453; John W. Foster, *American Diplomacy in the Orient*, pp. 313–17. For an account more favorable to Low, see Sheppard, "Low," pp. 146–48. See also James A. Field, Jr., *History of United States Naval Operations: Korea*, pp. 1–4.

51. Low to Fish, 6 July 1871, China Despatches. Admiral Rodgers's account of the mission and its results essentially corresponds with that of Low. See Charles O. Paullin, *Diplomatic Negotiations of American Naval Officers, 1778–1883*, pp. 287–91.

52. John King Fairbank, "The Early Treaty System in the Chinese World Order," pp. 260–63.

53. Ibid.; Tseng-tsai Wang, "The Audience Question: Foreign Representatives and the Emperor of China, 1858–1873," pp. 623–26; Sheppard, "Low," pp. 144–45.

54. Low to Fish, 25 March 1872, China Despatches.

55. Low to Fish, 24 March 1873, 30 June 1873 (unofficial), 10 July 1873, ibid.

56. Low to Fish, 30 May 1872, 8 August 1873, ibid.; Fish to Low, 9 April 1874, China Instructions.

57. "James B. Angell Diaries concerning His Service in China from 1880 to 1881," Vol. 1, p. 13, James B. Angell Papers, Michigan Historical Collections of the University of Michigan; Sheppard, "Low," pp. 150–51; Melendy and Gilbert, *Governors of California*, p. 139.

58. Fairbank, Bruner, and Matheson, *I. G. in Peking*, Vol. 1, p. 187.

59. Benjamin P. Avery to Fish, 21 June 1874, 12 August 1874, 30 October 1874, 9 December 1874, China Despatches; Avery to Williams, 20 May 1874, Samuel Wells Williams Family Papers.

60. Ernest R. May, "Benjamin Parke Avery: Including a Review of the Office of State Printer, 1850–72," pp. 125–41; Fish to Avery, 7 May 1874, China Instructions; Andrew F. Rolle, *California*, p. 270.

61. Immanuel C. Y. Hsü, *China's Entrance into the Family of Nations*, p. 107; Immanuel C. Y. Hsü, *The Rise of Modern China*, p. 335.

62. Memorandum enclosed in Avery to Fish, 5 November 1874, China Despatches; Hsü, *Modern China*, pp. 386–90; John O. P. Bland, *Li Hungchang*, pp. 77–78, 157–58.

63. Memorandum enclosed in Avery to Fish, 5 November 1874, China Despatches.

64. Ibid.; Avery to Williams, 22 October 1874, Williams Family Papers.

65. Avery to Fish, 31 August 1875 (confidential), China Despatches.

66. Ibid.; Avery to Fish, 17 February 1875, 6 October 1875, ibid.; Nevins, *Hamilton Fish*, p. 915; J. O. P. Bland and E. Backhouse, *China under the Empress Dowager*, pp. 74–85.

67. Avery to Fish, 10 December 1874, 29 March 1875, 17 May 1875, 13 June 1875, 13 July 1875, China Despatches; Albert Feuerwerker, *China's Early Industrialization*, pp. 97–99, 172.

68. Avery to Fish, 12 November 1874, China Despatches.

69. Avery to Fish, 20 December 1874, ibid.

70. Ibid.

71. Ibid.

72. Ibid.

73. Avery to Fish, 27 January 1875, ibid.

74. Avery to Fish, 19 March 1875, ibid.

75. Ibid.; Avery to Fish, 28 February 1875, 14 May 1875, ibid.; Dennett, *Americans in Eastern Asia*, p. 592.

76. Cordier, *Histoire*, Vol. 1, pp. 557–65; Pelcovits, *Old China Hands*, p. 122; Arthur W. Hummel, ed., *Eminent Chinese of the Ch'ing Period (1644–1912)*, pp. 744–45; Samuel Wells Williams, *The Middle Kingdom*, Vol. 2, pp. 721–22.

77. Avery to Fish, 12 May 1875, 1 April 1875, China Despatches.

78. Avery to Fish, 12 May 1875, ibid.

79. Avery to Fish, 20 October 1875, ibid.

80. Ibid.

81. Ibid.; Chester Holcombe to Fish, 8 November 1875 (telegram), 10 November 1875, ibid.; May, "Avery," p. 141.

82. William H. Seward, *Travels around the World*, p. 216.

83. Ibid., p. 258.

5. THE DIPLOMACY OF EXPEDIENCY

1. Allen Johnson and Dumas Malone, eds., *Dictionary of American Biography*, Vol. 16, pp. 613–14; *Monthly Bulletin of the Fidelity and Casualty Company of New York*, pp. 6–7; Burlingame to W. Seward, 12 November 1862 (private), William Henry Seward Papers, University of Rochester Library; G. Seward to W. Seward, 20 November 1862, 8 December 1863, ibid.

2. G. Seward to W. Seward, 24 November 1863, U.S., Department of State, Despatches from United States Consuls in Shanghai, 1847–1906 (hereafter cited as Shanghai Despatches).

3. G. Seward to Browne, 22 January 1869, William Henry Seward Papers.

4. G. Seward to Davis, 16 February 1870, Shanghai Despatches; G. Seward to W. Seward, 15 June 1864, 16 February 1869, ibid.; G. Seward to Fish, 13 October 1870, ibid.; Jane Burlingame to Livermore, 10–11 April 1863, Burlingame Family Papers, Library of Congress.

5. G. Seward to Fish, 22 April 1870, Shanghai Despatches.

6. Ibid.

7. Ibid.

8. Ibid.

9. Ibid.

10. Low to Williams, 7 January 1876, 15 August 1876, Samuel Wells Williams Family Papers.

11. G. Seward to Davis, 26 May 1874, Shanghai Despatches.

12. G. Seward to Cadwalader, 25 November 1875 (telegram), ibid.

13. Quoted in Allan Nevins, *Hamilton Fish*, pp. 862–63.

14. Fish to G. Seward, 10 January 1876 (telegram), U.S., Department of State, Diplomatic Instructions of the Department of State, 1801–1906, China (hereafter cited as China Instructions); G. Seward to Fish, 9 November 1871 (telegram), Shanghai Despatches; G. Seward to Davis, 26 May 1874, ibid.; G. Seward to Cadwalader, 11 December 1875 (telegram), ibid.

15. G. Seward to Fish, 5 May 1876, U.S., Department of State, Despatches from United States Ministers to China, 1843–1906 (hereafter cited as China Despatches).

16. Ibid.; G. Seward to Fish, 6 May 1876, ibid.

17. Fish to G. Seward, 22 July 1876, China Instructions.

18. Ibid.; Fish to G. Seward, 19 December 1876, ibid.

19. G. Seward to Fish, 20 June 1876, 1 July 1876, 6 July 1876, China Despatches.

20. U.S., Department of State, *Foreign Relations of the United States*, 1877, pp. 74–77; Nathan A. Pelcovits, *Old China Hands and the Foreign Office*, p. 123; G. Seward to Fish, 8 August 1876, China Despatches. Mary Wright argues that the Chefoo Convention demonstrated unilateral treaty making similar to the treaties of 1858. See Mary Wright, *The Last Stand of Chinese Conservatism*, pp. 294–95. Immanuel Hsü contends, however, that Li successfully softened Wade's demands. See Immanuel C. Y. Hsü, *China's Entrance into the Family of Nations*, pp. 178–79.

21. G. Seward to Fish, 14 October 1876, China Despatches.

22. Ibid.; G. Seward to Fish, 3 October 1876, ibid.

23. G. Seward to Fish, 23 August 1876, 5 September 1876, ibid.; Hsü, *China's Entrance*, pp. 177–79; Stanley F. Wright, *Hart and the Chinese Customs*, pp. 410–11; John King Fairbank, Katherine Frost Bruner, and Elizabeth MacLeod Matheson, eds., *The I. G. in Peking*, Vol. 1, p. 422. Paul H. Clyde, "Attitudes and Policies of George F. Seward, American Minister at Peking, 1876–1880," p. 392, points out that Hart better understood how to deal with both the Chinese and the British than did Seward.

24. G. Seward to Fish, 30 October 1876, 22 November 1876, China Despatches; G. Seward to William M. Evarts, 12 July 1879, ibid.

25. T'ung-tsu Ch'ü, *Law and Society in Traditional China*, pp. 23–25, 40–41.

26. G. Seward to Fish, 5 December 1876, China Despatches; Seward to

Evarts, 12 May 1877, 18 September 1879, 18 November 1879, ibid.; Charles I. Bevans, ed., *Treaties and Other International Agreements of the United States of America, 1776–1949*, Vol. 6, pp. 690, 736–43.

27. G. Seward to Evarts, 21 November 1879, China Despatches.

28. Ibid.; G. Seward to Fish, 5 December 1876, ibid.; G. Seward to Evarts, 10 February 1880, ibid.; Clyde, "Attitudes and Policies," p. 404.

29. U.S., Congress, House, Report 134, 45th Cong., 3d sess., pp. 1–7.

30. Ibid., pp. 7–20; Frederick W. Seward, *Reminiscences of a War-time Statesman and Diplomat, 1830–1915*, p. 433; Evarts to G. Seward, 6 June 1877, China Instructions.

31. G. Seward to Fish, 4 April 1877 (separate and confidential), China Despatches.

32. Ibid.; G. Seward to Fish, 21 March 1877 (separate and confidential), 28 March 1877 (telegram), ibid.; G. Seward to Evarts, 17 May 1877, ibid.; Oliver B. Bradford to Campbell, 28 April 1877 (special), Shanghai Despatches.

33. G. Seward to Fish, 4 April 1877 (separate and confidential), China Despatches; G. Seward to Evarts, 12 July 1877, ibid.; G. Seward to Davis, 12 June 1871, 11 July 1871, Shanghai Despatches; G. Seward to Cadwalader, 1 October 1874, ibid.; John C. Myers to Campbell, 5 March 1877, 11 April 1877, ibid.; *New York Times*, 15 April 1878.

34. Myers to Cadwalader, 13 January 1877, 31 January 1877, Shanghai Despatches; G. Wiley Wells to Campbell, 23 October 1877, ibid.; U.S., Congress, House, Miscellaneous Document 31, 45th Cong., 2d sess., Vol. 1, pp. 11–13; Low to Williams, 27 September 1878, Williams Family Papers; *New York Times*, 10 December 1878.

35. *Congressional Record*, 45th Cong., 3d sess., pp. 2138–44; U.S., Congress, House, Report 141, 45th Cong., 3d sess.

36. G. Seward to Davis, 10 September 1873, Shanghai Despatches.

37. G. Seward to W. Seward, 27 May 1867, ibid.; G. Seward to Davis, 9 December 1871, 10 September 1873, 28 January 1874, ibid.; G. Seward to Cadwalader, 17 October 1874, ibid.; Tyler Dennett, *Americans in Eastern Asia*, p. 597; Ssu-yü Teng and John K. Fairbank, *China's Response to the West*, pp. 116–17.

38. G. Seward to Bradford, 2 February 1876, enclosed in G. Seward to Fish, 2 February 1876, China Despatches.

39. Ibid.; Fairbank, Bruner, and Matheson, *I. G. in Peking*, Vol. 1, p. 121.

40. Fish to G. Seward, 8 April 1876, China Instructions.

41. Ibid.; Avery to Fish, 12 November 1874, 18 March 1875, China Despatches; Dennett, *Americans in Eastern Asia*, p. 595.

42. G. Seward to Fish, 15 June 1876, 29 November 1876, China Despatches.

43. G. Seward to Fish, 29 November 1876, ibid.; G. Seward to Evarts, 16 October 1877, 21 December 1877, ibid.; Evarts to G. Seward, 14 November 1877, China Instructions; Wells to Campbell, 20 November 1877, Shanghai Despatches.

44. C. P. Blethen to G. Seward, 3 April 1877, enclosed in G. Seward to Fish, 4 April 1877 (separate and confidential), China Despatches.

45. Ibid.; G. Seward to Evarts, 8 May 1877, 29 June 1877, ibid.; Frederick Seward to G. Seward, 11 May 1877, China Instructions.

46. The final roll call vote was 106 yeas, 2 nays, and 182 not voting (79 of

that number absent). *Congressional Record*, 45th Cong., 3d sess., pp. 2349–85; *New York Times*, 5 March 1879.

47. For Myers's charges, see House, Miscellaneous Document 31, 45th Cong., 2d sess., Vol. 1, pp. 11–13. See also DeBenneville Randolph Keim, *A Report to the Hon. George S. Boutwell, Secretary of the Treasury, upon the Conditions of the Consular Service of the United States of America*, pp. 67–71, 124–28; Wells to Campbell, 23 October 1877, 20 November 1877, Shanghai Despatches; *New York Times*, 10 December 1878. For Seward's land holdings, see G. Seward to Evarts, 12 July 1877, China Despatches. Seward's personal files provide no information on his China career, because his "China papers" were "lost by fire." See G. Seward to Professor J. C. Schwab, 7 March 1897, George Frederick Seward Papers, New York Historical Society.

48. Neil L. Shumsky, "San Francisco's Workingmen Respond to the Modern City," pp. 46–51, and the accompanying pictorial history, "The Workingman's Party in California, 1877–1882," pp. 58–73; Roger Olmsted, "The Chinese Must Go!" pp. 285–94.

49. G. Seward to Fish, 22 March 1876, China Despatches.

50. The statistics on Chinese immigration are approximate. See Mary R. Coolidge, *Chinese Immigration*, pp. 425, 501; Elmer C. Sandmeyer, *The Anti-Chinese Movement in California*, p. 17.

51. Sandmeyer, *Anti-Chinese Movement*, pp. 25–39; Alexander Saxton, *The Indispensable Enemy*, pp. 258–65; Robert McClellan, *The Heathen Chinee*, pp. 1–6; Dennett, *Americans in Eastern Asia*, pp. 535–40; Stuart Creighton Miller, *The Unwelcome Immigrant*, pp. 3–15; Philip P. Choy, "Golden Mountain of Lead: The Chinese Experience in California," pp. 267–76.

52. G. Seward to Fish, 29 June 1876, China Despatches.

53. California, Legislature, Senate, Special Committee on Chinese Immigration, *Chinese Immigration*, pp. 6, 24.

54. Low to Williams, 16 June 1876, Williams Family Papers; Gary Pennanen, "Public Opinion and the Chinese Question, 1876–1879," p. 141.

55. Coolidge, *Chinese Immigration*, pp. 96–104, 132–33; John W. Foster, *American Diplomacy in the Orient*, pp. 283–93. For Sargent's report, see U.S., Congress, Senate, Report 689, 44th Cong., 2d sess. For Morton's notes, see U.S., Congress, Senate, Miscellaneous Document 20, 45th Cong., 2d sess.

56. G. Seward to Fish, 13 March 1878, China Despatches; Coolidge, *Chinese Immigration*, pp. 83–84, 114–16, 133–34; Pennanen, "Public Opinion," pp. 141–43.

57. G. Seward to Evarts, 22 March 1878, China Despatches; U.S., Congress, House, Report 240, 45th Cong., 2d sess.

58. G. Seward to Evarts, 22 March 1878, China Despatches.

59. *Congressional Record*, 45th Cong., 3d sess., pp. 791–801, 1264–76, 1299–316, 1383–400, 1796–97; U.S., Congress, House, Report 62, 45th Cong., 3d sess.

60. *New York Times*, 24 February 1879.

61. Pennanen, "Public Opinion," pp. 143–45.

62. T. Harry Williams, ed., *Hayes*, p. 189.

63. Ibid., pp. 187–89; James D. Richardson, comp., *A Compilation of the Messages and Papers of the Presidents*, Vol. 6, pp. 4466–72.

64. Williams, *Hayes*, p. 192 (emphasis added).

65. Evarts to G. Seward, 23 April 1879, China Instructions.

66. G. Seward to Evarts, 21 July 1879, China Despatches.

67. Ibid.

68. G. Seward to Evarts, 1 August 1879, ibid.

69. O. N. Denny to Angell, 10 August 1880, James B. Angell Papers, Michigan Historical Collections of the University of Michigan; "James B. Angell Diaries concerning His Service in China from 1880 to 1881," Vol. 1, p. 8, ibid.; Evarts to G. Seward, 27 December 1879 (telegram), 5 June 1880, China Instructions; G. Seward to Evarts, 26 January 1880, China Despatches; Commission to Evarts, 11 October 1880, ibid.

70. George F. Seward, *Chinese Immigration, in Its Social and Economical Aspects*, p. 158.

71. G. Seward to Davis, 18 July 1874, Shanghai Despatches.

72. Ibid.; G. Seward, *Chinese Immigration*, pp. v–vi, 11–13.

73. G. Seward to Evarts, 6 May 1880, China Despatches.

74. Ibid.; G. Seward to Evarts, 11 March 1876, ibid.; *Monthly Bulletin of the Fidelity and Casualty Company of New York*, pp. 8–12; *Insurance Press*, 4 December 1895.

6. ATTEMPTS AT AN INDEPENDENT POLICY

1. "James B. Angell Diaries concerning His Service in China from 1880 to 1881," Vol. 1, pp. 3, 59 (hereafter cited as Angell Diaries), James B. Angell Papers, Michigan Historical Collections of the University of Michigan.

2. Shirley W. Smith, *James Burrill Angell*, pp. 7–55, 267, 328.

3. Ibid., pp. 56–115; *New York Times*, 25 March 1880.

4. James Burrill Angell, *Reminiscences*, p. 131; Smith, *Angell*, pp. 116–22; Mary R. Coolidge, *Chinese Immigration*, p. 152.

5. Smith, *Angell*, pp. 118, 338–43; Angell Diaries, Vol. 1, pp. 69, 71, and passim, Angell Papers.

6. Smith, *Angell*, pp. 122–23; Coolidge, *Chinese Immigration*, p. 153.

7. Angell Diaries, Vol. 1, pp. 7–11, Angell Papers; Smith, *Angell*, pp. 124–25; Brainerd Dyer, *The Public Career of William M. Evarts*, p. 222.

8. Angell Diaries, Vol. 1, p. 8, Angell Papers.

9. Ibid., p. 9.

10. Evarts to Commission, 7 June 1880, 23 July 1880, U.S., Department of State, Diplomatic Instructions of the Department of State, 1801–1906, China (hereafter cited as China Instructions).

11. Angell Diaries, Vol. 1, pp. 17–18, Angell Papers.

12. William H. Trescot to Evarts, 3 September 1880, 21 August 1880, U.S., Department of State, Despatches from United States Ministers to China, 1843–1906 (hereafter cited as China Despatches).

13. Memorandum enclosed in Commission to Evarts, 11 October 1880, ibid.; Angell Diaries, Vol. 1, pp. 59–60, Angell Papers.

14. Commission to Evarts, 27 September 1880, 23 October 1880, China Despatches; Angell Diaries, Vol. 1, pp. 66–67, Angell Papers; Arthur W. Hummel, ed., *Eminent Chinese of the Ch'ing Period (1644–1912)*, pp. 472, 854–55.

15. Commission to Evarts, 3 November 1880, China Despatches; Angell Diaries, Vol. 1, pp. 70–72, Angell Papers.

16. Angell Diaries, Vol. 1, pp. 72–75, Angell Papers; Angell, *Reminiscences*, pp. 143–45; Commission to Evarts, 6 November 1880, China Despatches.

17. Angell to Alexis Angell, 14 August 1880, 21 November 1880, Angell Papers; Jerome Ch'en, *China and the West*, pp. 234, 254–55.

18. Charles I. Bevans, ed., *Treaties and Other International Agreements of the United States of America*, Vol. 6, pp. 685–87.

19. Commission to Evarts, 17 November 1880, China Despatches.

20. Angell Diaries, Vol. 1, p. 80, Angell Papers.

21. Commission to Evarts, 17 November 1880, China Despatches.

22. Ibid.; Bevans, *Treaties*, Vol. 6, pp. 688–90; Angell Diaries, Vol. 1, p. 77, Angell Papers.

23. E. V. G. Kiernan, *British Diplomacy in China, 1880 to 1885*, p. 277.

24. Angell, *Reminiscences*, p. 133; Smith, *Angell*, pp. 140–55, 195–205, 232–41, 251–71, 301–305.

25. Angell Diaries, Vol. 1, p. 80, Angell Papers.

26. Coolidge, *Chinese Immigration*, pp. 164–69.

27. *Congressional Record*, 47th Cong., 1st sess., p. 1739.

28. Thomas C. Reeves, *Gentleman Boss*, pp. 278–79; Coolidge, *Chinese Immigration*, pp. 169–78; U.S., Congress, Senate, Executive Document 148, 47th Cong., 1st sess.

29. Ch'en, *China and the West*, pp. 256–57.

30. John Russell Young, *Men and Memories*, Vol. 1, pp. 151–55, 164, 207, Vol. 2, pp. 294–96; David M. Pletcher, *The Awkward Years*, p. 198; *New York Tribune*, 14 March 1882.

31. "John Russell Young: His Life and Correspondence," unpublished manuscript, John Russell Young Papers, Library of Congress. The authorship of this four-volume manuscript is unknown, although the work appears to be largely autobiographical. Frederick T. Frelinghuysen to Ulysses S. Grant, 21 February 1882, ibid.

32. Tyler Dennett, "American Choices in the Far East in 1882," pp. 84–85; John Russell Young, *Around the World with General Grant*, Vol. 2, pp. 371–74, 432–33; Young, *Men and Memories*, Vol. 2, p. 325. For a detailed study of Young's diplomacy, see Victoria M. Cha-tsu Siu, "Sino-American Relations, 1882–1885: The Mission of John Russell Young" (Ph.D. dissertation).

33. Immanuel C. Y. Hsü, *The Ili Crisis*, pp. 1, 187–92; Hummel, *Eminent Chinese*, pp. 746–47.

34. Lloyd E. Eastman, *Throne and Mandarins*, pp. 104–105; Henri Cordier, *Histoire des Relations de la Chine avec des Puissances Occidentales, 1860–1900*, Vol. 2, p. 322; Tony Yung-yuan Teng, "Prince Kung and the Survival of the Ch'ing Rule, 1858–1898" (Ph.D. dissertation), pp. 146–66; J. O. P. Bland and E. Backhouse, *China under the Empress Dowager*, pp. 103–105.

35. John Russell Young to Frelinghuysen, 18 October 1882, China Despatches.

36. Young to Frelinghuysen, 6 December 1882, ibid.; Yen-p'ing Hao, *The Comprador in Nineteenth Century China*, pp. 1, 210; Hummel, *Eminent Chinese*, pp. 766–67.

37. Young to Frelinghuysen, 6 December 1882, China Despatches.

38. Ibid.

39. Ibid.

40. Ibid.

41. Ibid.; Young to Frelinghuysen, 21 December 1882, ibid.; Kiernan, *British Diplomacy*, p. 242; Ssu-yü Teng and John K. Fairbank, *China's Response to the West*, pp. 79–83.

42. Young to Frelinghuysen, 6 December 1882, China Despatches.

43. Ibid.

44. Young to Frelinghuysen, 19 December 1882, 6 December 1882, 12 December 1882, ibid.

45. Young to Frelinghuysen, 3 January 1883, 6 January 1883, ibid.

46. Young to Frelinghuysen, 4 January 1883, 19 January 1883, 30 January 1883, ibid.

47. Young to Frelinghuysen, 4 February 1883, ibid.

48. Ibid.

49. Ibid.

50. Frelinghuysen to Young, 26 February 1883, China Instructions; Frelinghuysen to Young, 27 February 1883 (private), Young Papers.

51. Young to Frelinghuysen, 4 February 1883, China Despatches.

52. Young to Frelinghuysen, 25 August 1883, 27 April 1883, ibid.; Pletcher, *Awkward Years*, pp. 202–205, describes Young's concern about future American interests in China but does not note the minister's final decision.

53. Young to Admiral Pierce Crosby, 8 May 1883, Young Papers.

54. John F. Cady, *The Roots of French Imperialism in Eastern Asia*, pp. 267–96; Joseph Buttinger, *Vietnam*, pp. 75–98.

55. Eastman, *Throne and Mandarins*, pp. 57–84; Cordier, *Histoire*, Vol. 2, pp. 362–66, 393–99; John O. P. Bland, *Li Hung-chang*, pp. 145–49.

56. Young to Frelinghuysen, 8 August 1883, China Despatches.

57. Ibid.

58. Frelinghuysen to Young, 4 August 1883 (telegram), 12 July 1883 (telegram), China Instructions; Young to Frelinghuysen, 5 July 1883 (telegram), 16 August 1883, China Despatches; Hummel, *Eminent Chinese*, pp. 467–68; Pletcher, *Awkward Years*, pp. 214–15; Eastman, *Throne and Mandarins*, pp. 108–73.

59. Young to Frelinghuysen, 8 October 1883, 24 December 1883, 9 December 1884, China Despatches; Young to Li Hung-chang, 15 August 1883, Young Papers.

60. "John Russell Young Diary," 23 October 1883, Young Papers.

61. Quoted in "John Russell Young: His Life and Correspondence," Vol. 4, p. 27, ibid.; "Young Diary," 19 April 1883, 2 August 1883, 13 October–31 December 1883, ibid.

62. Young to Frelinghuysen, 20 July 1884 (telegram), 30 July 1884 (telegram), 21 August 1884, 23 September 1884 (telegram), 9 December 1884, China Despatches; Frelinghuysen to Young, 23 July 1884 (telegram), 5 August 1884 (telegram), 13 September 1884 (telegram), 7 November 1884 (telegram), China Instructions; Nathan A. Pelcovits, *Old China Hands and the Foreign Office*, pp. 142–49; Kiernan, *British Diplomacy*, pp. 148–59, 310–11; Stanley F. Wright, *Hart and the Chinese Customs*, pp. 513–32; Pletcher, *Awkward Years*,

pp. 216–17; Bland, *Li Hung-chang*, pp. 149–54; Cordier, *Histoire*, Vol. 2, pp. 452–76; Hummel, *Eminent Chinese*, pp. 48, 245–46, 527; China, Imperial Maritime Customs, *Treaties, Conventions, etc., between China and Foreign States*, Vol. 1, pp. 897–907.

63. Young to Frelinghuysen, 18 June 1884, 22 December 1884, China Despatches; Eastman, *Throne and Mandarins*, pp. 85–107; Teng, "Prince Kung," pp. 192–94; Bland and Backhouse, *China under the Empress Dowager*, pp. 105–106.

64. Young to Frelinghuysen, 8 August 1883, China Despatches.

65. Young to Frelinghuysen, 22 December 1884, 24 December 1883, 10 January 1885, ibid.

66. Young to Frelinghuysen, 24 December 1883, ibid.

67. Ibid.; Young to Frelinghuysen, 8 August 1883, 11 September 1884, ibid.; Paul A. Varg, *Open Door Diplomat*, p. 11.

68. Young to Frelinghuysen, 22 December 1884, China Despatches; Young to James Young, 16 December 1884, Young Papers.

69. Young, *Men and Memories*, Vol. 2, p. 312.

70. Ibid.; Young to Frelinghuysen, 4 September 1884, 9 December 1884, China Despatches; Pletcher, *Awkward Years*, pp. 216–17.

71. Quoted in Young to Frelinghuysen, 26 December 1884, China Despatches.

72. Ibid.

73. Young to Frelinghuysen, 27 January 1885, ibid.; Thomas F. Bayard to Young, 30 March 1885 (telegram), China Instructions; David Mearns, *The Story Up to Now*, pp. 136–66; "John Russell Young: His Life and Correspondence," Vol. 4, pp. 30–33, Young Papers.

7. TWO CHINA POLICIES

1. Charles Denby, *China and Her People*, Vol. 1, pp. ix–xii; Charles Callan Tansill, *The Foreign Policy of Thomas F. Bayard, 1885–1897*, pp. 422–23; David Healy, *US Expansionism*, p. 179.

2. Denby, *China and Her People*, Vol. 1, pp. v, xv; Tyler Dennett, *Americans in Eastern Asia*, p. 548; Jeffery M. Dorwart, *The Pigtail War*, p. 11.

3. Paul A. Varg, *Open Door Diplomat*, pp. 12–13; Charles Denby to William W. Rockhill, 10 May 1886, 9 January 1887, 11 March 1887, 6 April 1887, William Woodville Rockhill Papers, Houghton Library, Harvard University; Denby to Bayard, [January?] 1887, ibid.; Denby to Bayard, 18 December 1885, U.S., Department of State, Despatches from United States Ministers to China, 1843–1906 (hereafter cited as China Despatches).

4. Denby, *China and Her People*, Vol. 1, pp. 7–8.

5. Ibid., Vol. 1, pp. 7–11, Vol. 2, pp. 21, 87–88; Julius Pratt, *The Expansionists of 1898*, pp. 5–20; Walter LaFeber, *The New Empire*, pp. 99–100.

6. Denby, *China and Her People*, Vol. 2, pp. 88–89.

7. Ibid., pp. 89–90.

8. Ibid., p. 90.

9. Denby to Bayard, 20 July 1888, 8 March 1886, 14 October 1886, China

Despatches; Denby to John Sherman, 15 March 1897, ibid.; Bayard to Denby, 15 December 1887, U.S., Department of State, Diplomatic Instructions of the Department of State, 1801–1906, China (hereafter cited as China Instructions); Denby, *China and Her People*, Vol. 1, pp. 91–99; Healy, *US Expansionism*, p. 180.

10. Denby to Bayard, 3 June 1887, 13 July 1886, 12 January 1887, 25 March 1887, 5 April 1887, China Despatches; Denby, *China and Her People*, Vol. 2, p. 41; Tansill, *Bayard*, p. 424; Marilyn Blatt Young, *The Rhetoric of Empire*, pp. 34–52; James H. Wilson, *China*, pp. xi, 294.

11. Denby to Bayard, 17 September 1888, 19 September 1888, 21 September 1888, 23 September 1888, 22 October 1888, 1 December 1888, China Despatches; Denby, *China and Her People*, Vol. 2, p. 97; Mary R. Coolidge, *Chinese Immigration*, pp. 188–202; Tansill, *Bayard*, pp. 137–81; Dennett, *Americans in Eastern Asia*, pp. 546–47; John A. S. Grenville and George Berkeley Young, *Politics, Strategy, and American Diplomacy*, pp. 54–63.

12. Manuscript of remarks made by George Seward, no date, filed with 1894 correspondence, George Frederick Seward Papers, New York Historical Society.

13. Denby to John W. Foster, 3 November 1892, China Despatches; Denby to Walter Q. Gresham, 2 June 1894, ibid.; Coolidge, *Chinese Immigration*, pp. 202–40; Dennett, *Americans in Eastern Asia*, pp. 547–49; Alice Felt Tyler, *The Foreign Policy of James G. Blaine*, pp. 255–61.

14. Denby to Bayard, 18 December 1885, 25 February 1887, China Despatches; Denby, *China and Her People*, Vol. 2, pp. 9–15, 28–31, 42–43; Paul A. Varg, *The Making of a Myth*, pp. 14–16; Charles S. Campbell, Jr., *Special Business Interests and the Open Door Policy*, pp. 1–9; Thomas J. McCormick, *China Market*, pp. 21–52; LaFeber, *New Empire*, pp. 176–96.

15. Richard Olney to Denby, 22 June 1895, China Instructions.

16. Ibid.; Gresham to Denby, 15 April 1895 (telegram), ibid.; Denby to Gresham, 26 December 1894, 5 March 1895, China Despatches; Dennett, *Americans in Eastern Asia*, pp. 579–81; Dorwart, *Pigtail War*, p. 35.

17. Olney to Denby, 19 December 1896, China Instructions.

18. Ibid.; Denby to Olney, 5 November 1896, China Despatches.

19. Denby to Olney, 10 January 1897, 15 February 1897, ibid.; Sherman to Denby, 8 March 1897, China Instructions; William R. Braisted, "The United States and the American China Development Company," pp. 147–50; Campbell, *Special Business Interests*, pp. 26–29; Dennett, *Americans in Eastern Asia*, p. 602; Young, *Rhetoric of Empire*, pp. 64–68, 88–92; McCormick, *China Market*, pp. 74–76, 87–89, overstates when he labels the lame-duck Cleveland administration's efforts a "major turning point" in American China policy.

20. Campbell, *Special Business Interests*, pp. 10–11; Dennett, *Americans in Eastern Asia*, pp. 579–82; William Woodruff, *America's Impact on the World*, pp. 159–60, 268–69.

21. Denby to Bayard, 1 October 1888, China Despatches; Denby to Olney, 29 January 1897, ibid.; Denby to Sherman, 20 October 1897, ibid.; Healy, *US Expansionism*, p. 183; Varg, *Making of a Myth*, p. 50; David M. Pletcher, "Rhetoric and Results: A Pragmatic View of American Economic Expansionism, 1865–98," pp. 101–105; John William Cassey, "The Mission of Charles

Denby and International Rivalries in the Far East, 1885–1898" (Ph.D. dissertation), p. 295.

22. Denby, *China and Her People*, Vol. 1, p. 234.

23. Denby to Gresham, 22 March 1895, China Despatches.

24. Denby, *China and Her People*, Vol. 1, p. 220.

25. Denby to Gresham, 22 March 1895, China Despatches; Denby to Bayard, 9 October 1886, ibid.; Paul A. Varg, *Missionaries, Chinese, and Diplomats*, pp. 84–85.

26. John King Fairbank, Katherine Frost Bruner, and Elizabeth MacLeod Matheson, eds., *The I. G. in Peking*, Vol. 2, p. 845.

27. *Official Papers of the Chinese Legation*, p. 27.

28. Varg, *Missionaries, Chinese, and Diplomats*, pp. 12–13; Edmund S. Wehrle, *Britain, China, and the Antimissionary Riots, 1891–1900*, pp. 12–15; Kenneth Scott Latourette, *A History of Christian Missions in China*, pp. 329, 405–407, 479, 537–38; Thomas A. Breslin, *China, American Catholicism, and the Missionary*, pp. 15–18.

29. Denby, *China and Her People*, Vol. 1, p. 225.

30. Denby to James G. Blaine, 14 March 1892, China Despatches.

31. Ibid.; Denby to Bayard, 13 February 1889, ibid.; Denby, *China and Her People*, Vol. 2, p. 71; Varg, *Missionaries, Chinese, and Diplomats*, p. 41.

32. Denby to Blaine, 5 December 1891, 19 November 1889, 26 January 1890, China Despatches; Denby to Bayard, 10 October 1887, 13 April 1888, ibid.; Denby to Rockhill, 20 May 1886, 6 September 1886, Rockhill Papers.

33. Denby, *China and Her People*, Vol. 2, p. 91.

34. Denby to Bayard, 31 July 1886, 21 September 1886, 20 December 1886, China Despatches; Bayard to Denby, 25 September 1886, China Instructions.

35. Denby to Blaine, 20 May 1891, 27 May 1891, 24 October 1891, 5 March 1892, China Despatches; Denby to Bayard, 18 January 1889, ibid.; Varg, *Missionaries, Chinese, and Diplomats*, p. 38; Wehrle, *Britain, China, and the Antimissionary Riots*, pp. 19–28.

36. Denby to Blaine, 8 June 1891, China Despatches.

37. Blaine to Denby, 25 November 1891 (telegram), China Instructions.

38. Denby to Blaine, 14 August 1891, 17 September 1891, 31 December 1891, 30 January 1892, China Despatches.

39. Denby to Olney, 3 August 1895, ibid.

40. Denby to Edwin F. Uhl, 20 June 1895, ibid.; Denby to Olney, 19 August 1895, ibid.; Varg, *Missionaries, Chinese, and Diplomats*, pp. 39–41.

41. Olney did not rule out the use of force in all cases but would not approve it in this particular situation. Olney to Denby, 10 August 1895, China Instructions.

42. Denby, *China and Her People*, Vol. 2, p. 75.

43. Adee to Denby, 19 July 1895, China Instructions; Rockhill to Charles Denby, Jr., 28 July 1896, ibid.; Olney to Denby, 25 November 1896, ibid.

44. Denby to Olney, 15 August 1895, 26 July 1895, 19 August 1895, China Despatches. Young, *Rhetoric of Empire*, pp. 79–80, implies erroneously that Denby abandoned support for an international investigation after receiving the missionaries' petition in July. For example, she quotes Denby's telegram to Olney (13 August 1895, U.S., Department of State, *Foreign Relations of the United States*, 1895, p. 104 [hereafter cited as FRUS, followed by the appro-

priate year]): "Will you appoint a commission of Americans exclusively to investigate Szechuan riots as asked by Americans in China?" She omits the last part of the telegram: "or create international commission?"

45. Quoted in Wehrle, *Britain, China, and the Antimissionary Riots*, p. 95.

46. Contrary to Gérard's allegations, British policy was to seek protection of missionaries without a burdensome involvement in China's internal affairs. Ibid., pp. 28–44; Denby to Olney, 30 September 1895, China Despatches; FRUS, 1895, pp. 173–89; George E. Paulson, "The Szechwan Riots of 1895 and American 'Missionary Diplomacy,'" pp. 285–98.

47. Adee to Denby, 12 August 1895 (telegram), China Instructions.

48. Olney to Denby, 17 September 1895 (telegram), ibid.

49. Olney to Denby, 19 September 1895, China Instructions; Dennett, *Americans in Eastern Asia*, p. 500. For an analysis of the Cleveland-Olney policy on Venezuela, see Charles S. Campbell, Jr., *The Transformation of American Foreign Relations, 1865–1900*, pp. 198–205; Charles S. Campbell, Jr., *From Revolution to Rapprochement*, pp. 175–81.

50. Olney to Denby, 19 September 1895, China Instructions.

51. Edwin O. Reischauer, *Japan*, pp. 114–47.

52. Hilary Conroy, *The Japanese Seizure of Korea*, pp. 65–67, 107–11, 169–260; Arthur W. Hummel, ed., *Eminent Chinese of the Ch'ing Period (1644–1912)*, pp. 468–69.

53. Gresham to Bayard, 20 July 1894, FRUS, 1894, Appendix 1, p. 37.

54. Ibid., pp. 36–39; John M. B. Sill to Gresham, 25 June 1894, 29 June 1894, ibid., pp. 24–28; Denby, Jr. to Gresham, 6 July 1894, 8 July 1894, China Despatches; Payson J. Treat, *Diplomatic Relations between the United States and Japan, 1853–1895*, Vol. 2, pp. 457–66; Dorwart, *Pigtail War*, pp. 11, 20–26; Dennett, *Americans in Eastern Asia*, p. 489.

55. Gresham to Denby, 24 November 1894, China Instructions.

56. Ibid.; Gresham to Denby, 6 November 1894 (two telegrams), ibid.; Denby to Gresham, 3 November 1894 (telegram), 4 November 1894, 10 November 1894, China Despatches; W. E. Goschen to Gresham, 6 October 1894, FRUS, 1894, Appendix 1, p. 70; Gresham to Goschen, 12 October 1894, ibid.; Gresham to Edwin Dun, 6 November 1894, ibid., p. 76; *Journal of Commerce and Commercial Bulletin*, 17 November 1894, 9 April 1895, 4 October 1895; *Washington Post*, 11 November 1894, 12 December 1894, 15 December 1894; Dorwart, *Pigtail War*, pp. 73–76; William L. Langer, *The Diplomacy of Imperialism, 1890–1902*, pp. 174–75.

57. Denby to Thomas Edgar Garvin, 24 November 1894, in David M. Silver, ed., "Charles Denby and the Sino-Japanese War, 1894–1895," pp. 285–88.

58. Ibid.; Denby to Gresham, 31 October 1894, 4 November 1894, 8 December 1894, 26 February 1895, China Despatches; Young, *Rhetoric of Empire*, pp. 20–21, 30–31.

59. Denby to Gresham, 22 November 1894, 23 November 1894 (telegram), 19 February 1895 (telegram), China Despatches; FRUS, 1895, pp. 199–203; Hummel, *Eminent Chinese*, pp. 469–70; Dorwart, *Pigtail War*, pp. 76–88; Treat, *United States and Japan*, Vol. 2, pp. 498–530.

60. Denby, *China and Her People*, Vol. 2, pp. 147–48.

61. Conroy, *Japanese Seizure of Korea*, pp. 285–92; Langer, *Diplomacy of Imperialism*, pp. 180–87.

62. Denby to Sherman, 9 March 1898, 29 March 1898, 5 April 1898, 20 April 1898, China Despatches; Varg, *Making of a Myth*, pp. 19–21; Langer, *Diplomacy of Imperialism*, pp. 445–80; Pelcovits, *Old China Hands*, pp. 220–24.

63. Denby, *China and Her People*, Vol. 2, pp. 1–2, 23–24, 92–96, 166.

64. Denby to Sherman, 31 January 1898, China Despatches.

65. Denby to Sherman, 3 April 1898, ibid.; Sherman to Denby, 25 March 1898, China Instructions; Campbell, *Special Business Interests*, p. 30; Denby, *China and Her People*, Vol. 2, p. 152; Charles Denby, Jr., "America's Opportunity in Asia," pp. 32–39.

66. Denby, *China and Her People*, Vol. 2, p. 238.

67. McCormick, *China Market*, pp. 89–115; Campbell, *Transformation of American Foreign Relations*, pp. 280–95; Allen Johnson and Dumas Malone, eds., *Dictionary of American Biography*, Vol. 5, p. 234.

68. Denby, *China and Her People*, Vol. 2, pp. 237, 151–52.

69. Paul A. Varg, "The Myth of the China Market, 1890–1914," pp. 742–58; Marilyn Blatt Young, "American Expansion, 1870–1900: The Far East," p. 186; Samuel Flagg Bemis, ed., *The American Secretaries of State and Their Diplomacy*, Vol. 8, pp. vii–ix.

70. Denby, *China and Her People*, Vol. 2, p. 235.

71. Ibid., pp. 234–35.

72. These choices are suggested in Michael H. Hunt, *Frontier Defense and the Open Door*, pp. 25–29. See also Michael H. Hunt, *The Making of a Special Relationship*, pp. 177–81.

8. EPILOGUE

1. U.S., Department of State, *Foreign Relations of the United States*, 1900, p. 299 (hereafter cited as FRUS, followed by appropriate year).

2. H. Wayne Morgan, *William McKinley and His America*, p. 400.

3. Kenton J. Clymer, *John Hay*, pp. 86–91, 143–44; Tyler Dennett, *John Hay*, p. 286.

4. Edwin H. Conger to John Hay, 3 November 1898, U.S., Department of State, Despatches from United States Ministers to China, 1843–1906 (hereafter cited as China Despatches).

5. Conger to Hay, 1 March 1899, ibid.

6. *New York Times*, 8 March 1899.

7. Ibid., 8 March 1899, 14 April 1899, 14 May 1899; Conger to Hay, 26 November 1898, 30 November 1898, China Despatches; Dennett, *John Hay*, p. 288; Charles S. Campbell, Jr., *Special Business Interests and the Open Door Policy*, pp. 50–51.

8. *New York Times*, 4 August 1899.

9. Campbell, *Special Business Interests*, pp. 10–18, 30–44; Thomas J. McCormick, *China Market*, p. 131.

10. Charles Denby, *China and Her People*, Vol. 2, pp. 237–38.

11. Ibid., p. 240; *New York Times*, 2 May 1899, 26 October 1899; H. Wayne Morgan, *America's Road to Empire*, pp. 100, 109.

12. William L. Langer, *The Diplomacy of Imperialism, 1890–1902*, pp. 682–86; Nathan A. Pelcovits, *Old China Hands and the Foreign Office*, pp. 241–42, 301–302; Chester C. Tan, *The Boxer Catastrophe*, pp. 30–31.

13. *New York Times*, 16 August 1899.

14. McCormick, *China Market*, pp. 140–43; Marilyn Blatt Young, *The Rhetoric of Empire*, pp. 125–26.

15. Hay to Rockhill, 24 August 1899, John Hay Papers, Library of Congress; A. Whitney Griswold, *The Far Eastern Policy of the United States*, pp. 62–75; George F. Kennan, *American Diplomacy, 1900–1950*, pp. 23–32; Young, *Rhetoric of Empire*, pp. 123–31; Stanley F. Wright, *Hart and the Chinese Customs*, p. 785; Paul A. Varg, *Open Door Diplomat*, pp. 26–32; Dennett, *John Hay*, pp. 289–91; U.S., Congress, House, Document 547, 56th Cong., 1st sess.

16. A. R. Colquhoun to Hay, 12 January 1899, Hay Papers; McCormick, *China Market*, p. 144; Dennett, *John Hay*, p. 198; Graham H. Stuart, *The Department of State*, p. 207.

17. Hay to Paul Dana, 16 March 1899, Hay Papers; Hay to Conger, 4 March 1899, U.S., Department of State, Diplomatic Instructions of the Department of State, 1801–1906, China (hereafter cited as China Instructions).

18. Memorandum of reply to British embassy, [March 1898,] Hay Papers; Sherman to Denby, 25 March 1898, China Instructions; Dennett, *John Hay*, pp. 188–89, 285–86; Clymer, *John Hay*, pp. 86–91.

19. Hay to Foster, 23 June 1900, Hay Papers. Although Hay wrote this letter several months after the first Open Door Note was sent, he expressed similar views in a letter to Andrew White, 9 September 1899, ibid.

20. Rockhill to Hay, 28 August 1899, ibid.; Hay to Andrew White, 9 September 1899, ibid.; Rockhill to Alfred E. Hippisley, 3 August 1899, William Woodville Rockhill Papers, Houghton Library, Harvard University; Charles S. Campbell, Jr., *Anglo-American Understanding, 1898–1903*, pp. 1–13, 161–66.

21. FRUS, 1899, pp. 131–33; Rockhill to Hay, 3 August 1899, 28 August 1899, Hay Papers; Rockhill to Adee, 19 August 1899, ibid.; Hay to Rockhill, 24 August 1899, ibid.; Hippisley to Rockhill, 21 August 1899, Rockhill Papers; Clymer, *John Hay*, p. 147; McCormick, *China Market*, pp. 144–45; Varg, *Open Door Diplomat*, pp. 32–33; Harvey Pressman, "Hay, Rockhill, and China's Integrity: A Reappraisal," pp. 71–73.

22. FRUS, 1899, pp. 141–42.

23. Ibid., pp. 128–43.

24. Hay to Joseph H. Choate, 13 November 1899, Hay Papers; Hay to Wu Ting-fang, 11 November 1899, ibid.; Michael H. Hunt, *The Making of a Special Relationship*, pp. 190–97.

25. George F. Seward, "The Open Door," *Monthly Bulletin of the Fidelity and Casualty Company of New York*, 14 February 1900, George Frederick Seward Papers, New York Historical Society.

26. FRUS, 1899, pp. 132, 140–41.

27. Hay to Henry White, 2 April 1900, Hay Papers.

28. Dennett, *John Hay*, pp. 293–95, 317; Campbell, *Anglo-American Understanding*, pp. 168–69.

29. Secretary of Agriculture James Wilson, quoted in *New York Times*, 6 January 1900.

30. S. Chamberlain to Hay, 23 June 1900, Hay Papers; James J. Hooker to Hay, 26 June 1900, ibid.; Hay to Andrew White, 9 September 1899, ibid.; Dennett, *John Hay*, pp. 298–99; Marilyn Blatt Young, "American Expansion,

1870–1900: The Far East," p. 197; Henry Cranbrook Allen, *Great Britain and the United States*, p. 588.

31. Quoted in Li Chien-nung, *The Political History of China, 1840–1928*, p. 167.

32. Ibid., pp. 155–73; Frederick Wakeman, Jr., *The Fall of Imperial China*, pp. 206–216.

33. Li, *Political History of China*, pp. 173–79; Wakeman, *Fall of Imperial China*, pp. 216–21; Tan, *Boxer Catastrophe*, pp. 75–83, 93–116.

34. Hay to "My Dear Boy," 1 July 1900, Hay Papers; *New York Times*, 4 July 1900, 5 July 1900; Dennett, *John Hay*, pp. 298–301; Thomas Beer, *Hanna*, pp. 234–35; Ernest R. May, *American Imperialism*, pp. 209–210; Göran Rystad, *Ambiguous Imperialism*, pp. 211–14.

35. FRUS, 1900, p. 299.

36. Hay to Henry Adams, 8 July 1900, Hay Papers; J. H. Woodward to Hay, 22 July 1900, ibid.; Dennett, *John Hay*, pp. 302–307; May, *American Imperialism*, pp. 210–11.

37. Choate to Hay, 20 June 1900, 27 June 1900, Hay Papers; Hay to Henry Adams, 15 June 1900, ibid.; Hay to Foster, 23 June 1900, ibid.; Hay to Conger, 10 June 1900 (telegram), China Instructions.

38. Hay to Henry Adams, 15 June 1900, Hay Papers.

39. FRUS, 1900, p. 299.

40. Hay to St. Clair McKelway, 12 July 1900, Hay Papers.

41. Hay to J. F. Goodnow, 1 July 1900, ibid.; Hay to Henry Adams, 8 July 1900, ibid.; Hay to Choate, 17 July 1900, ibid.; Dennett, *John Hay*, pp. 308–309, 323; Clymer, *John Hay*, pp. 148–51; John King Fairbank, *The United States and China*, pp. 314–23; Pressman, "Hay, Rockhill, and China's Integrity," p. 72; Foster Rhea Dulles, "John Hay (1898–1905)," pp. 30–33; James A. LeRoy, *The Americans in the Philippines*, Vol. 2, p. 217.

42. Brooks Adams to Hay, 17 August 1900, Hay Papers.

43. Patrick A. Curtis to Hay, 5 July 1900, ibid.

44. Denby, *China and Her People*, Vol. 2, pp. 59–63; Michael H. Hunt, *Frontier Defense and the Open Door*, pp. 32–33.

45. Josiah Quincy, "China and Russia," *North American Review* 171 (October 1900), excerpted in Norman A. Graebner, ed., *Ideas and Diplomacy*, pp. 373–77.

46. William Appleman Williams, *The Tragedy of American Diplomacy*, p. 38; Kennan, *American Diplomacy*, p. 36.

47. Kennan, *American Diplomacy*, pp. 32–37; Griswold, *Far Eastern Policy*, pp. 62–76; Young, *Rhetoric of Empire*, pp. 123–36, 230–31; John A. S. Grenville and George Berkeley Young, *Politics, Strategy, and American Diplomacy*, pp. 308–309.

48. McCormick, *China Market*, p. 128; Williams, *Tragedy of American Diplomacy*, pp. 39–43, 300; Campbell, *Special Business Interests*, pp. 53–74; Walter LaFeber, *The New Empire*, pp. 407–417; Robert L. Beisner, *From the Old Diplomacy to the New, 1865–1900*, pp. 28–33, 126–39; Ian J. Bickerton, "John Hay's Open Door Policy: A Re-examination," pp. 54–66; James C. Thomson, Jr., Peter W. Stanley, and John Curtis Perry, *Sentimental Imperialists*, pp. 121–33.

49. Hay to Henry Adams, 8 July 1900, Hay Papers.

50. Quoted in Dennett, *John Hay,* p. 320.

51. Quoted in ibid., p. 321.

52. Hay to Dana, 16 March 1899, Hay Papers.

53. Hay to Conger, 10 March 1899, China Instructions; Paul A. Varg, *The Making of a Myth,* pp. 50–53; Beisner, *Old Diplomacy to the New,* pp. 17–26; Hunt, *Frontier Defense,* p. 34.

54. Tyler Dennett, *Americans in Eastern Asia,* p. 678, asserts, on the contrary, that "the principles of American policy were entirely consistent from the days of [William] Seward onward." Hunt, *Making of a Special Relationship,* pp. 170–76, also discerns a "remarkable consistency" in the persistent paternalism of American diplomats in China.

55. Akira Iriye, *Across the Pacific,* pp. 80–82; Raymond A. Esthus, "The Changing Concept of the Open Door, 1899–1910," pp. 435–54; Hunt, *Making of a Special Relationship,* pp. 181–83.

56. *Congressional Record,* 56th Cong., 1st sess., pp. 704–12.

57. Langer, *Diplomacy of Imperialism,* pp. 67–96; May, *American Imperialism,* pp. 172–91; Graebner, *Ideas and Diplomacy,* pp. vii–xi; H. Wayne Morgan, *America's Road to Empire,* pp. 110–15; Julius Pratt, *The Expansionists of 1898,* pp. 293–98; Williams, *Tragedy of American Diplomacy,* pp. 53–56; Wolfgang Franke, *China and the West,* pp. 126–28; Arthur A. Ekirch, Jr., *Ideas, Ideals, and American Diplomacy,* pp. 79–99; Edward McNall Burns, *The American Idea of Mission,* pp. 3–32, 262–66; Thomson, Stanley, and Perry, *Sentimental Imperialists,* p. 311.

BIBLIOGRAPHY

Government Documents

Bevans, Charles I., ed. *Treaties and Other International Agreements of the United States of America, 1776–1949*. Washington: U.S. Government Printing Office, 1968–72.

California. Legislature. Senate. Special Committee on Chinese Immigration. *Chinese Immigration: The Social, Moral, and Political Effect of Chinese Immigration*. Sacramento: State Printing Office, 1876.

China. Imperial Maritime Customs. *Treaties, Conventions, etc., between China and Foreign States*. Shanghai: Inspectorate General of Customs, 1908.

Great Britain. Parliament. *Correspondence respecting the Relations between Great Britain and China*. China, no. 1 (1869).

Keim, DeBenneville Randolph. *A Report to the Hon. George S. Boutwell, Secretary of the Treasury, upon the Conditions of the Consular Service of the United States of America*. Washington: U.S. Government Printing Office, 1872.

Richardson, James D., comp. *A Compilation of the Messages and Papers of the Presidents*. Washington: Bureau of National Literature, 1913.

U.S. Congress. *Congressional Globe*, 34th Cong., 1st sess.; and 35th Cong., 1st sess.

————. *Congressional Record*, 45th Cong., 3d sess.; 47th Cong., 1st sess.; and 56th Cong., 1st sess.

————. House. Document 547, 56th Cong., 1st sess.

————. House. Miscellaneous Document 31, 45th Cong., 2d sess.

————. House. Report 62, 45th Cong., 3d sess.

————. House. Report 134, 45th Cong., 3d sess.

————. House. Report 141, 45th Cong., 3d sess.

————. House. Report 240, 45th Cong., 2d sess.

————. Senate. Executive Document 148, 47th Cong., 1st sess.

————. Senate. Miscellaneous Document 20, 45th Cong., 2d sess.

————. Senate. Report 689, 44th Cong., 2d sess.

U.S. Department of the Navy. Area File of the Naval Records Collection, 1775–1910. Naval Records Collection of the Office of Naval Records and Library, Record Group 45, National Archives.

————. Letters Received by the Secretary of the Navy from Commanding Officers of Squadrons, 1841–1886. Naval Records Collection of the Office of Naval Records and Library, Record Group 45, National Archives.

U.S. Department of State. Despatches from United States Consuls in Shanghai, 1847–1906. General Records of the Department of State, Record Group 59, National Archives.

————. Despatches from United States Ministers to China, 1843–1906. General Records of the Department of State, Record Group 59, National Archives.

————. Diplomatic Instructions of the Department of State, 1801–1906, China. General Records of the Department of State, Record Group 59, National Archives.

————. Diplomatic Instructions of the Department of State, 1801–1906, Great Britain. General Records of the Department of State, Record Group 59, National Archives.

————. *Foreign Relations of the United States.* Washington: U.S. Government Printing Office, 1861–1900.

————. Notes from the Chinese Legation in the United States to the Department of State, 1868–1906. General Records of the Department of State, Record Group 59, National Archives.

————. Notes to Foreign Legations in the United States from the Department of State, 1834–1906, China. General Records of the Department of State, Record Group 59, National Archives.

Manuscript Collections

Adams Family Papers. Massachusetts Historical Society.

Angell, James B., Papers. Michigan Historical Collections of the University of Michigan.

Bancroft, George, Papers. Massachusetts Historical Society.

Burlingame Family Papers. Library of Congress.

Burlingame Family Papers. Syracuse University Library.

Hay, John, Papers. Library of Congress.

Poston, Charles D. "Reminiscences." Arizona Historical Society Library.

Rockhill, William Woodville, Papers. Houghton Library, Harvard University.

Seward, George Frederick, Papers. New York Historical Society.

Seward, William Henry, Papers. University of Rochester Library.

Williams, Samuel Wells, Family Papers. Yale University Library.

Young, John Russell, Papers. Library of Congress.

Newspapers

Boston Daily Advertiser. 1854, 1860.

Insurance Press. 1895.

Journal of Commerce and Commercial Bulletin (New York). 1894–1895.

New York Times. 1878–1880, 1899–1900.

New York Tribune. 1884.

North China Herald (Shanghai). 1867.

San Francisco Daily Examiner. 1870–1871.

San Francisco Newsletter and California Advertiser. 1868.

Washington Post. 1894.

Books

Allen, Henry Cranbrook. *Great Britain and the United States: A History of Anglo-American Relations (1783–1952).* London: Odhams Press, 1954.

Angell, James Burrill. *Reminiscences.* New York: Longmans, Green, & Co., 1912.

Arlington, L. C., and Lewisohn, William. *In Search of Old Peking*. Peking: Henri Vetch, 1935.

Bancroft, Hubert Howe. *History of California*. San Francisco: History Co., 1890.

Beer, Thomas. *Hanna*. New York: Alfred A. Knopf, 1929.

Beisner, Robert L. *From the Old Diplomacy to the New, 1865–1900*. New York: Thomas Y. Crowell Co., 1975.

Bemis, Samuel Flagg, ed. *The American Secretaries of State and Their Diplomacy*. New York: Alfred A. Knopf, 1928.

Bland, John O. P. *Li Hung-chang*. Freeport, N.Y.: Books for Libraries Press, 1971.

Bland, J. O. P., and Backhouse, E. *China under the Empress Dowager: Being the History of the Life and Times of Tzu Hsi*. Boston: Houghton Mifflin Co., 1914.

Bredon, Juliet. *Peking: A Historical and Intimate Description of Its Chief Places of Interest*. Shanghai: Kelly & Walsh, 1922.

Breslin, Thomas A. *China, American Catholicism, and the Missionary*. University Park, Pa.: Pennsylvania State University Press, 1980.

Browne, Lina Fergusson, ed. *J. Ross Browne: His Letters, Journals, and Writings*. Albuquerque: University of New Mexico Press, 1969.

Burns, Edward McNall. *The American Idea of Mission: Concepts of National Purpose and Destiny*. New Brunswick, N.J.: Rutgers University Press, 1957.

Buttinger, Joseph. *Vietnam: A Political History*. New York: Praeger, 1968.

Cady, John F. *The Roots of French Imperialism in Eastern Asia*. Ithaca, N.Y.: Cornell University Press, 1954.

Campbell, Charles S., Jr. *Anglo-American Understanding, 1898–1903*. Baltimore: Johns Hopkins Press, 1957.

———. *From Revolution to Rapprochement: The United States and Great Britain, 1783–1900*. New York: John Wiley & Sons, 1974.

———. *Special Business Interests and the Open Door Policy*. New Haven: Yale University Press, 1951.

———. *The Transformation of American Foreign Relations, 1865–1900*. New York: Harper & Row, 1976.

Ch'en, Jerome. *China and the West: Society and Culture, 1815–1937*. Bloomington: Indiana University Press, 1979.

Ch'ü, T'ung-tsu. *Law and Society in Traditional China*. Paris and The Hague: Mouton & Co., 1961.

Clymer, Kenton J. *John Hay: The Gentleman as Diplomat*. Ann Arbor: University of Michigan Press, 1975.

Cohen, Paul. *China and Christianity: The Missionary Movement and the Growth of Chinese Antiforeignism, 1860–1870*. Cambridge: Harvard University Press, 1963.

Cohen, Warren I. *America's Response to China: An Interpretative History of Sino-American Relations*. 2d ed. New York: John Wiley & Sons, 1980.

Conger, Sarah Pike. *Letters from China*. Chicago: A. C. McClurg & Co., 1909.

Conroy, Hilary. *The Japanese Seizure of Korea: 1868–1910*. Philadelphia: University of Pennsylvania Press, 1960.

Coolidge, Mary R. *Chinese Immigration.* New York: Henry Holt & Co., 1909.

Cordier, Henri. *Histoire des Relations de la Chine avec des Puissances Occidentales, 1860–1900.* Paris: Felix Alcan, 1901–02.

Dean, Britten. *China and Great Britain: The Diplomacy of Commercial Relations, 1860–1864.* Cambridge: Harvard University Press, 1974.

Denby, Charles. *China and Her People.* Boston: L. C. Page & Co., 1906.

Dennett, Tyler. *Americans in Eastern Asia: A Critical Study of the Policy of the United States with Reference to China, Japan, and Korea in the Nineteenth Century.* New York: Macmillan Co., 1922.

———. *John Hay: From Poetry to Politics.* Port Washington, N.Y.: Kennikat Press, 1963.

Dillon, Richard H. *J. Ross Browne: Confidential Agent in Old California.* Norman: University of Oklahoma Press, 1965.

Dorwart, Jeffery M. *The Pigtail War: American Involvement in the Sino-Japanese War of 1894–1895.* Amherst: University of Massachusetts Press, 1975.

Dulles, Foster Rhea. *China and America.* Princeton: Princeton University Press, 1946.

Dyer, Brainerd. *The Public Career of William M. Evarts.* Berkeley: University of California Press, 1933.

Eastman, Lloyd E. *Throne and Mandarins: China's Search for a Policy during the Sino-French Controversy, 1880–1885.* Cambridge: Harvard University Press, 1967.

Ekirch, Arthur A., Jr. *Ideas, Ideals, and American Diplomacy: A History of Their Growth and Interaction.* New York: Appleton-Century-Crofts, 1966.

Ellison, Joseph. *California and the Nation, 1850–1869.* Berkeley: University of California Press, 1927.

Fairbank, John King. *China Perceived: Images and Policies in Chinese-American Relations.* New York: Alfred A. Knopf, 1974.

———. *Trade and Diplomacy on the China Coast: The Opening of the Treaty Ports, 1842–1854.* Stanford: Stanford University Press, 1969.

———. *The United States and China.* 4th ed. Cambridge: Harvard University Press, 1979.

Fairbank, John King; Bruner, Katherine Frost; and Matheson, Elizabeth MacLeod, eds. *The I. G. in Peking: Letters of Robert Hart, Chinese Maritime Customs, 1868–1907.* Cambridge: Harvard University Press, Belknap Press, 1975.

Fairbank, John K.; Reischauer, Edwin O.; and Craig, Albert M. *East Asia: Tradition and Transformation.* Boston: Houghton Mifflin Co., 1978.

Feuerwerker, Albert. *China's Early Industrialization: Shang Hsuan-huai (1844–1916) and Mandarin Enterprise.* Cambridge: Harvard University Press, 1958.

Field, James A., Jr. *History of United States Naval Operations: Korea.* Washington: U.S. Government Printing Office, 1962.

Foster, John W. *American Diplomacy in the Orient.* Boston: Houghton Mifflin Co., 1903.

Franke, Wolfgang. *China and the West: The Cultural Encounter, Thirteenth to Twentieth Centuries.* Translated by R. A. Wilson. New York: Harper Torchbooks, 1967.

Gerson, Jack J. *Horatio Nelson Lay and Sino-British Relations, 1854–1864.* Cambridge: Harvard University Press, 1972.

Gilbert, Felix. *The Beginnings of American Foreign Policy: To the Farewell Address.* New York: Harper Torchbooks, 1965.

Goetzmann, William H. *When The Eagle Screamed: The Romantic Horizon in American Diplomacy, 1800–1860.* New York: John Wiley & Sons, 1966.

Goodman, Michael. *A Western Panorama, 1849–1875: The Travels, Writings, and Influence of J. Ross Browne on the Pacific Coast, and in Texas, Nevada, Arizona, and Baja California, as the First Mining Commissioner, and Minister to China.* Glendale, Calif.: Arthur H. Clark Co., 1966.

Graebner, Norman A., ed. *Ideas and Diplomacy: Readings in the Intellectual Tradition of American Foreign Policy.* New York: Oxford University Press, 1964.

Grenville, John A. S., and Young, George Berkeley. *Politics, Strategy, and American Diplomacy: Studies in Foreign Policy, 1873–1917.* New Haven: Yale University Press, 1966.

Griswold, A. Whitney. *The Far Eastern Policy of the United States.* New Haven: Yale University Press, 1962.

Gumpach, Johannes von. *The Burlingame Mission.* Shanghai: [no publisher], 1872.

Hao, Yen-p'ing. *The Comprador in Nineteenth Century China: Bridge between East and West.* Cambridge: Harvard University Press, 1970.

Heald, Morrell, and Kaplan, Lawrence S. *Culture and Diplomacy: The American Experience.* Westport, Conn.: Greenwood Press, 1977.

Healy, David. *US Expansionism: The Imperialist Urge in the 1890's.* Madison: University of Wisconsin Press, 1970.

Hittell, Theodore H. *History of California.* San Francisco: N. J. Stone & Co., 1897.

Holcombe, Chester. *The Real Chinaman.* New York: Dodd, Mead & Co., 1895.

Hsü, Immanuel C. Y. *China's Entrance into the Family of Nations.* Cambridge: Harvard University Press, 1960.

———. *The Ili Crisis: A Study of Sino-Russian Diplomacy, 1871–1881.* Oxford: Clarendon Press, 1965.

———. *The Rise of Modern China.* 2d ed. New York: Oxford University Press, 1975.

Hummel, Arthur W., ed. *Eminent Chinese of the Ch'ing Period (1644–1912).* Washington: U.S. Government Printing Office, 1943.

Hunt, Michael H. *Frontier Defense and the Open Door: Manchuria in Chinese-American Relations, 1895–1911.* New Haven: Yale University Press, 1973.

———. *The Making of a Special Relationship: The United States and China to 1914.* New York: Columbia University Press, 1983.

Iriye, Akira. *Across the Pacific: An Inner History of American-East Asian Relations.* New York: Harcourt Brace Jovanovich, 1967.

Johnson, Allen, and Malone, Dumas, eds. *Dictionary of American Biography.* New York: Charles Scribner's Sons, 1928–36.

Kammen, Michael. *People of Paradox: An Inquiry concerning the Origins of American Civilization.* New York: Vintage Books, 1973.

Kennan, George F. *American Diplomacy, 1900–1950.* Chicago: University of Chicago Press, 1951.

Kiernan, E. V. G. *British Diplomacy in China, 1880 to 1885.* New York: Octagon Books, 1970.

Kossuth in New England. Boston: John P. Jewett & Co., 1852.

LaFeber, Walter. *The New Empire: An Interpretation of American Expansion.* Ithaca, N.Y.: Cornell University Press for the American Historical Association, 1963.

Langer, William L. *The Diplomacy of Imperialism, 1890–1902.* 2d ed. New York: Alfred A. Knopf, 1951.

Latourette, Kenneth Scott. *A History of Christian Missions in China.* New York: Macmillan Co., 1929.

LeRoy, James A. *The Americans in the Philippines: A History of the Conquest and First Years of Occupation with an Introductory Account of the Spanish Rule.* New York: AMS Press, 1970.

Li Chien-nung. *The Political History of China, 1840–1928.* Translated and edited by Ssu-yü Teng and Jeremy Ingalls. Stanford: Stanford University Press, 1967.

Lucid, Robert F., ed. *The Journal of Richard Henry Dana, Jr.* Cambridge: Harvard University Press, Belknap Press, 1968.

McClellan, Robert. *The Heathen Chinee.* Columbus: Ohio State University Press, 1971.

McCormick, Thomas J. *China Market: America's Quest for Informal Empire, 1893–1901.* Chicago: Quadrangle Books, 1967.

Martin, W. A. P. *A Cycle of Cathay or China.* New York: Fleming H. Revell Co., 1900.

Mason, Mary Gertrude. *Western Concepts of China and the Chinese.* New York: Russell & Russell, 1939.

May, Ernest R. *American Imperialism: A Speculative Essay.* New York: Atheneum, 1968.

Mearns, David. *The Story Up to Now: The Library of Congress, 1800–1946.* Washington: U.S. Government Printing Office, 1947.

Melendy, H. Brett, and Gilbert, Benjamin F. *The Governors of California: Peter H. Burnett to Edmund G. Brown.* Georgetown, Calif.: Talisman Press, 1965.

Merk, Frederick. *Manifest Destiny and Mission in American History.* New York: Vintage Books, 1966.

Michael, Franz. *The Taiping Rebellion: History.* Seattle: University of Washington Press, 1966.

Michie, Alexander. *The Englishman in China.* Edinburgh: William Blackwood & Sons, 1900.

Miller, Stuart Creighton. *The Unwelcome Immigrant: The American Image of the Chinese, 1785–1882.* Berkeley: University of California Press, 1969.

Morgan, H. Wayne. *America's Road to Empire: The War with Spain and Overseas Expansion.* New York: John Wiley & Sons, 1965.

————. *William McKinley and His America.* Syracuse: Syracuse University Press, 1963.

Nevins, Allan. *Hamilton Fish: The Inner History of the Grant Administration.* New York: Dodd, Mead & Co., 1936.

O'Conner, Richard. *Pacific Destiny: An Informal History of U.S. in the Far East, 1776–1968.* Boston: Little, Brown & Co., 1969.

Official Papers of the Chinese Legation. Berlin: S. Calvary & Co., [1870].

Paullin, Charles O. *Diplomatic Negotiations of American Naval Officers, 1778–1883.* Baltimore: Johns Hopkins Press, 1912.

Pelcovits, Nathan A. *Old China Hands and the Foreign Office.* New York: King's Crown Press for the American Institute of Pacific Relations, 1948.

Plesur, Milton. *America's Outward Thrust: Approaches to Foreign Affairs, 1865–1890.* DeKalb, Ill.: Northern Illinois University Press, 1971.

Pletcher, David M. *The Awkward Years: American Foreign Relations under Garfield and Arthur.* Columbia: University of Missouri Press, 1962.

Pratt, Julius. *The Expansionists of 1898: The Acquisition of Hawaii and the Spanish Islands.* Baltimore: Johns Hopkins Press, 1936.

Pumpelly, Raphael. *My Reminiscences.* New York: Henry Holt & Co., 1918.

Rather, Lois. *J. Ross Browne, Adventurer.* Oakland, Calif.: Rather Press, 1978.

Reeves, Thomas C. *Gentleman Boss: The Life of Chester Alan Arthur.* New York: Alfred A. Knopf, 1975.

Reischauer, Edwin O. *Japan: The Story of a Nation.* New York: Alfred A. Knopf, 1970.

Robinson, William Stevens. *"Warrington" Pen Portraits.* Edited by Mrs. W. S. Robinson. Boston: Mrs. W. S. Robinson, 1887.

Rolle, Andrew F. *California: A History.* New York: Thomas Y. Crowell Co., 1969.

Rystad, Göran. *Ambiguous Imperialism: American Foreign Policy and Domestic Politics at the Turn of the Century.* [Stockholm]: Esselte Studium, 1975.

Sandmeyer, Elmer C. *The Anti-Chinese Movement in California.* Urbana: University of Illinois Press, 1939.

Saxton, Alexander. *The Indispensable Enemy: Labor and the Anti-Chinese Movement in California.* Berkeley: University of California Press, 1971.

Seward, Frederick W. *Reminiscences of a War-time Statesman and Diplomat, 1830–1915.* New York: G. P. Putnam's Sons, 1916.

Seward, George F. *Chinese Immigration, in Its Social and Economical Aspects.* New York: Charles Scribner's Sons, 1881.

Seward, William H. *Travels around the World.* Edited by Olive Risley Seward. New York: D. Appleton & Co., 1873.

Smith, Richard J. *Mercenaries and Mandarins: The Ever-Victorious Army of Nineteenth Century China.* Millwood, N.Y.: KTO Press, 1978.

Smith, Shirley W. *James Burrill Angell: An American Influence.* Ann Arbor: University of Michigan Press, 1954.

Stuart, Graham H. *The Department of State: A History of Its Organization, Procedures, and Personnel.* New York: Macmillan Co., 1949.

Swisher, Earl. *China's Management of the American Barbarians: A Study of Sino-American Relations, 1841–1861, with Documents.* New Haven: Far Eastern Publications for the Far Eastern Association, 1951.

———. *Chinese Representation in the United States, 1861–1912.* University of Colorado Studies, Series in History, no. 5. Boulder: University of Colorado Press, 1967.

Tan, Chester C. *The Boxer Catastrophe*. New York: W. W. Norton & Co., 1971.
Tansill, Charles Callan. *The Foreign Policy of Thomas F. Bayard, 1885–1897*. New York: Fordham University Press, 1940.
Teng, Ssu-yü, and Fairbank, John K. *China's Response to the West: A Documentary Survey, 1839–1923*. New York: Atheneum, 1968.
Thomson, James C., Jr.; Stanley, Peter W.; and Perry, John Curtis. *Sentimental Imperialists: The American Experience in East Asia*. New York: Harper & Row, 1981.
Tong, Te-kong. *United States Diplomacy in China, 1844–60*. Seattle: University of Washington Press, 1964.
Treat, Payson J. *Diplomatic Relations between the United States and Japan, 1853–1895*. Stanford: Stanford University Press, 1932.
Tyler, Alice Felt. *The Foreign Policy of James G. Blaine*. Minneapolis: University of Minnesota Press, 1927.
Van Alstyne, Richard W. *Genesis of American Nationalism*. Waltham, Mass.: Blaisdell Publishing Co., 1970.
Varg, Paul A. *The Making of a Myth: The United States and China, 1897–1912*. East Lansing: Michigan State University Press, 1968.
———. *Missionaries, Chinese, and Diplomats: The American Protestant Missionary Movement in China, 1890–1952*. Princeton: Princeton University Press, 1958.
———. *Open Door Diplomat: The Life of W. W. Rockhill*. Illinois Studies in the Social Sciences 33:4. Urbana: University of Illinois Press, 1952.
Wakeman, Frederick, Jr. *The Fall of Imperial China*. New York: Free Press, 1975.
Wehrle, Edmund S. *Britain, China, and the Antimissionary Riots, 1891–1900*. Minneapolis: University of Minnesota Press, 1966.
Welter, Rush. *The Mind of America, 1820–1860*. New York: Columbia University Press, 1975.
Williams, Frederick Wells. *Anson Burlingame and the First Chinese Mission to Foreign Powers*. New York: Charles Scribner's Sons, 1912.
———. *The Life and Letters of Samuel Wells Williams, LLD*. New York: G. P. Putnam's Son, 1889.
Williams, Samuel Wells. *The Middle Kingdom*. New York: Charles Scribner's Sons, 1883.
Williams, T. Harry, ed. *Hayes: The Diary of a President, 1875–1881*. New York: David McKay Co., 1964.
Williams, William Appleman. *The Tragedy of American Diplomacy*. Rev. ed. New York: Delta, 1962.
Wilson, Henry. *History of the Rise and Fall of the Slave Power in America*. Boston: James R. Osgood & Co., 1874.
Wilson, James H. *China: Travels and Investigations in the "Middle Kingdom."* New York: D. Appleton & Co., 1887.
Woodruff, William. *America's Impact on the World: A Study of the Role of the United States in the World Economy, 1750–1970*. New York: John Wiley & Sons, 1975.
Wright, Mary. *The Last Stand of Chinese Conservatism: The T'ung-Chih Restoration, 1862–1874*. New York: Atheneum, 1967.

Wright, Stanley F. *Hart and the Chinese Customs.* Belfast: Wm. Mullan & Sons for the Queen's University, 1950.

Young, John Russell. *Around the World with General Grant.* New York: American News Co., 1879.

———. *Men and Memories.* Edited by Mary D. Russell Young. New York: F. Tennyson Neely, 1901.

Young, Marilyn Blatt. *The Rhetoric of Empire: American China Policy, 1895–1901.* Cambridge: Harvard University Press, 1968.

Articles

Bickerton, Ian J. "John Hay's Open Door Policy: A Re-examination." *Australian Journal of Politics and History* 23, no. 1 (April 1977): 54–66.

Biggerstaff, Knight. "Anson Burlingame's Instructions from the Chinese Foreign Office." *Far Eastern Quarterly* 1, no. 3 (May 1942): 277–79.

———. "The Official Chinese Attitude toward the Burlingame Mission." *American Historical Review* 41, no. 4 (July 1936): 682–702.

———. "The Secret Correspondence of 1867–1868: Views of Leading Chinese Statesmen regarding the Further Opening of China to Western Influence." *Journal of Modern History* 22, no. 2 (June 1950): 122–36.

Braisted, William R. "The United States and the American China Development Company." *Far Eastern Quarterly* 11, no. 2 (February 1952): 147–65.

Browne, J. Ross. "Under the Dragon's Footstool." *Overland Monthly* 6, no. 2 (February 1871): 155–64, and 6, no. 3 (March 1871): 233–43.

Campbell, James E. "Sumner-Brooks-Burlingame or the Last of the Great Challenges." *Ohio Archeological and Historical Quarterly* 24 (1925): 435–73.

Choy, Philip P. "Golden Mountain of Lead: The Chinese Experience in California." *California Historical Quarterly* 50, no. 3 (September 1971): 267–76.

Clyde, Paul H. "Attitudes and Policies of George F. Seward, American Minister at Peking, 1876–1880." *Pacific Historical Review* 2, no. 4 (December 1933): 387–404.

———. "The China Policy of J. Ross Browne, American Minister to Peking, 1868–1869." *Pacific Historical Review* 1, no. 3 (September 1932): 312–33.

———. "Frederick F. Low and the Tientsin Massacre." *Pacific Historical Review* 2, no. 1 (March 1933): 100–108.

Curti, Merle, and Stalker, John. "'The Flowery Flag Devils'—The American Image in China, 1840–1900." *Proceedings of the American Philosophical Society* 96, no. 6 (December 1952): 663–90.

Denby, Charles, Jr. "America's Opportunity in Asia." *North American Review* 166 (January 1898): 32–39.

Dennett, Tyler. "American Choices in the Far East in 1882." *American Historical Review* 30, no. 1 (October 1924): 84–108.

———. "Seward's Far Eastern Policy." *American Historical Review* 28, no. 1 (October 1922): 45–62.

Dulles, Foster Rhea. "John Hay (1898–1905)." In *An Uncertain Tradition: American Secretaries of State in the Twentieth Century,* edited by Norman A. Graebner. New York: McGraw-Hill Book Co., 1961.

Esthus, Raymond A. "The Changing Concept of the Open Door, 1899–1910." *Mississippi Valley Historical Review* 46, no. 3 (December 1959): 434–54.

Fairbank, John King. "The Early Treaty System in the Chinese World Order." In *The Chinese World Order*, edited by John King Fairbank. Cambridge: Harvard University Press, 1968.

———. "A Preliminary Framework." In *The Chinese World Order*, edited by John King Fairbank. Cambridge: Harvard University Press, 1968.

Field, James A., Jr. "American Imperialism: The Worst Chapter in Almost Any Book." *American Historical Review* 83, no. 3 (June 1978): 644–68.

Hofstadter, Richard. "Manifest Destiny and the Philippines." In *America in Crisis*, edited by Daniel Aaron. New York: Alfred A. Knopf, 1952.

Iriye, Akira. "Imperialism in East Asia." In *Modern East Asia: Essays in Interpretation*, edited by James B. Crowley. New York: Harcourt, Brace & World, 1970.

Kibby, Leo P. "Union Loyalty of California's Civil War Governors." *California Historical Society Quarterly* 44, no. 4 (December 1965): 311–21.

Kim, Samuel S. "America's First Minister to China: Anson Burlingame and the Tsungli Yamen." *Maryland Historian* 3 (Fall 1972): 87–104.

———. "Burlingame and the Inauguration of the Cooperative Policy." *Modern Asian Studies* 5, no. 4 (October 1971): 337–54.

Liu, Kwang-ching. "America and China: The Late Nineteenth Century." In *American-East Asian Relations: A Survey*, edited by Ernest R. May and James C. Thomson, Jr. Cambridge: Harvard University Press, 1972.

Mancall, Mark. "The Persistence of Tradition in Chinese Foreign Policy." *Annals of the American Academy of Political and Social Sciences* 349 (September 1963): 16–22.

May, Ernest R. "Benjamin Parke Avery: Including a Review of the Office of State Printer, 1850–72." *California Historical Society Quarterly* 30, no. 2 (June 1951): 125–49.

Monthly Bulletin of the Fidelity and Casualty Company of New York 16, no. 1 (January 1911): 6–12.

Olmsted, Roger. "The Chinese Must Go!" *California Historical Quarterly* 50, no. 3 (September 1971): 285–94.

Paulson, George E. "The Szechwan Riots of 1895 and American 'Missionary Diplomacy.'" *Journal of Asian Studies* 28, no. 2 (February 1969): 285–98.

Pennanen, Gary. "Public Opinion and the Chinese Question, 1876–1879." *Ohio History* 77, nos. 1, 2, 3 (Winter, Spring, Summer 1968): 139–48.

Pletcher, David M. "Rhetoric and Results: A Pragmatic View of American Economic Expansionism, 1865–98." *Diplomatic History* 5, no. 2 (Spring 1981): 93–105.

Pressman, Harvey. "Hay, Rockhill, and China's Integrity: A Reappraisal." *Papers on China* 13 (Harvard University, East Asian Research Center, 1959): 61–79.

Rawlinson, John L. "The Lay-Osborn Flotilla: Its Development and Significance." *Papers on China* 4 (Harvard University, East Asian Research Center, 1950): 58–93.

Ring, Martin R. "The Burgevine Case and Extrality in China, 1863–1866." *Papers on China* 20 (Harvard University, East Asian Research Center, 1969): 136–48.

Sheppard, Eli T. "Frederick Ferdinand Low, Ninth Governor of California." *University of California Chronicle* 19, no. 2 (April 1917): 109–53.

Shumsky, Neil L. "San Francisco's Workingmen Respond to the Modern City." *California Historical Quarterly* 55, no. 1 (Spring 1976): 46–57.

Silver, David M., ed. "Charles Denby and the Sino-Japanese War, 1894–1895." *Indiana Magazine of History* 52, no. 3 (September 1956): 285–88.

Tate, E. Mowbray. "U.S. Gunboats on the Yangtze: History and Political Aspects, 1842–1922." *Studies on Asia* 7 (1966): 121–32.

Varg, Paul A. "The Myth of the China Market, 1890–1914." *American Historical Review* 73, no. 3 (February 1968): 742–58.

Wang, Tseng-tsai. "The Audience Question: Foreign Representatives and the Emperor of China, 1858–1873." *Historical Journal* 14, no. 3 (September 1971): 617–33.

Winks, Robin W. "Imperialism." In *The Comparative Approach to American History*, edited by C. Vann Woodward. New York: Basic Books, 1968.

"The Workingman's Party in California, 1877–1882." *California Historical Quarterly* 55, no. 1 (Spring 1976): 58–73.

Young, Marilyn Blatt. "American Expansion, 1870–1900: The Far East." In *Towards a New Past: Dissenting Essays in American History*, edited by Barton J. Bernstein. New York: Vintage Books, 1969.

———. "The Quest for Empire." In *American-East Asian Relations: A Survey*, edited by Ernest R. May and James C. Thomson, Jr. Cambridge: Harvard University Press, 1972.

Dissertations

Cassey, John William. "The Mission of Charles Denby and International Rivalries in the Far East, 1885–1898." Ph.D. dissertation, University of Southern California, 1959.

Kim, Samuel Soonki. "Anson Burlingame: A Study in Personal Diplomacy." Ph.D. dissertation, Columbia University, 1966.

Koo, Telly Howard. "The Life of Anson Burlingame." Ph.D. dissertation, Harvard University, 1922.

Ring, Martin R. "Anson Burlingame, S. Wells Williams, and China, 1861–1870: A Great Era in Chinese-American Relations." Ph.D. dissertation, Tulane University, 1972.

Rock, Francis J. "J. Ross Browne: A Biography." Ph.D. dissertation, Catholic University of America, 1929.

Siu, Victoria M. Cha-tsu. "Sino-American Relations, 1882–1885: The Mission of John Russell Young." Ph.D. dissertation, Georgetown University, 1975.

Teng, Tony Yung-yuan. "Prince Kung and the Survival of the Ch'ing Rule, 1858–1898." Ph.D. dissertation, University of Wisconsin, 1972.

INDEX

Adams, Brooks, 185

Adee, Alvey A., 159, 175

Alcock, Rutherford B.: and treaty revision, 49–50; negotiated Alcock Convention, 63–64, 204n; compared with Burlingame and Browne, 64; George Seward's views of, 94; mentioned, 33, 198n

American Asiatic Association, 173, 177, 187

American China Development Company, 152–53, 166

Angell, James B.: compared with Young, 1, 142, 168, 188; met with Low, 80, 120; appointed minister and treaty commissioner, 115, 116, 118; early life, 116–17; teacher of John Hay and Richard Olney, 116–17; president of University of Michigan, 116, 117–18, 124; recommended by Sen. George Edwards, 118; and missionaries, 118–19; on Chinese in California, 120; negotiated commercial articles, 123–24; and British, 123–24; on opium trade, 123–24, 147; later life, 124; compared with George Seward, 188. See also Angell Treaty

Angell Treaty: and Burlingame's ideals, 116; Evarts's instructions on, 119–20; Chinese negotiators, 121; and George Seward's proposals, 121; negotiations, 121–23; provisions, 123; and exclusion legislation, 124–26, 149

Arrow War, 9, 21, 35

Arthur, Chester A., 125

Austria-Hungary, 183

Avery, Benjamin P.: compared with Browne, 1, 62, 86, 89, 142, 188; compared with Burlingame, 1, 62, 142, 188, 190; appointed minister, 80–81, 82; early life and career, 81–82; fatal illness, 81, 89; and cooperative policy, 81, 82–89; met with Li Hung-chang on Taiwan dispute, 83, and audience question, 84; promoted commerce, 84; promoted Fukien telegraph construction, 84–87; and Margary murder, 87–89; criticized Wade's diplomacy, 88–89; compared with Low, 89, 142, 188

Balluzeck, L. D., 25

Bayard, Thomas F., 146, 149, 150, 155–56

Bell, H. H., Admiral, 33–34, 36, 199n

Beresford, Lord Charles, 172–73, 176

Berthemy, Jules, 25, 33–34

Beveridge, Albert J., 191

Bismarck, Count Otto von, 45

Blaine, James G., 150, 156

Blair, Henry W., 146

Bourée, Frederick A., 135–36

Boxer Uprising, 180–83

Bradford, Oliver B., 100–104

Britain: legation in Peking, 7, 121; and treaty system, 8–10, 20; diplomats compared with American diplomats, 12; force policy, 22, 158–59, 217n; interest in China compared with American, 24–26, 35, 139, 188; and Burlingame Mission, 45; and Angell negotiations, 119–20, 121, 123–24; Olney on, 159–60; and Sino-Japanese War, 162; concessions, 165, 174, 189–90; and Open Door Notes, 175, 178–79, 184–85, 186; Hay on, 176–77, 184–85; mentioned, 4. See also Alcock, Rutherford B.; Wade, Thomas

Browne, John Ross: compared with Burlingame, 1, 13, 38, 55–56, 60–61, 142, 168–70, 188; appointed minister, 46–47, 49; early life, 47; career as author and government agent, 47–49; and Burlingame Treaty, 49–50, 51–52; and Alcock negotiations, 50; criticized Burlingame's policies and mission, 52, 57–60; on China's need for Western technology, 53–56; on gunboat diplomacy, 55–56, 189; resigned as minister, 59–60, 203n; Fish's view of, 60, 169. See also Cooperative policy

Bruce, Frederick: relationship with Burlingame, 20, 22, 26, 31–32; and cooperative policy, 25–26, 62, 169, 198n; and Lay-Osborn affair, 31–32; transferred to Washington, 32

Burgevine, Henry Andrea, 28–30

Burlingame, Anson: compared with Browne, 1, 13, 38, 55–56, 60–61, 168–70; established U.S. legation in Peking, 7–8, 19; established cooperative policy, 11–12, 16, 24–37, 62, 168–69, 188, 190, 200n; early life, 18; antislavery congressman, 18–19; and Sumner-Brooks affair, 18–19; appointed minister to Austria, 19; appointed minister to China, 19; relationship with Bruce, 20, 22, 26, 31–32; opposed gunboat diplomacy, 21, 33–36, 189; and Robert Hart, 31, 57–58; appointed Chinese envoy to Western nations, 36–39; on commerce, 37, 43, 44, 54, 93; death in Russia, 46; view of Browne, 60; legacy in U.S. China policy, 89, 113, 116, 142; mentioned, 72, 154. *See also* Burlingame Mission; Burlingame Treaty

Burlingame Mission: and cooperative policy, 38–39, 43–45; and Tsungli Yamen's instructions to Burlingame, 40–42, 200n; Chinese coleaders of, 41; controversy surrounding, 42–43, 45, 52; and Lord Clarendon's letter, 45, 52; and Bismarck, 45; mentioned, 16. *See also* Burlingame Treaty

Burlingame Treaty: result of Burlingame-Seward negotiations, 43; provisions, 43–45; criticized, 45, 50; compared with Alcock Convention, 49, 63; ratification by China, 51–52; and Fish, 64, 103; Avery's view of, 85–86, 88; George Seward's view of, 92, 111; and immigration, 106–107, 109, 113; revised by Angell, 115, 118–23

Chefoo Convention, 96–97, 208n
Cheshire, F. D., 129–30
China market. *See* Commerce
Chinese antiforeignism: Tientsin massacre, 68–74, 205n; Margary murder, 87–88; during 1880s, 115, 127–32, 138; antimissionary riots of 1890s, 144, 154–60, 168; Boxer Uprising, 180–83

Chinese immigration: Fish on, 65; Low on, 67–68; and California, 67–68, 105–109, 120; U.S. controversy over 105–12, 189; protected by Burlingame Treaty, 106–107; and treaty system, 107, 109–11, 118; opposed by Sargent, 108; defended by Morton, 108; and Angell Treaty, 115–16,

118–26, 149; Scott Act, 149–50; Geary Act, 150

Chinese traditional world view, 5–7, 22, 78–79, 88

Chinese views of U.S., 12, 77

Choate, Joseph H., 178, 184

Civil War, U.S., 13, 21, 24, 27, 35, 66–67, 146

Clarendon, Lord, 45, 52

Cleveland, Grover, 124, 141, 146, 149–50, 159, 163

Commerce: as objective in U.S. China policy, 8–9, 65–66, 190; and treaty system, 10; the China market, 14, 150–53, 168, 173, 187; and Tientsin massacre, 71; promoted by George Seward, 92–93; promoted by Denby, 148–49, 150–53, 167–69; and Open Door Notes, 172–86 *passim*

Concessions, 164–66, 167, 174, 189–90

Confucianism, 3, 5–6, 20–21, 53

Conger, Edwin H., 166, 172, 176

Cooperative policy: pre-1861, 9; defined, 11, 24–26, 37, 50, 83, 133; and Chinese government, 11, 28, 188; and Browne, 11–12, 38, 49–51, 63, 188; and Burgevine case, 29–30; and Lay-Osborn affair, 30–33; contrasted with force policy, 34–35, 37; and Burlingame Mission, 38–39, 43–45; and Fish, 52, 64, 95–96; and Robert Hart, 57; and Alcock Convention, 62–64; Mary Wright on, 63, 198n; and Low, 68; and Avery, 81, 82–89; and George Seward, 90, 92, 99, 140–41; and Young, 132–33, 140, 141; and Bayard, 155–56; and Denby, 168–69; and Open Door Notes, 190. *See also* Burlingame, Anson; Seward, William H.

Crosby, Pierce, Admiral, 130–31

Cushing, Caleb, 8, 11

DeLano, M. M., 85, 87

Democratic party, 107, 119, 146, 180, 183

Denby, Charles: on use of force, 1, 147–48, 155–58, 169, 189; on missionaries, 3–4, 153–60; on commerce, 3–4, 148–49, 150–54, 166–67; early life, 145–46; and railroads, 146, 148–49, 152, 169; appointed minister, 146; belief in Social Darwinism, 147; on treaty system, 147–48, 169, 189; compared with Browne, 149, 169; compared with Seward, 149, 169; on immigration, 149–50; and Sino-Japanese War, 160, 163–65; on concessions, 164–66, 167;

replaced by Conger, 166; on Spanish-American War, 167, 174; later life, 167; and cooperative policy, 168–69; compared with Burlingame, 169; on Open Door Notes, 185

Denby, Charles, Jr., 147, 162

Dun, Edwin, 164

Evarts, William M.: and immigration, 109–11, 115, 119–20, 168; asked for George Seward's resignation, 112; appointed Angell minister, 116, 118; views of Britain, 119–20, 190; on commerce, 120. *See also* Angell Treaty

Ever-Victorious Army, 28–29

Extraterritoriality. *See* Treaty system

Fish, Hamilton: on cooperative policy, 52, 64, 95–96; and Browne, 60, 63–65, 168; on Alcock's diplomacy, 63–65; and Burlingame Treaty, 64; on immigration, 65; on commerce, 65–66, 71; on Low and Tientsin massacre, 71, 168, 205*n*; and Low's mission to Korea, 75; recommended George Seward as minister, 94–95

Forbidden City, 5, 78

Formosa, 9, 29, 83, 148, 164

Fournier, Francois E., 137–38

France: legation in Peking, 7; and treaty system, 8, 9–10; interest in China compared with American, 24–26, 35, 139; *General Sherman* incident, 33–34; and Burlingame Mission, 45; and Tientsin massacre, 68–72, 205*n*; Henri Cordier on French policy, 71; Sino-French War, 115, 135–40; and Sino-Japanese War, 162–64; concessions, 165, 189–90; and Open Door Notes, 175, 178

Frelinghuysen, Frederick T., 133–34

Gérard, Auguste, 159

Germany: Prince Wittgenstein as minister to China, 27; and Burlingame Mission, 45; and Tientsin massacre, 69, 205*n*; use of naval force at Amoy, 131–32, 134–35; interest in China compared with American, 139; and Sino-Japanese War, 162–64; concessions, 165, 174, 189–90; and Open Door Notes, 175, 178–80, 186

Gordon, Charles G. (Chinese), 29

Grant, Ulysses S., 66, 95, 126–27

Gresham, Walter Q., 146, 151, 162–64

Harrison, Benjamin, 146, 149–50

Hart, Robert: became head of Chinese Customs, 31; on Burlingame's policies, 57–59, 154; role in Chefoo Convention, 96–97, 208*n*; and Sino-French War, 138; and cooperative policy, 198*n*

Hay, John: student of Angell, 116–17; appointed secretary of state, 172; and Britain, 176–77, 184–85, 190; and Russia, 179–80; compared with Denby, 180, 187; and Boxer Uprising, 182–83. *See also* Open Door Notes

Hayes, Rutherford B., 96, 105, 107–108, 110–11, 112

Hippisley, Alfred E., 175–77, 186

Howard, William A., 56, 60

Idealism: in U.S. China policy, 2, 15, 16, 89, 114, 116, 148, 170, 188–92; and American culture, 2–4, 191; and Burlingame, 46, 89, 114

Ili crisis, 122, 127–28

Imperialism: in U.S. China policy, 2, 13, 15, 89, 114, 116, 133–34, 148, 170, 188–92; and American culture, 2–4, 191; defined, 4; and missionaries, 155

Imperial Palace, 5, 78

Italy, 174, 175, 178

Japan: Matthew Perry's mission to, 75, 161; dispute with China over Taiwan, 83; and Open Door Notes, 175, 178, 188; and concessions, 189–90. *See also* Sino-Japanese War

Johnson, Andrew, 46–47, 67, 126

Korea: *General Sherman* incident, 33–34; Low's mission to, 74–78; in Sino-Japanese War, 161–62, 164; mentioned, 5, 10, 192

Kung, Prince: head of Tsungli Yamen, 22; audience question, 78–79; and Tz'u-hsi, 128, 138; cooperative policy, 132–33; removed from office, 138. *See also* Tsungli Yamen

Lay, Horatio Nelson, 26, 30–32

Lay-Osborn flotilla, 30–32

Legation Quarter. *See* Peking

LeGendre, Charles W., 55

Li Hung-chang: and Avery, 83; negotiated Chefoo Convention, 96–97; and Young, 127, 136; and Sino-French War, 135–38;

negotiations with Bourée and Tricou, 135–36; Li-Fournier convention, 137–38; interest in railroads, 149; signed Treaty of Shimonoseki, 164; mentioned, 112, 129

Lincoln, Abraham, 19, 66–67, 117

Livermore, Isaac, 54

Low, Frederick F.: compared with Burlingame, 1, 62, 72–73, 74, 78, 89, 142, 188; compared with Browne, 1, 62, 74, 78, 142, 188; compared with Avery, 1, 89, 188; and Tientsin massacre, 62, 68–74; early life, 66; appointed minister, 66, 68; governor of California, 66–68; and Chinese immigration, 67–68, 80, 108; and cooperative policy, 68; on force policy, 72–74, 80, 189; mission to Korea, 74–78, 94; audience with emperor, 78–79; resigned as minister and later life, 80

McKinley, William, 141, 151, 172

McLane, Robert, 9

Margary, Augustus R., 87–89, 95–96

Marshall, Humphrey, 9

Martin, W. A. P., 20, 57

Merchants, 3, 73. See also Commerce

Missionaries: and treaty system, 10; and Tientsin massacre, 68–70, 73, 154, 156; Denby on, 3–4, 153–60; increase in number of, 154; as targets of riots, 156–59, 181; mentioned, 36

Morton, Oliver P., 108

Most-favored-nation. See Treaty system

Muraviev, Count Michael, 178–79

Myers, John C., 99–102, 104

Nanking, Treaty of, 8, 10, 98

O'Conor, Nicholas, 158–59

Olney, Richard: student of Angell, 116–17; gave Denby qualified support on commerce, 151–52; restrained Denby on use of force, 158–60, 216n; on Britain, 159–60, 190

Open Door Notes: and U.S. dilemma in China, 1–2, 12, 15, 171, 187, 190–92; and cooperative policy, 11–12, 190; and Hay, 171, 175–78, 183, 186–88; and commerce, 172–88 passim; and U.S. politics, 176–87 passim; contents of first note (1899), 177–79; responses to, 178–80; and China's sovereignty, 178–79, 182–83, 188, 190; contents of second note (1900), 183–85; historical interpretations, 185–86; compared with Burlingame's policy, 190; compared with Browne's policy, 190

Opium War, 8–9, 21, 35

Osborn, Sherard, 25, 29, 30–32

Parker, Peter, 9

Peking: description, 4–5; foreign legations in, 7–8, 19–20, 121, 181–82

Philippine Islands, 12, 167, 173–74, 183–84

Poston, Charles D., 56

Prussia. See Germany

Quincy, Josiah, 185

Raasloff, General (Danish minister), 85–87

Railroad construction, 55, 93, 102–104, 148–49, 152

Reed, William B., 9

Republican party: and Burlingame, 19; and Browne, 46; and Low, 66–68; and Avery, 81; and George Seward, 100–101, 105, 112; position on immigration, 107–108, 119; and Open Door Notes, 180, 183

Rochechouart, Count, 69–72, 76

Rockhill, William W.: and Young, 139; and Denby, 146–47; and Open Door Notes, 175–77, 184, 186

Rodgers, John, Rear Admiral, 75–77

Russia: legation in Peking, 7; and treaty system, 9–10; and Ili crisis, 127–28; interest in China compared with American, 139, 188; and Sino-Japanese War, 162–64; concessions, 165, 174, 189–90; and Open Door Notes, 175, 178–80, 185

Sargent, Aaron A., 66, 82, 108

Self-strengthening movement, 53, 130

Seward, George F.: and Burgevine case, 29; and Korea, 34; on Alcock's diplomacy, 63–64, 94; compared with Burlingame, 90, 92, 93, 94, 99, 105, 113, 141; compared with Browne, 90, 92, 93, 94, 99, 112–13; compared with Low, 90, 99, 105; compared with Avery, 90, 95, 99, 105; and cooperative policy, 90, 92, 99, 140–41; on treaty system, 90, 94, 95–99, 103–104, 188; early life, 90–91; consul general at Shanghai, 91, 99–105; and promotion of commerce, 92–93, 103–104, 141; supported Burlingame Treaty, 92, 111, 113; and railroad development, 93, 102–104; on force policy, 93–94, 189; appointed minister, 94–95; and Wade, 95–97, 190; on Chefoo Convention, 96–97; impeachment effort against, 99–105; on Chinese immigration, 106–13, 120, 121, 140–41, 150, 168; relieved as minister, 112; wrote

Chinese Immigration, 112; later life, 113; criticized Hay, 179; mentioned, 1, 123, 142, 163, 169

Seward, William H.: and cooperative policy, 11–12, 22–27, 168, 190; on *General Sherman* incident, 34, 74; and Burlingame Treaty, 43–44, 49–50; on telegraph construction, 54; on Alcock's diplomacy, 63; visit to China, 89; mentioned, 91, 92

Shanghai, 5, 91, 99–105, 128–32

Sherman, John, 152, 166

Shimonoseki, Treaty of, 164

Shurman, Jacob Gould, 174–75, 176

Sino-French War, 115, 135–40

Sino-Japanese War, 144, 151, 160–64

Spanish-American War, 166–67, 170, 173–74

Springer, William M., 100–102, 104–105

Stanford, Leland, 66, 81–82

Swift, John F., 119–24

Taiping Rebellion, 13, 21, 25

Taiwan, 9, 29, 83, 148, 164

Tariffs. *See* Treaty system

Telegraph construction, 54–55, 84–87

Tientsin, Treaties of: result of Arrow War, 9; and U.S. China policy, 9–10; and Burlingame Mission, 40; supplemented by Burlingame Treaty, 43–44; Alcock's efforts to revise, 49, 63–64; mentioned, 28, 93, 128

Tientsin massacre, 62, 68–74, 154, 156

Treaty system: establishment of, 8–9; most-favored-nation provision, 8, 11, 99, 120, 128; provisions as of 1861, 9–10; extraterritoriality, 10, 29–30, 98–99, 155; tariffs, 10, 120, 123; and Chinese sovereignty, 11, 133, 142, 188; George Seward on, 90, 94, 95–99, 103–104, 188; *likin*, 97–98, 120; and immigration controversy, 107, 109–11, 118; and opium trade, 123–24, 147; and Angell Treaty, 125–26, 188; and manufacturing, 128–35; Young on, 130–34, 188; Denby on, 147–48, 169; mentioned, 12, 143. *See also* Nanking, Treaty of; Tientsin, Treaties of; Wanghia, Treaty of

Trescot, William H., 119–24

Tribute system. *See* Chinese traditional world view

Tricou, Arthur, 136

Tseng Kuo-fan, 53

Tso Tsung-t'ang, 129–31

Tsungli Yamen: established, 22; on cooperative policy, 26, 36; Chinese critics of, 27,

32–33, 42; and Lay-Osborn affair, 31–33; and Burlingame Mission, 39–42; and Burlingame Treaty, 43, 51–52; and Tientsin massacre, 70–72; and Li Hung-chang, 83; and telegraph construction, 85–87; and Chinese immigration, 107, 121; opposed Western manufacturing, 130–32; and railroads, 152; and Denby, 163–64

T'ung-chih Restoration, 21, 42

Tz'u-an, Empress Dowager, 128

Tz'u-hsi, Empress Dowager, 84, 128, 138, 181–82

Unequal treaties. *See* Treaty system

Vietnam, 5, 135–38, 192

Vlangaly, George, 33

Von Brandt (German minister), 131–32, 133–34

Von Ketteler, Clemens, 181–82

Wade, Thomas, 87–89, 95–97

Walker, Robert J., 48

Wanghia, Treaty of, 8, 10, 11

Ward, Frederick T., 28

Washington, George, Farewell Address, 8, 166

Wells, G. Wiley, 102

Wetmore, W. S., 128–32

Williams, Samuel Wells: secretary of U.S. legation in Peking, 19; and Burgevine case, 29–30; and Burlingame's instructions as China's envoy, 41; favored by Burlingame as successor, 46; favored by Low as Avery's successor, 94; mentioned, 91

Wilson, James H., 146, 149

Woosung railroad, 102–104

Wu Ting-fang, 179

Young, John Russell: compared with Angell, 1, 142–43, 168; appointed minister, 115, 126–27; and Grant, 126–27; early life, 126; newspaper career, 126–27, 141; and Li Hung-chang, 127, 136; and Wetmore factory case, 128–32; on commerce and industry, 128–34; on cooperative policy, 132–33, 140, 141; compared with Burlingame, 133, 141–42; rejected force policy, 134, 189; and Sino-French War, 135–40; wife's death, 137; on Western imperialism, 138–39; and Open Door Notes, 139; and George Seward, 141; resigned as minister, 141; later career, 141